THE NONPROFIT SECTOR IN CANADA
Roles and Relationships

The Public Policy and the Third Sector Series

The Nonprofit Sector in Canada: Roles and Relationships
Keith G. Banting, editor

THE NONPROFIT SECTOR IN CANADA

Roles and Relationships

Edited by Keith G. Banting

Published by the School of Policy Studies, Queen's University
Distributed by McGill-Queen's University Press
Montreal & Kingston • London • Ithaca

Canadian Cataloguing in Publication Data

Main entry under title:

The nonprofit sector in Canada : roles and relationships

(The public policy and the third sector series)
Includes bibliographical references.
ISBN 0-88911-815-9 (bound) ISBN 0-88911-813-2 (pbk.)

1. Nonprofit organizations – Canada. I. Banting, Keith G., 1947-
II. Queen's University (Kingston, Ont.). School of Policy Studies.
III. Series.

HD2769.2.C3N66 2000   361.7'63'0971   C99-932712-7

© School of Policy Studies, 2000

Contents

Tables and Figures	vii
Preface	ix
1. The Nonprofit Sector in Canada: An Introduction *Michael Hall and Keith G. Banting*	1
2. Distinctive Trajectories: Homecare and the Voluntary Sector in Quebec and Ontario *Jane Jenson and Susan D. Phillips*	29
3. Religious Nonprofits: Social Service Provision by Congregations in Ontario *Femida Handy and Ram A. Cnaan*	69
4. After Government Cuts: Insights from Two Ontario "Enterprising Nonprofits" *Raymond Dart and Brenda Zimmerman*	107
5. Hand-in-Hand: When Accountability Meets Collaboration in the Voluntary Sector *Susan D. Phillips and Katherine A. Graham*	149
6. The Nonprofit Sector in Manitoba: A Baseline Survey *Laura K. Brown, Elizabeth S. Troutt and Attah K. Boame*	191
7. Advocacy from the Margins: The Role of Minority Ethnocultural Associations in Affecting Public Policy in Canada *Audrey Kobayashi*	229
Contributors	267

Tables and Figures

Tables

Types of Charities and Distribution of Revenues	12
Sources of Revenues of Charitable Organizations	14
Sources of Revenue for Nonprofit Organizations: Selected Countries	17
Congregations by Denomination	74
Ethnic Composition of Congregations by City	74
Operating Budgets of Congregations by City	76
Number of Paid Clergy	76
Most Commonly Offered Programs	77
Persons/Groups as Initiators of Programs by City	84
Reasons for Initiating a Program by City	84
Programs Reported by at Least 25 Percent of Congregations in at Least One City	93
Assessed Averaged Monetary Value per Month per Program for all Programs	102
Assessed Net Contribution	104
Emergent Outcomes	110
Overall Results Summary	118
Emergent Outcomes: The Resources Dimension	119
Relationships	129
Reputation Outcomes	132

Emergent Outcomes: The Responsiveness Dimension	137
Average Number of Volunteers and Volunteer Hours by Primary Service Category	204
Average 1997 Expenditures by NPOs in Primary Service Categories	205
Number of NPOs Receiving Funds from Federal, Provincial and Local Governments	205
Average Percentage of Funds from Different Levels of Government, by NPOs with Varying Levels of Reliance on Government Funding	209
Average Reliance by NPOs in Different Primary Service Categories on Funds from Different Sources	210
Reliance on Government Funding by NPOs Who Target Specific Groups in their Activities	211
Average Perceived Influence Over Decision Making Wielded by Five Different Groups	213
Average Perceived Influence Over Decision Making Wielded by Government Funding Sources Overall, in Non-Quasi-Governmental NPOs and in Quasi-Governmental NPOs	215
Average Decision-Making Influence by Major Funding Source	217

Figures

Typology Framework for Charities	135
Organizational Collaboration: A Continuum	157
Number of Sampled NPOs in Primary Service Categories	202
Number of NPOs with 1997 Expenditures in Specified Ranges	204
Number of Sample NPOs with Varying Dependence on Government Funding	207
Structural Relations of Ethnocultural Nonprofit Associations in Canada	239

Preface

The nonprofit sector suddenly finds itself at the centre of social and political debates in Canada. Governments see nonprofit agencies as an alternative mechanism for delivering public services to citizens. Activists see voluntary organizations as instruments of social change. Communities see civic groups as a means of mobilizing local resources to tackle problems often ignored by others. Theorists see a rich network of community organizations as building public trust, strengthening democratic governance and reinforcing social cohesion.

Despite such heady expectations, we know remarkably little about the nonprofit sector in Canada. In comparison with the massive research efforts that have been devoted to the roles of the state and the market in Canadian life, we have only a partial understanding of the nature of the nonprofit sector, its capacities and limitations, the roles that it plays, and its relations with governments and private corporations.

This book represents a collaborative effort to extend our understanding of the Canadian nonprofit sector. The effort was made possible by generous support from The Nonprofit Sector Research Initiative established by the Kahanoff Foundation to promote research and scholarship on nonprofit sector issues and to broaden the formal body of knowledge on the nonprofit sector.

With financial support from the Foundation, the School of Policy Studies at Queen's University sponsored a national research grants program. Applications for research funding were invited from researchers across the country, and grants were awarded by a peer-review panel organized by the School. To date, three waves of research grants have been awarded in annual competitions. This book incorporates papers flowing from the first wave of projects, and we hope that successive waves of research will appear in subsequent books in this series.

The overall shape of this book reflects its origins in a competitive research grants program. No overall design was established at the outset, and the topics were determined by the intuitions and curiosity of the researchers. As a result, the book does not purport to provide a comprehensive overview of the nonprofit sector in Canada. Nevertheless, the book does focus on critical issues in contemporary debates about the nonprofit sector. Both individually and collectively, the papers extend our understanding in important directions.

A collaborative project of this complexity depends on the contributions of many people. In thanking them, it is important to begin at the beginning. I would like to acknowledge the support of Shira Herzog of the Kahanoff Foundation, who has encouraged this effort at each stage of its evolution. The Foundation's foresight and commitment has represented a significant affirmation of the importance of the nonprofit sector, and has energized many researchers to think about the challenges it poses. Thanks are also due to Michael Hall for his support both as coordinator of the various components of the Foundation's Nonprofit Sector Research Initiative and as co-author of the introduction to this book.

I also wish to thank the authors for their enthusiasm for the project, and for their patience with the demands of an extended editorial process. In addition, the organizational skills of Shelley Pilon contributed to the success of a workshop at which the first drafts of the papers were presented and discussed. During the workshop, we benefited from the wise comments and suggestions of David Cameron, Kevin Davis, Roger Gibbins, Michael Hall, Daiva Stasiulis, Al Roberts, and Tom Williams. Finally, the skills and professionalism of Mark Howes and his colleagues in the Publications Unit of the School of Policy Studies were critical to the transition from papers to book; and the commitment of McGill-Queen's University Press to the *Queen's Policy Studies Series*, in which this book appears, remains a foundation on which we build.

The many strengths of this book are undoubtedly due to these people. Any remaining errors are my own.

Keith G. Banting

1

The Nonprofit Sector in Canada: An Introduction

Michael Hall and Keith G. Banting

There is a large group of organizations in Canada that are often unrecognized and until recently have been largely ignored in public policy debates. Variously described as nonprofit or voluntary or third sector organizations, they include hospitals, universities, social service organizations, shelters for the homeless, arts councils, food banks, organizations that raise funds to support medical research, self-help groups such as Alcoholics Anonymous, bodies that provide recreation to youth, places of worship, social clubs, trade associations, and advocacy groups. Although widely disparate in terms of their area of activity, these organizations share a common space between the state and the market, and represent a distinctive instrument for the conduct of collective action in contemporary life. Nonprofit organizations have long been privileged by governments. They are exempt from income taxes and other taxes and are also able, in the case of those that are registered charities, to provide receipts for donations that donors can use to claim tax credits.

Recent interest in nonprofit organizations in Canada has been driven by a number of changes in our politics and our social structure. The nonprofit sector appears to be emerging as a chosen instrument of collective action in a new century. Government retrenchment in the 1990s has led to reductions in many community and social services and a renewed interest in the potential role of nonprofit organizations in filling the resulting gaps in our social safety net. Such retrenchment has often been accompanied by a call for communities to do more on their own through voluntary action. Governments have also begun to explore the potential for nonprofits to deliver public services more cost effectively. For example, the federal government created NAV Canada to operate the country's air traffic control system. Other federal initiatives have included the creation of foundations to support health research (the Canadian Health Services Research Foundation) and to provide educational scholarships (the Canadian Millennium Scholarship Fund). Provincial governments have also turned increasingly to nonprofit structures. In Ontario, for example, the government has recently created regional Community Care Access Centres, nonprofit organizations which channel access to health services in local communities. It is worth noting that many of these government-created nonprofits have been developed with the expectation that they will be supported, in part, through private donations. The increase in government interest in the nonprofit sector has also been demonstrated at the federal level by improvements in tax incentives for donations to registered charities in three successive federal budgets (from 1995 through 1997). Some provinces, such as British Columbia and Ontario, have also created special initiatives to support the nonprofit sector within the past five years.

There also appears to be a growing interest among the Canadian public in using nonprofit organizations as a vehicle for voluntary action. According to the 1997 National Survey of Giving, Volunteering and Participating (Hall *et al.* 1998), the percentage of the population volunteering with a nonprofit organization increased from 26.8 percent to 31.4 percent in the ten-year period from 1987 to 1997. In addition, one in two Canadians was found to be a member of a community group.[1] Canada is also witnessing the steady creation of new charitable nonprofit organizations, with the number of charities registered with Revenue Canada increasing at an annual rate of 3 percent since 1987. Such growth in the numbers of nonprofit organizations is not unique to Canada. Salamon (1995) notes that there has been a dramatic rise in the formation and activism of nonprofit organizations around the world. In his view, the scope and scale of this rise constitutes a global "associational revolution" that could be as significant a social and political development as the rise of the nation state in earlier centuries.

The economic and social contributions of the nonprofit sector are also capturing attention. Drucker (1994) points to its growing importance in a post-industrial society and Rifkin (1995) argues that it will be the engine of future employment growth. Moreover, in the most prominent contribution to current debates, Putnam (1993, 1995*a*, 1995*b*) argues that a dense, vibrant community of civic associations builds networks and trust among citizens, and thereby enhances a society's capacity for collaboration and cooperative endeavours. This capacity for collective action represents a form of social capital which, according to Putnam, is every bit as important as financial capital or human capital. High levels of social capital, he insists, contribute both to strong economic performance and to effective democratic governance. Although not everyone shares Putnam's faith in the importance of social capital (Jenson 1998), the widespread debate about the idea has planted the nonprofit sector at the centre of social and political discourse.

Nonprofit organizations have a number of features that make them an attractive alternative to market-driven enterprises or state agencies. The lack of a primary profit motive strengthens the sense that they are more trustworthy than for-profit commercial firms in the delivery of sensitive public services. Nonprofit organizations also appear to have advantages over large, complex government bureaucracies. Because nonprofits are often formed by volunteers and, if incorporated, must by law be governed by a volunteer board of directors, they are often seen as having closer ties to their local communities. They also seem to be more flexible than government because they operate on a smaller scale, and they are able to attract voluntary contributions of time and money in a way that government and business cannot. Nonprofit organizations provide an organizational vehicle for citizens to respond to community, social or personal needs outside the public and the commercial sector. As a result, the nonprofit sector as a whole often acts as a social seismograph, leading the way in identifying new social problems, developing novel responses to emerging issues, and tackling issues that may be too sensitive or controversial for public officialdom.

Despite the growing interest in the nonprofit sector, we know surprisingly little about it and the role that it plays in our society. Research on the nonprofit sector lags well behind that on the public and private sectors in virtually all countries, but this is especially true in Canada. The various papers in this volume attempt to shed greater light on a number of dimensions of the sector. This introductory paper sets the context for their contributions by briefly outlining the current state of knowledge about the nonprofit sector, its role in Canadian society, and the forces that are restructuring the sector today. In addition, some of the current policy issues that confront the sector are outlined and the difficulties that policymakers face in developing policy in the face of a limited understanding of the sector are highlighted. We begin, however, by clarifying some of the terminology that is employed in the literature on the nonprofit, voluntary, or third sector.

THE CHALLENGE OF TERMINOLOGY AND DEFINITION

There is a lack of consensus about the appropriate terminology to describe the group of organizations that are the subject of this volume. Terms such as nonprofit sector, voluntary sector and third sector are often used to describe the field of inquiry. While these may be used interchangeably by different authors, sometimes within the same paper, these terms differ in their connotations. As a result, an investigation of nonprofit organizations may imply a slightly different focus than a study of voluntary organizations or third sector organizations. All of these terms are an attempt to describe those organizations that are not part of government and that are not motivated primarily by a profit motive. Each term has its origins in different academic disciplines, and each has its limitations (Lohman 1992; Thayer Scott 1997).

Generally speaking the term "nonprofit" is the language of economists, and is derived from a model of market economics that views nonprofit organizations as a residual category of organizations in an economy that otherwise has only two actors, market-driven producers and government. From this perspective, the defining characteristic of a nonprofit organization is that it operates with a non-distribution constraint. This means that, although many nonprofit organizations derive revenues from the sale of services or products, they cannot distribute any profits or surpluses to owners or shareholders. The term "nonprofit" is widely employed in the North American literature but is often criticized because it is a residual definition which defines the sector by what it is not rather than by any positive attributes, a critique captured nicely in the title of Lohman's article "And lettuce is a non-animal" (Lohman 1989).

The term "voluntary sector" has its origins in the work of sociological studies of voluntary associations and appears to be predominant in the British literature. It draws attention to the donations of time and money associated with these organizations; voluntary organizations can be distinguished by the fact that members of their governing boards serve without pay and that these organizations often benefit from the contributions of large numbers of individual volunteers. Without denying the importance of the voluntary impulse to the nonprofit sector, however, some critics object that the term might imply that these organizations are run entirely by volunteers, contrary to current realities.

The term "third sector" and the less used "independent sector" have their origins in political science. The third sector attempts to highlight the distinction between government and the private or business sector by focusing on its independence from government and its differences from the private sector. In this framework, government is the first sector, business organizations comprise the second sector and the rest of organizational life occurs in the third sector. One of the objections to the use of this term is that it might seem to imply that third sector organizations are less important than other types of organizations.

Although the terms nonprofit, voluntary, and third sector are perhaps most frequently used to describe those organizations that are non-state and non-market, other terms are also employed. For example, the term non-governmental organization (NGO) has primacy in the international development community and social economy (*économie sociale*) provides another framework that is used more often in Europe as well as in Quebec, as the paper in this volume by Jenson and Phillips highlights.

Fuzzy and Permeable Boundaries

Associated with diversity in terminology is a lack of consensus about what to include in the nonprofit, voluntary, or third sector. Most would agree that governments and for-profit organizations should not be included and that a defining characteristic of an organization in the nonprofit sector is that it is subject to a non-distribution constraint. Nevertheless, boundary lines are difficult to draw with precision, and vary with the analyst and the context. Certainly, the boundary line between the state and the nonprofit sector is fuzzy. Some organizations, such as hospitals and universities, although incorporated as nonprofit organizations and subject to the non-distribution constraint, are so strongly influenced by government that they may be better considered to be government institutions for some purposes. For example, when developing their budgets, provincial governments tend to lump universities and hospitals together with municipalities and school boards as part of the "MUSH" sector of transfer agencies that are dependent on public funding. Similarly, the boundary line between the private sector and the nonprofit sector is not simple. On the one hand, some nonprofit organizations exist primarily to engage in a commercial activity, such as operating health clubs or sports facilities, and depend on the fees that they charge to survive. Many charitable organizations sell services or products, ranging from Girl Guide cookies to sophisticated environmental assessments of private homes, in order to generate profits which can be used to subsidize the organization's social mission. On the other hand, some for-profit firms operate with mandates that go beyond the simple pursuit of profit to a broader view of the responsibilities of corporate citizenship which may include providing support to community causes and partnering with non-profit organizations. And in some contexts, the distinction between for-profit firms, cooperatives, and self-help groups is a subtle one.

One widely used definition is that offered by the International Classification of Nonprofit Organizations (ICNPO). Developed by the Johns Hopkins Comparative Nonprofit Sector Project, a 22-nation comparative study, the ICNPO employs a broadly inclusive "structural-operational" definition that identifies five key features that organizations must have in order to be included in the nonprofit sector:

> Organized. The organization must be institutionalized to some extent. The key concept is not that the organization be legally recognized but that it has some institutional reality (e.g., some degree of internal structure, relative persistence of goals) to give it a degree of organizational permanence.

Private. The organization must be institutionally separate from government. It must be 'non-governmental' in the sense of being structurally separate from the instrumentalities of government and in not exercising government authority.

Non-profit-distributing. The organization must not return any profits generated to the owners or directors.

Self-governing. The organization must be equipped to control their own activities and not be so tightly controlled by government or private business that they essentially function as parts of these institutions.

Voluntary. The organization must have a significant degree of voluntary participation, either in the conduct of its activities (program volunteers) or the management of its affairs (voluntary members of the board of directors). Membership must also be free of coercion so that organizations in which membership is required by law would be excluded. This would include some professional associations that require membership in order to be licensed to practice a trade or profession (Salamon, Anheir and Associates 1998).

Under the strict use of these criteria, cooperatives, mutuals, and self-help groups would be excluded because they would not meet the "non-profit distributing" requirement. However, these and similar types of organizations are sometimes included in the sector if their profit motive is secondary to the primary concern for offering services that benefit the broader local community.

Clearly, those with an interest in this topic must be prepared to tolerate substantial ambiguity in the language that is employed and the boundaries of the subject. In part, such ambiguity is a reflection of the relatively nascent state of our knowledge in this area. In part, however, ambiguity is simply a characteristic shared with other areas of social inquiry, where definitions and boundaries are regularly debated and contested, both in academic research and in policy debates.

Organizing Frameworks

The extreme diversity of nonprofit organizations makes them difficult to study in the abstract and has led to a number of attempts to develop classifications of distinct types. The most common approach is to develop typologies of nonprofit organizations according to their primary area of activity. For example, the ICNPO divides organizations into 12 major activity groups according to the *primary* type of goods or services each one provides (e.g., health, social services, environment). The major groups are:

1. *Culture and Recreation:* includes organizations and activities in general and specialized fields of culture and recreation.
2. *Education and Research:* includes organizations and activities administering, providing, promoting, conducting, supporting, and servicing education and research.
3. *Health:* includes organizations that engage in health-related activities, providing health care, both general and specialized services, administration of health-care services, and health support services.
4. *Social Services:* includes organizations and institutions providing human and social services to a community or target population.
5. *Environment:* includes organizations promoting and providing services in environmental conservation, pollution control and prevention, environmental education and health, and animal protection.
6. *Development and Housing:* includes organizations promoting programs and providing services to help improve communities and promote the economic and social well-being of society.
7. *Law, Advocacy, and Politics:* includes organizations and groups that work to protect and promote civil and other rights, advocate the social and political interests of general or special constituencies, offer legal services, and promote public safety.
8. *Philanthropic Intermediaries and Voluntarism:* includes philanthropic organizations and organizations promoting charity and charitable activities including grant-making foundations, voluntarism promotion and support, and fundraising organizations.
9. *International:* includes organizations promoting cultural understanding between peoples of various countries and historical backgrounds and also those providing relief during emergencies, and promoting development and welfare abroad.
10. *Religion:* organizations promoting religious beliefs and administering religious services and rituals; includes churches, mosques,

synagogues, temples, shrines, seminaries, monasteries, and similar religious institutions, in addition to related organizations and auxiliaries of such organizations.

11. *Business and Professional Associations, Unions:* includes organizations promoting, regulating, and safeguarding business, professional, and labour interests.

12. *Groups not elsewhere classified.*

Other classifications have also been employed. For example, the distinction is often made between *mutual benefit* organizations that exist primarily to provide services exclusively to their own members, such as professional associations and social clubs, and *public benefit* organizations that exist primarily to serve the wider community. Organizations can also be classified according to the *beneficiaries* of their services (such as youth, seniors or animals), according to their *function* (service delivery or political advocacy), or on the basis of the primary source of their *revenues*, distinguishing between commercial nonprofits that rely on sales of goods or services and donative nonprofits that rely on donations (Hansmann 1987).

In Canada, the distinction is often made between those nonprofits that are registered as charities and those that are not. The distinction between charities and other nonprofits is important for two reasons. First, registered charities are able to issue tax receipts for donations that can be used by donors to obtain tax credits while non-charities are not. Second, all registered charities must file annual Public Information Returns (T3010 Forms)[2] which are the only readily available source of detailed information about nonprofits in Canada.[3] Analysts of Revenue Canada data on registered charities usually employ a typology derived from Revenue Canada's classification of organizations that is based upon their major purpose at the time of registration.

By any measure, the nonprofit sector is diverse, potentially incorporating organizations as large and complex as a major teaching hospital and organizations as small and vulnerable as a local service and advocacy group. Whether this sector is more internally diverse than the public or private sectors is an interesting question, as is the question of whether the sector is capable of forming a common conception of itself. Do nonprofit organizations, large and small, think of themselves as sharing the same essential characteristics? Do they recognize themselves as a single community, potentially capable of sustaining common representative organizations and professional associations, developing common conceptions of best practices, and benefiting from common training and educational programs? Whether the phrase "nonprofit sector" is exclusively an analytical category used by students of organizational life, or whether it also refers to a real self-aware social community depends heavily on the answers to questions such as these.

WHAT DO WE KNOW ABOUT THE NONPROFIT SECTOR IN CANADA?

As noted earlier, we know surprisingly little about the nonprofit sector and the role it plays in Canada. This lack of knowledge limits our understanding of an important component of the world in which we live, and weakens our collective ability to develop sound public policy on the sector. For example, it would be useful to know: how many nonprofits there are and what they do; what resources they have; what is their contribution to the economy; what social needs do they address; how they govern themselves and how are they accountable to the communities they serve.

What little information we have about nonprofit organizations primarily pertains to registered charities. Data available from Revenue Canada has allowed a detailed understanding of their size, scope, finances, and operations (Sharpe 1994; Day and Devlin 1997). There is, however, no central registry for nonprofit organizations that are not registered charities. No one can say with any certainty how many of these organizations exist, what resources they depend upon or what their contributions are. Despite the fact that most of the data available covers only one part of the nonprofit sector, it is useful to review the findings about registered charities.

How Many?

There were 77,926 registered charities in June 1999 according to Revenue Canada and an estimated additional 100,000 other legally incorporated nonprofits (Quarter 1992). There are also substantially more numbers of grass-roots associations or unincorporated forms of organizations that should probably be included in any estimate of the size of the nonprofit sector. Smith (1997) suggests that a reasonable estimate of the number of grass-root associations in the United States is about 30 per 1,000 population which would yield a count of 870,000 grass-roots associations in Canada. As noted earlier, the number of registered charities has been growing by about 3 percent a year for the past ten years and one can assume that there is also a growing number of nonprofits that are not registered charities as well as grass-roots associations.

What Do Nonprofits Do?

Relying on data from Revenue Canada, we can obtain some understanding of what charities do in Canada. Revenue Canada classifies charities according to their stated purpose at the time of their registration. Using a modified version of Revenue Canada's classification system, charities can be grouped into 14 types.[4] Table 1 shows these charity types, their numbers and the estimated size of their revenues. As can be seen, 36 percent of all charities are classified as Places of Worship, making it the largest single category of charities. Social Service charities are the second largest category, accounting for 14 percent of charities followed by Community Benefit charities which comprise 7 percent of charities. The smallest category is Hospitals, which consists of only about 1 percent of charities.

Day and Devlin's (1997) analysis of the information returns filed by nonprofits that are not registered charities provides some insight into their activities. Their data is limited because only 4,490 of an estimated 100,000 nonprofits filed returns for the year that they studied (1994) and because Revenue Canada employs a very crude classification system for these organizations. Nevertheless, their analysis reveals a broad variety of nonprofits that are not registered charities which include the following types of organizations: agricultural (10 percent), recreational (7 percent), professional (8 percent), boards of trade (1 percent), civic improvement (2.5 percent), educational (3 percent), multicultural (0.4 percent), arts and cultural (2.3 percent) and a large polyglot "other" category (66 percent).

Table 1: Types of Charities and Distribution of Revenues

Type of Charity	Number	% of All Charities	Total Revenue (millions)	% Total Revenue
Arts and Culture	3,187	4.5	2.0	2.2
Community Benefit (e.g., human societies John Howard Society, Meals-on-Wheels)	5,238	7.3	2.5	2.8
Education (e.g., organizations supporting schools and education)	4,158	5.8	3.5	3.9
Health (e.g., organizations supporting medical research, public health)	3,180	4.5	6.4	7.1
Hospitals	978	1.4	27.4	30.4
Libraries and Museums	1,615	2.3	1.3	1.4
Places of Worship (e.g., churches, synagogues, mosques, etc.)	25,458	35.6	5.3	5.9
Private Foundation (organizations disbursing private funds)	3,356	4.7	1.5	1.6
Public Foundations (e.g., United Way, Centraide, hospital foundations)	3,466	4.9	4.7	5.2
Recreation	2,753	3.9	0.7	0.7
Religion (e.g., convents, monasteries, missionary organizations)	3,978	5.6	2.8	3.1
Social Services (child, youth, family and disabled welfare and services, international assistance, relief, etc.)	10,317	14.4	8.8	9.7
Teaching Institutions (universities and colleges)	2,642	3.7	23.5	25.9
Other (e.g., service clubs, employee charitable trusts)	1,087	1.5	0.1	0.1
Total	71,413	100.0	90.5	100.0

Note: Revenues expressed in thousands.
Source: Hall and Macpherson (1997).

What Resources Do They Have?

In the aggregate, the nonprofit sector commands significant resources, and represents a major component of the Canadian economy. The Canadian Centre for Philanthropy estimates that Canadian charities received $90.5 billion in revenues in 1994 (Hall and Macpherson 1997). However, the bulk of these revenues (56 percent) go to the two charity types that are the smallest in number, hospitals and teaching institutions which together comprise only 5 percent of all charities. The remaining 44 percent or $39.6 billion is divided among the remaining charities. Social service organizations receive about 10 percent of all revenues ($8.8 billion) while health organizations receive about 7 percent ($6.4 billion). Places of worship, which make up 36 percent of all charities, receive only 6 percent of the sector's revenues.

Where does the $90.5 billion in revenues come from? Almost 60 percent was reported to be in the form of government grants and payments; earned income accounted for 26 percent of all revenues and private giving accounted for 14 percent. Table 2 sets out the sources of revenues for different types of charitable organizations. Although the sector, as a whole, is very dependent upon government grants and payments, most government grants and payments go to two types of charities: hospitals receive 37 percent and teaching institutions receive 30 percent.

Many charitable nonprofits rely heavily on government for funding and as such are very vulnerable to changes in government spending. Hospitals, teaching institutions, libraries and museums are most dependent, with government accounting for over 70 percent of their revenues. Charities engaged in community services, education, health, and social services follow closely behind, relying on government for over 60 percent of their revenues. At the other extreme, religious congregations and private foundation charities receive very little revenue from government sources.

Other types of charities rely more heavily on earning income from fees and the sale of goods and services. This is more likely to be the case for recreational organizations, private foundations, arts and cultural charities where earned income accounts for from 40 percent to 58 percent of their revenues. In contrast, libraries, museums, places of worship, and health charities receive only from 17 to 20 percent of their income from this source.

Table 2: Sources of Revenues of Charitable Organizations

Type of Charity	Revenues from Government (%)	Revenues from Earned Income (%)	Revenues from Private Giving (%)
Arts and Culture	50	40	10
Community Benefit	64	24	12
Education	61	31	8
Health	64	20	16
Libraries and Museums	74	17	9
Other	6	28	66
Places of Worship	1	18	81
Private Foundations	11	54	35
Public Foundations	41	22	37
Recreation	27	58	15
Religion	13	46	41
Social Services	64	25	15
Teaching Institution	71	26	3

Source: Hall and Macpherson (1997).

Private giving is the largest source of income for places of worship (comprising 81 percent of all of their revenues) and other charities (66 percent). It is also a relatively larger source of revenue for public and private foundations and religion charities than it is for other types of charities, accounting for from 35 to 41 percent of their revenues. In contrast, despite their high-profile fundraising campaigns, hospitals and teaching institutions receive only a modest percentage of their revenues from this source (2 to 3 percent).

The nonprofit sector receives a substantial amount of support from the Canadian public in the form of donations of money and time. According to the 1997 National Survey of Giving, Volunteering, and Participating, 78 percent of Canadians aged 15 and over contributed $4.44 billion in financial donations to charitable and nonprofit organizations over a one-year period (Hall *et al.* 1998). Almost one-third of Canadians volunteered their time to a nonprofit organization over the same period of time. The total number of hours contributed amounted to 1.11 billion hours, or the equivalent of 578,000 full-time jobs, an amount roughly equivalent to the labour force of Manitoba.

What Contributions Do Nonprofits Make?

Because of the lack of data on nonprofit organizations in Canada, it is virtually impossible to develop a comprehensive picture of their contributions to Canadian society. Nonprofit organizations and their activities are hidden from view in virtually all of the government data that map the important dimensions of Canadian life. This is primarily because governments have yet to see the value in differentiating for-profit and nonprofit organizational forms in their analyses of organizational and business activities. As a result, one can readily determine from government statistics the number of food processing plants in Canada, the size of their labour force, and their levels of production. It is, however, impossible to find out how many food banks are operating in Canada and the amount of food they distribute to those in need without initiating a specific study to do so.

Information about the contributions that nonprofits make is primarily restricted to their economic contributions. Day and Devlin (1997) estimate that the nonprofit sector, at a minimum, accounts for 4 percent of GDP in Canada. The Canadian Centre for Philanthropy estimated the GDP contribution of charities alone as being between around 13 percent of Canada's Gross Domestic Product (GDP), approximately the size of the GDP of British Columbia and estimated that it employed about 9 percent of Canada's labour force or 1.3 million (Sharpe 1994). Ekos Research Associates estimate that nonprofits provided 1.6 million jobs in 1994-95 (Browne 1996).

There is little comprehensive evidence of the social contributions of the nonprofit sector. Until government statistical agencies develop an integrated system of social accounts to parallel the national economic accounts established in the first half of the twentieth century, data on the social contributions of the nonprofit sector will remain partial and based on studies of particular organizations and communities. A number of the papers in this volume contribute to this ground-up picture of the social role of nonprofit agencies, adding to the work of other researchers (see also Rekart

1997; Municipality of Metropolitan Toronto, City of Toronto, Social Planning Council of Metropolitan Toronto 1997). A similar approach is inevitable when assessing the political role of nonprofits through their advocacy of social and economic causes. In this case, however, social scientists and other researchers have already contributed to a substantial literature on social movements and interest groups in Canadian politics, to which Kobayashi's paper in this volume makes an important addition.

How Distinctive Is the Canadian Nonprofit Sector?

The nonprofit sector plays a critical role in all liberal democratic societies, and common features of the organizational form appear in different countries. Nevertheless, the nonprofit sector in each individual country is also shaped by the economic, cultural, and political features of the society of which it is part. It is highly unlikely that the structure and role of the nonprofit sector in Canada are identical to the nonprofit sectors of the United States or Europe, let alone other countries. However, the precise dimensions of the distinctiveness of the Canadian sector have not been well explored by comparative studies; Canada, for example, was not included in the sample of 22 countries examined in the Johns Hopkins Comparative Nonprofit Sector Project.

Some distinctive features of Canadian experience do stand out. For example, the greater role that the state has played in the development of economic and social life throughout Canadian history, in comparison with the pattern south of the border and in many other countries, is clearly reflected in the sources of funding of the nonprofit sector (Table 3). In addition, the regional and linguistic dimensions of Canadian society and the federal structure of our political institutions are important to the shape of the nonprofit sector. There is considerable variation in the number of charities per 1,000 population across the provinces, from a high of 4.4 per 1,000 in Saskatchewan to a low of 1.8 per 1,000 in Quebec and Newfoundland (Hall and Macpherson 1997). Moreover, the role of the nonprofit sector also varies considerably across the country. The Jenson and Phillips contribution to this volume, for example, highlights the different role played by voluntary organizations in the provision of long-term care in Quebec and Ontario. Multiculturalism represents another defining feature of contemporary Canada, but much less is known about the role played by nonprofit

Table 3: Sources of Revenue for Nonprofit Organizations: Selected Countries

Country	Government (%)	Earned Income (Fees, Charges) (%)	Private Giving (%)
Canada[1]	60	26	14
United Kingdom	47	45	9
France	58	35	7
Australia	31	62	6
United States	30	57	13

Note: [1]Canadian data for registered charities only.
Sources: Hall and Macpherson (1997); Salamon, Anheier and Associates (1998).

organizations rooted in distinctive ethnic communities. Kobayashi's paper analyzes the role of the Canadian Ethnocultural Council as an advocacy organization, but this is one more dimension of the Canadian experience that cries out for further work.

AN ERA OF TRANSITION AND TURBULENCE?

The last decades of the twentieth century have been a period of sweeping restructuring in the organizations of modern societies. The private corporation has been reshaped by the globalization of the economy, the revolution in communications and information processing, changing technology of production, new forms of marketing, the expansion of non-traditional forms of employment, and a host of other factors. Restructuring, mergers, and new types of alliances characterize the corporate sector in the modern era. Similar changes have swept through the public sector, driven by many of the same factors and reinforced by fiscal constraints, shifts in prevailing ideologies, and the expectations of a less deferential and more sceptical public.

The nonprofit sector has not been immune from organizational turmoil. It is easy to overstate the extent of change today, in part because we lack benchmarks of the pace of change in nonprofit organizations in earlier periods. Just as some economic historians deny that technological innovation today is any faster or more disruptive than the changes in earlier periods, so might analysts argue that change has always been a hallmark of the nonprofit sector. Moreover, there are important islands of continuity and stability in the nonprofit sector, as Handy and Cnaan's study of the role of religious congregations in this volume reminds us. Indeed, some would argue that, in comparison with the experience of public and private sectors in the last two decades, the restructuring and rationalization of the nonprofit sector are only just beginning.

Nevertheless, when all the qualifications are noted, the contemporary reality of change and turmoil in the nonprofit sector cannot be denied. The most powerful pressures for change have come from the public sector. However, the implications of government actions for the nonprofit sector have been decidedly Janus-faced. On one side, the restructuring of government seems to create historic opportunities for an expansion of the role for the nonprofit sector. Indeed, at first glance, the nonprofit organization would seem to be emerging as the new instrument of collective action in a new millennium. On the other hand, many governments have also reduced their funding to nonprofit organizations, or changed the form in which funding is provided, with dramatic consequences for the sector. In particular, the politics of fiscal constraint has had a major impact on those nonprofit organizations that receive a high proportion of their revenues from government, such as health, education, and social service organizations.

Government retrenchment can initiate a complex chain reaction for the nonprofit sector (Hall and Reed 1998). In the initial stage, the elimination or retrenchment of public social service increases demand for nonprofit services, but reductions in government funding for many social service nonprofits simultaneously weaken their capacity to respond. The second stage is dominated by a series of ripple effects, as social service nonprofits seek to compensate for the lost revenues by seeking alternative funding from private donors or increasing the revenues they earn on their own. The drive to increase earned income will lead some nonprofits to institute fees for services, increase existing fees or search for new revenue-generating opportunities, some of which may be commercial in nature. The drive to substitute government funding with private donations leads to increased competition among nonprofits and increased fundraising costs. The need for funding also leads to overtures to the business sector for sponsorship, some of which can carry risks for the credibility of the nonprofit organization, especially if the nonprofit explicitly associates its name with a commercial product.

Change in the relationship with the public sector is not limited to the level of funding. In order to reduce their costs and increase their control, governments have often changed the form of their funding arrangements with nonprofit organizations. A shift from grants to contracts is ubiquitous, with powerful consequences. Rekart (1993), for example, illustrates the effects in British Columbia of governments moving from providing grants, which enable the nonprofits to deliver services according to their own judgement and experience, to contracts, which require nonprofits to deliver services according to government mandates. As she shows, such changes in funding may lead to changes in the types of services offered and the types of clients they serve. In Ontario, nonprofit organizations have found themselves competing with for-profit companies for contracts to deliver social services. Once again, the effects are powerful. It is too early to know whether nonprofit organizations will be able to compete effectively over the long term in this new world. However, the papers by Dart and Zimmerman, Jenson and Phillips, and Graham and Phillips in this volume highlight some of the immediate consequences for nonprofit organizations in Ontario: restructuring, mergers, and alliances; changes toward more entrepreneurial leadership styles; and narrowed mandates and changes in the mix of services provided and clients served. The wider impact of these changes on the clients of the nonprofit sector and the social needs of their communities remains to be studied.

Governments have also begun to compete with the limited pool of private funds available to nonprofits by creating nonprofit organizations of their own with the expectation that they will be supported by private donations. Examples of this further blurring of the lines between the public and nonprofit sectors include the federal government's Millennium Scholarship Foundation and the Ontario government's Community Care Access Centres and Great Lakes Renewal Foundation. In other instances, government departments and agencies, such as Parks Canada, have begun to seek private donations to support government services. This more competitive environment is further complicated by changes in the approach of the corporate sector. Although corporate contributions have never been a significant element in the revenue base of the nonprofit sector as a whole, they have been important to some types of organizations. However, corporate strategies have been evolving from traditional philanthropy toward more targeted contributions, cause marketing, and joint promotional campaigns, a trend that raises both opportunities and potential risks for some nonprofit organizations.

Shifts in the level and nature of funding have not been the only source of change in the nonprofit sector. Longer term social and cultural trends are also transforming the context in which nonprofit organizations operate. The dramatic expansion of the educated middle classes and the spread of postmaterialist values emphasizing personal development and empowerment have contributed to a new social ethos sympathetic to voluntary action. As noted earlier, the proportion of Canadians volunteering their time has risen over the past ten years. This pattern has been reinforced by the emergence of new social movements representing women, aboriginal communities, consumers, environmental concerns, and other social groups that question deference to, and reliance on large-scale bureaucracies. However, many of these changes also pose critical challenges for the nonprofit sector. Volunteers have increasingly sophisticated expectations about their role as volunteers, and many new volunteers anticipate that they will be able to use and develop their training and skills through engagement in the nonprofit sector. Moreover, the less trusting attitudes about organizations among the public at large apply to nonprofit ones as well. This trend has been reinforced by a more aggressive media which pounces on any hint of scandal and misuse of funds, and by neo-conservative criticisms of many social groups and advocacy organizations as "special interests." As a result, nonprofit organizations are under pressure to be more transparent and accountable about their management of the public trust, and advocacy organizations often must operate in a less sympathetic environment.

Clearly, the nonprofit sector is under pressure in the contemporary period. What is much more difficult to discern at this early stage is the overall direction of change. Is turmoil a sign of a general weakening of the sector?

Or do these stresses and shifting relationships represent early signs of the institutionalization of the nonprofit sector, different perhaps from the nonprofit sector of the past but potentially a more significant component of Canadian society?

In thinking about these questions, it is interesting to ask whether there are analogies to be found in the early history of public administration in Western nations. During the second half of the nineteenth century and the first part of the twentieth century, the structure of the public sector underwent a profound revolution. The process began at different times and proceeded at different speeds in different countries, but central trends were similar. The sprawling, ad hoc assemblage of bureaus and agencies inherited from the pre-industrial era was consolidated into a more coherent pattern. Standard organization forms were established; new budgetary systems and consolidated revenue accounts were put in place; recruitment was professionalized as patronage gave way to merit selection; and the lines of political accountability were tightened. Although no single organizational form emerged, even in any one country, widely accepted norms developed. In the Canadian case, the norm was the departmental structure with a deputy minister reporting directly to a minister; and other organizational forms, such as Crown corporations and regulatory agencies, were recognized, in Hodgetts revealing language, as "structural heretics" (Hodgetts 1973).

This structural transition was accompanied by the emergence of a self-conscious professional community associated with the public sector. Intermediary associations were established to represent the interests of public servants, and to conduct debates about best practices. University programs, special departments and *grand écoles* emerged in various countries to train officials for an expanded public bureaucracy. Public administration became a specialized area of research, with foundations and research councils funding programs designed to enhance the quality of administration and governance. In the United States, for example, "the staff of the Rockerfeller philanthropies wished to support the public administration community because of their worry that federal, state and local governments could not carry the burdens which the Depression had cast on them" (Roberts 1994, p. 222). This professionalization of administration was accompanied, especially in North America, with an attempt to draw a strict — although inevitably artificial — line between politics and administration, as a means of depoliticizing the profession and insulating it from political challenge (ibid).

Obviously, the current restructuring of the nonprofit sector is different in many ways, and it is much too early to know whether the turmoil heralds the early stages of a similar process of institutionalization, complete with greater standardization of form and practice. But it is not difficult to see parallels. Nonprofits are taking on expanded functions, and heightened public expectations swirl around them. Many nonprofit organizations are undergoing dramatic restructuring, and their relationships with the centres of political and economic power in contemporary society are being redefined. One sign of this is the emergence of new mechanisms for consultation between government and the nonprofit sector, including the new federal roundtables, the establishment of a Ministry of Community Development, Cooperatives and Volunteers in British Columbia, and the Premier's Roundtable on Voluntary Action in Ontario, an advisory body consisting of representatives of the voluntary sector, business leaders and government.

One can also detect the development of a professional nonprofit community. Mechanisms are emerging for the conduct of debates about best practices within the sector, such as the Voluntary Sector Roundtable — an unincorporated group of national voluntary organizations. Specialized research and training programs are developing in colleges and universities, often funded by foundations and granting councils concerned about the capacity of the nonprofit sector to fulfil the greater responsibilities being expected of it. Moreover, the sector is caught up in a controversy about the balance between its administrative and political roles, in the form of a debate about political advocacy and the terms governing eligibility for charitable status for tax purposes.

Undoubtedly, the evolution of the nonprofit sector will be distinctive from the historic trajectory of the public sector in many ways. Moreover, such transitions do not follow some inexorable process. The future scope of the nonprofit sector, its structure and the nature of its economic and social roles remain open questions, and the outcomes will be shaped by continuing political and social debates in the decades to come. In that context, the sector will be powerfully shaped by the public policies adopted by the governments of Canada, and by the quality of the information, research, and analysis on which those policies are based.

THE NEED FOR BETTER UNDERSTANDING TO INFORM POLICY DEBATES

Our overview of the current state of knowledge about the nonprofit sector demonstrates a large number of gaps. Clearly a better understanding of nonprofit organizations is required if one is to have any informed discussion of the policy issues that deserve the attention of governments in Canada. The list of policy issues is lengthy. In recent years, proposals have emerged from researchers, think tanks and, most recently, the Panel on Accountability on Governance in the Voluntary Sector (PAGVS 1999) established by the Voluntary Sector Roundtable. Recent policy recommendations include calls for:

- improvements in organizational laws to facilitate the creation of nonprofit organizations (Hirshorn and Stevens 1997);
- broadening the definition of charity to provide more nonprofits with the ability to issue tax receipts that can provide incentives for donations (Drache 1998; PAGVS 1999);
- increasing the supervision of nonprofits through the creation of a supervisory body to enforce standards of practice (Hirshorn and Stevens 1997);
- creating a new Voluntary Sector Commission that would provide information about best practices to voluntary organizations to improve accountability and governance, and collect and provide information to the public (PAGVS 1999);
- improving tax incentives to encourage donations to registered charities (Voluntary Sector Roundtable 1995, 1996).
- restricting the advocacy activities of nonprofit organizations (Bryden 1994); and
- restricting the commercial activities of nonprofits that enjoy preferential tax treatment, thereby reducing their ability to compete with for-profit organizations (Bryden 1996).

Informed responses to these and many other policy issues relevant to the sector would be enriched by a better understanding of the strengths and weaknesses of the nonprofit sector, its contributions to Canadian life, the factors that constrain its role, the impact of current government strategies toward the sector, the attitudes of the public, and so on. The research agenda is formidable.

This book represents one step in building a better understanding of the nonprofit sector. Although each of the papers addresses a different topic, there appear to be a number of themes that emerge when they are viewed collectively. First, the various contributions reflect the relatively nascent state of the body of knowledge on the nonprofit sector. The research is exploratory, and often represents one of the first efforts to study a particular dimension of the Canadian nonprofit experience. Although the researchers differ in the mix of qualitative and quantitative methodologies they employ, in virtually all cases their task is to map the contours of nonprofit organizations and their relationships with wider communities. The task of developing theories to explain and predict nonprofit activity still lies ahead.

Second, the papers reflect once again the rich diversity of the nonprofit sector. In this volume can be found studies of religious congregations (Handy and Cnaan), homecare organizations (Jenson and Phillips), health and social service organizations (Phillips and Graham), counselling organizations and environmental organizations (Dart and Zimmerman), a national advocacy organization (Kobayashi) along with a study that has as its focus the entire nonprofit sector of one province, Manitoba (Brown, Trout and Boame). The latter study further underscores the diversity of organizations ranging from those working in the areas of leisure services, health, education, poverty relief, crisis intervention, environmental causes as well as those engaging in advocacy, cat care, and artistic services. In addition, many of these papers attend to other sources of diversity among nonprofits such as the size of the organization, the extent of paid staff, and the type of relationship with funders.

More importantly, the papers highlight the restructuring of the nonprofit sector, and illustrate its vulnerability to changes in government funding. Jenson and Phillips explore the ways in which different government philosophies and strategies have propelled the nonprofit sector along diverging trajectories in Ontario and Quebec. Dart and Zimmerman's case studies show how nonprofit organizations have turned to commercial ventures and the consequences for them. Phillips and Graham discuss the problems that arise when government funders attempt to force partnerships or collaboration among nonprofit organizations where a natural fit does not exist. And the data gathered by Handy and Cnaan document the extent to which the social agendas of churches in Ontario represent a response to cuts in federal, provincial, and municipal services. Although the paper by Brown, Trout and Boame does not examine the impact of government cuts directly, it does explore the perceived influence of government funders on the decisions of nonprofit organizations.

The papers in this book also underscore the extent to which the practice of dividing organizational activity into three sectors (nonprofit, for-profit, and government) obscures important similarities, and highlight the central role of networks and alliances among organizations, both within and across sectors. Phillips and Graham describe a variety of collaborative linkages among for-profits, governments, and nonprofits. The Community Care Access Centres (CCAC) and the *Centre local des services communautaires* (CLSC) that Jenson and Phillips study are organizations that straddle the border between the public and nonprofit sectors, with a multiplicity of nonprofit and government players performing interconnected roles. Dart and Zimmerman show that the nonprofit commercial enterprises they studied operate with a mission-related, pro-social orientation, while Handy and Cnaan document an extensive set of connections between religious congregations and other types of nonprofits. Moreover, Kobayashi focuses on the contradictory embrace between the state and advocacy organizations, and the growing importance of alliances among different advocacy organizations with similar purposes. These papers, taken together, present a picture of the nonprofit sector as a complex set of networks that spread across many traditional boundaries.

This book represents a contribution to the growing debate about the nonprofit sector, and about the mix of organizations that Canadians will rely on to achieve their collective purposes in a new century. The issues are critical, and we hope that the research reported here will encourage others to join in the process of building richer understandings of the nonprofit experience in Canada.

Notes

[1] The most common organizations or groups in which respondents were involved were work-related (e.g., unions or professional associations reported by 19 percent of respondents), sports and recreation organizations (18 percent), and groups affiliated with religious organizations (13 percent).

[2] Data contained in the T3010s are of unknown reliability and validity. Many of the forms are completed by volunteers who are guided by their own interpretations about what they are being requested to report. Revenue Canada does not perform any checks on their accuracy or validity.

[3] Some nonprofit organizations that are not registered charities are required to file tax returns (Form T1044), however, the usefulness of this information is limited. First, only those nonprofits that earn annual revenues of $10,000 or more, or that have assets of $100,000 are required to file. Second, many nonprofits may not be aware of their requirements to file because Revenue Canada is not able to identify them to inform them of the requirements. Finally, they are required to provide much less detailed information than are charities; and some of that information is not publicly available.

[4] Revenue Canada classifies charities on the basis of their stated purpose when application is made for registered charity status. However, it should be noted that an organization's purpose can change over time and organizations may have more than one purpose.

References

Browne, P.L. 1996. *The "Third Sector" and Employment: Final Report to the Department of Human Resources Development.* Ottawa: Canadian Centre for Policy Alternatives.

Bryden, J. 1994. "Special Interest Group Funding: MP's Report." Unpublished paper.

─────── 1996. "MP's Report Canada's Charities: A Need for Reform." Unpublished paper.

Day, K. and R.A. Devlin. 1997. *The Canadian Nonprofit Sector.* Ottawa: Canadian Policy Research Networks.

Drache, A. 1998. *Charities, Public Benefit and the Canadian Income Tax System: A Proposal for Reform.* Toronto: Kahanoff Foundation Nonprofit Sector Research Initiative.

Drucker, P. 1994. "The Age of Social Transformation." *Atlantic Monthly,* 274(5):53-80.

Hall, M.H. and L.G. Macpherson. 1997. "A Provincial Portrait of Canada's Charities," *Research Bulletin*, 4(2&3). Toronto: Canadian Centre for Philanthropy.

Hall, M.H. and M. Parmegiani. 1998. "Public Opinion and Accountability in the Charitable Sector," *Research Bulletin*, 5(2). Toronto: Canadian Centre for Philanthropy.

Hall, M.H. and P.B. Reed. 1998. "Shifting the Burden: How Much Can Government Download to the Non-Profit Sector," *Canadian Public Administration*, 4(1):1-20.

Hall, M.H., T. Knighton, P. Reed, P. Bussière, D. McRae and P. Bowen. 1998. *Caring Canadians, Involved Canadians: Highlights from the 1997 National Survey of Giving, Volunteering and Participating*, Cat. No. 71-542-XPE. Ottawa: Statistics Canada

Hansmann, H. 1987. "Economic Theories of Nonprofit Organization," in *The Non-Profit Sector: A Research Handbook*, ed. W. Powell. Hew Haven: Yale University Press.

Hirshorn, R. and D. Stevens. 1997. "Organizational and Supervisory Law in the Nonprofit Sector," Working Paper No. CPRN 01. Ottawa: Canadian Policy Research Networks.

Hodgetts, J.E. 1973. *The Canadian Public Service: A Physiology of Government, 1867-1970*. Toronto: University of Toronto Press.

Jenson, J. 1998. "Mapping Social Cohesion: The State of Canadian Research," CPRN Study No. F03. Ottawa: Canadian Policy Research Networks.

Lohmann, R.A. 1989. "And Lettuce is a Non-Animal: Towards a Positive Economics of Nonprofit Action," *Nonprofit and Voluntary Sector Quarterly*, 18(4):367-83.

_____ 1992. *The Commons: New Perspectives on Nonprofit Organizations and Voluntary Action*. San Francisco: Jossey-Bass.

Municipality of Metropolitan Toronto, City of Toronto, and Social Planning Council of Metropolitan Toronto. 1997. *Profile of a Changing World: 1996 Community Agency Survey*. Toronto: Municipality of Metropolitan Toronto.

Panel on Accountability and Governance in the Voluntary Sector. 1999. *Building on Strength: Improving Governance and Accountability in Canada's Voluntary Sector*. Ottawa: PAGVS.

Putnam, R. 1993. *Making Democracy Work: Civic Traditions in Modern Italy*. Princeton, NJ: Princeton University Press.

_____ 1995a. "Bowling Alone: America's Declining Social Capital." *Journal of Democracy*, 6(1):65-78.

———— 1995b. "Tuning In, Tuning Out." *PS: Political Science and Politics*, 28(4):664-84.

Quarter, J. 1992. *Canada's Social Economy.* Toronto: James Lorimer.

Rekart, J. 1993. *Public Funds, Private Provision: The Role of the Voluntary Sector.* Vancouver: UBC Press.

———— 1997. *The Transformation of the Voluntary Sector: From Grassroots to Shadow State.* Vancouver: Social Planning and Research Council of BC (SPARC).

Rifkin, J. 1995. *The End of Work: The Decline of the Global Labor Force and the Dawn of the Post-Market Era.* New York: Tarcher/Putnam.

Roberts, A. 1994. "Demonstrating Neutrality: The Rockefeller Philanthropies and the Evolution of Public Administration, 1927-1936," *Public Administration Review,* 54(3):221-28.

Salamon, L.M. 1995. *Partners in Public Service: Government-Nonprofit Relations in the Modern Welfare State.* Baltimore: Johns Hopkins University Press.

Salamon, L.M., H.K. Anheier and Associates. 1998. *The Emerging Sector Revisited: A Summary, Initial Estimates.* Baltimore: Johns Hopkins University, Institute for Policy Studies, Center for Civil Society Studies.

Sharpe, D.W. 1994. *A Portrait of Canada's Charities.* Toronto: Canadian Centre for Philanthropy.

Smith, D.H. 1997. "The Rest of the Nonprofit Sector: Grassroots Associations as the Dark Matter Ignored in Prevailing "Flat Earth" Maps of the Sector," *Nonprofit and Voluntary Sector Quarterly,* 26(2):114-31.

Thayer Scott, J. 1997. "Defining the Nonprofit Sector," in *The Emerging Sector in Search of a Framework*, ed. R. Hishorn. Ottawa: Renouf.

Voluntary Sector Roundtable. 1995. "Pre-Budget Submission to the House of Commons Standing Committee on Finance" [On-line]. Available: http://www.web.net/vsr-trsb/publications/prebudget96.html.

———— 1996. "Voluntary Sector Roundtable Pre-Budget Submission to the House of Commons Standing Committee on Finance" [On-line]. Available: http://www.web.net/vsr-trsb/publications/prebudget96.html.

2

Distinctive Trajectories: Homecare and the Voluntary Sector in Quebec and Ontario

Jane Jenson and Susan D. Phillips

Care for the dependent elderly has arrived as an issue on the governmental agenda primarily in the last decades. For example, it is only in recent years that the governments of OECD countries have come to recognize population ageing as a new policy challenge. If the OECD's 1981 publication, *The Welfare State in Crisis*, did not highlight care for the frail elderly at all, by the 1990s the issue was at the top of the policy list. Nor was this shift in attention a product of chance; altered population structures were producing rapid growth among the very elderly. "Although the size of the 80+ population remains small in relative terms, it is growing at a considerably faster rate than the population as a whole and faster than the 65+ population as a whole" (OECD 1996, p. 15). Moreover, the general policy direction has been very similar across jurisdictions. Policymakers have declared their intent to keep elderly persons in their homes and communities and with their families as long as and as much as possible. This is sometimes termed "ageing in place."

This goal has direct and obvious consequences for service needs. Demand for homecare, both medical and non-medical, is rising. It is important to note at the beginning that the overwhelming proportion of care for the dependent elderly person is provided "informally" (that is, privately and within the home) by family members. These family members are most frequently a spouse, closely followed by a child. Other family members, such as nieces or nephews, daughters-in-law, etc., also provide care.[1] The overwhelming majority of these "informal" carers are women. They do caring work by helping with everyday living (from personal hygiene to housekeeping and food preparation), by nursing the bedridden and housebound, and managing personal affairs (banking, insurance, and — very importantly — interfacing with the "formal" system of care). While the informal system covers the bulk of caring work provided, families, as well as elderly people without such support systems, frequently need to have their own caring work supplemented by that of the "formal" system. Care of this second type is the focus of this paper.

In the "formal" system, some care given in the home is publicly provided; visiting nurses have been part of the public health system for more than a century. Policymakers' commitment to "ageing in place" has intensified in recent years, however, as they have sought to redesign health service delivery and to reduce the costs of the hospital system. Quite simply, it often costs less to care for a dependent elderly person, even one with chronic health problems, in his or her home than in a hospital. Nonetheless, to say that the system is "formal" is not to say that it is either necessarily public or acquired through the market. It can be provided by volunteer labour, and indeed, much of such care is provided by volunteers or by nonprofit agencies in the voluntary sector. This paper focuses on this kind of care, by examining in detail the changing relationship between the voluntary sector and the public sector.

In the mid-1990s both Quebec and Ontario restructured health care, including that outside hospitals. Both made substantial cuts in the financing of health care, closing hospital beds, seeking to reduce the labour force, and relying more on the family or voluntary sector for caring work. Both reforms were driven in large part by financial goals, as the two provinces sought to control their own spending even as Ottawa was slicing huge amounts from its transfer payments for health care. Despite the similar financial goals, however, the two provinces did not make the same decisions about how to deliver homecare, nor about the role of the state, market, and voluntary sectors. Quebec's decisions involved reinforcement of an existing mixed model for community health in which the public sector maintains a significant role in the provision of services as well as the coordination of volunteers. Ontario's marked a change toward a "contractual model," forcing even voluntary sector care into a system that is competitive and market-mimicking if not completely market-based. The role of the provincial government became one of arm's-length coordinator and contractor of services. What has happened to the voluntary sector and its involvement in the care for dependent elderly in these two situations? How is this related to the new pluralism of social policy?[2]

RENDERING VISIBLE THE INVISIBLES: STATE-VOLUNTARY SECTOR RELATIONS IN THE CONTEXT OF HEALTH-CARE REFORM

Scholars have tended to describe postwar welfare states in terms of their impact on the wage relation, categorizing them according to their capacity for "decommodifying" labour.[3] Nonetheless, the postwar decades, in which new social policies and new state-society relations were constructed, were also ones in which caring and responsibility for care occupied policymakers. Providing health care was at the core of postwar welfare state development and competing visions of state-society relations. As Julia O'Connor (1997, p. 23) recently wrote, "the welfare state is about the care of dependent people. The crisis of the welfare state is at least in part ... a 'crisis of the care of the dependent'."

In the traditional welfare state literature, however, such programs have been treated as secondary, following *from* the fact that the wage relation was regulated and capital-labour postwar compromises were in place. The profound error of neglecting to see that the "other" programs were at least as much constitutive of postwar welfare states became evident exactly at the moment that the latter were remodelled in the 1980s and 1990s (Jenson 1997). There has been an explosion of attention to the "caring dimensions" of social policies. It has, in other words, become very visible, whereas before it was often hidden in the household or performed in large institutions organized according to the traditional labour processes of Fordism.[4]

Another, and closely related, upsurge in attention renders visible the centrality of the relationship between the state and the voluntary sector. In large part this has happened because neo-liberal governments themselves tend to turn to the voluntary sector — or as they sometimes say, "civil society" — in order to fill some of the "compassion gaps" opened by their more draconian economic policies as well as to save money on wage bills and other costs of public services.[5] But the work of social scientists is also focusing this attention. Challenged to rethink their own categories for understanding postwar welfare states and democracies, political scientists have begun to pay more attention to the voluntary sector and particularly its role in service delivery.

In doing so, they encounter accounts of the relationship between the state and voluntary sector proposed by economists and have frequently found them wanting. The dominant economic theories attribute voluntary sector provision of services to market failures (Hansmann 1980), or to an inherent conflict between state provision and voluntary action which suggests that the state must be pared back in order to make room for volunteers (Weisbrod 1988). These approaches have been widely criticized as empirically wanting (see Salamon 1995; Gidron, Kramer and Salamon 1992; Ware 1989). Recent work has uncovered an abundance of cases of partnerships between the state and voluntary sector and the active involvement of voluntary organizations in the provision of a diversity of social goods and services (often in direct competition with the private sector) at the height of the Keynesian welfare state. This hidden history of the welfare state is now being acknowledged by more and more research studies.

In the current conjuncture of years of deficit cutting and rethinking the role of the state, the issue of the relationship between public and voluntary sector remains a central one. As André Picard wrote:

> The issue is really one of choices. In building a social welfare system ... Canada has chosen ... to fund most basic services through tax collection, while contracting out much service provision to community-based groups. Unfortunately, many politicians today conveniently ignore the first part of the equation, promoting the fiction that charities can miraculously fill the gap if we all 'dig a little deeper'. The truth is that we have to lower expectations or make tough choices about our priorities as a society. Right now, those choices are being made in a back-handed fashion, by dumping programmes on groups that cannot afford to maintain them, rather than making strategic decisions (1998, p. 5).

Since the mid-1990s, however, we have observed some of these choices being made in the health-care system. In our area of particular concern, homecare, both the governments of Quebec and Ontario undertook to rearrange the way in which the service would be provided. These reforms were not simply technical adjustments. In both cases they reflected ideas about the way in which what used to be termed social rights of citizenship would be delivered as we enter the new millennium.

QUEBEC: INNOVATION WITHIN CONTINUITY

The Quiet Revolution that began in 1960 started Quebec down the road to a modern, secular society in which the state and its technocrats would play a major role in organizing social life and social services.[6] Health care was one of the areas that most changed in these years. If before 1960 services were provided privately by religious and other charitable agencies, by 1971 Quebec had a universal and free health-care system designed to be coordinated across a range of institutions to provide both prevention and cure, in large hospitals and local community clinics (White 1992). The system grew out of the Commission d'enquête sur la santé et le bien-être social (Castonguay-Nepveu Commission) as well as the incentives coming from the federal government's spending on health. Reform in health care was located in a much broader process, itself committed to new technocratic expertise and comprehensive reform to solve problems of poverty, education, and employment, as well as to economic development. The result across policy domains was a style of policy making that has been described as "far-reaching and visionary," a style that distinguished it from the more incremental one of Ontario.[7] It was, moreover, one in which the state — in the form of the government in Quebec City — had a crucial role to play.

Care for the Dependent Elderly

The health-care regime built after 1971 provided an integrated institutional complex designed to democratize access to services and foster community development, in addition to delivering health care. The Castonguay-Nepveu Commission described its goals as building a regime that would be universal and available to all citizens, no matter where they lived, would rationalize services and make their distribution more efficient, and would democratize health and social services by involving citizens and their representatives in everyday governance (Roy 1987, p. 16). Nonetheless, the commission was suspicious of community involvement in the *provision* of services. It railed against the "private sector," by which it meant both the commercial and the private nonprofit sector. If they had any place, it was simply to meet "special needs," not supported by government (Vaillancourt 1988, pp. 149-50).

A concrete institutional manifestation of the notion of coordinated and democratic services was the Centre local des services communautaires (CLSC). These neighbourhood centres were intended to be the gateway to the system and to deliver primary-care services. They were modelled on the *cliniques populaires* which had sprung up in poor neighbourhoods in the 1960s to provide better access to, and more democratic control over, health care.[8] The CLSCs are small; Quebec was originally supposed to have about 200; there are 151 today. However, they provide both medical care and certain social services; and the staff usually includes a community organizer or animator, responsible for "community health."

Despite such innovations, Quebec's health-care system was much criticized in the 1970s because it had failed to live up to the promises of the Castonguay-Nepveu Commission.[9] According to Marc Renaud, Quebec's system was no different from that of most Western countries, being overly statist and centralized, constructed on high technology solutions, excessively medicalized, emphasizing cure over prevention, and dominated by health-care professionals with a minimal role for citizen-users (cited in Mayer and Groulx 1987, p. 88). In the case of the elderly and others as well, this produced a great deal of institutionalized care and insufficient support for the non-medical services necessary for a healthy homecare system (Lesemann and Nahmiash 1993).

Eventually the criticisms settled into a debate about "privatization," although the word never meant the same thing to all participants. Indeed, this debate re-emerged as recently as the 1998 provincial election. In part this linguistic confusion about the role of the public and the private has allowed the CLSC to survive waves of reforms, each of which sought to eliminate it. Moreover, the ownership of the hopes for the CLSC by community activists and other progressive forces helps to explain why Quebec and Ontario are following different routes to reform in this time of cutbacks.

As Yves Vaillancourt described the privatization discussion of the 1980s, there were two distinct versions. The progressive version sought to reduce the excessive control of the public sector, to use health and social services as a terrain for pursuing goals of democratization and empowerment of the poor and weak. Thus, these intellectuals and activists preferred the CLSC to hospitals and nursing homes. They preferred to decentralize decision making and action into the community away from the large Fordist institutions of the post-1960 years.[10] This was the project of the leftists who in the 1960s had been anti-statist, and/or *autogestionnaire* ex-Catholics, and/or influenced by US-style community development politics. This position also influenced the government, including the Ministry of Social Affairs (MAS), the department responsible for health care. In 1979, the ministry wrote: "In order to help groups representing the elderly and handicapped, the state must ensure the survival of volunteer organisations, rather than looking to replace them" (quoted in Vaillancourt 1988, p. 154). The plan of the MAS for home care was to reduce institutionalization, making funds available as infra-structural grants to voluntary organizations providing services and support to the elderly.[11]

The second version of the privatization discourse promoted commercialization as the route to the value of liberal choice. Faced with an overly centralized system and active state, as well as rising costs, this discourse was promoted by the Quebec Liberal Party, parts of the business community, and Claude Castonguay, the former co-chair of the commission that recommended CLSCs in the first place.[12] This version of the debate had some resonance in policy circles. Indeed, in 1986 Minister Paul Gobeil issued a report in which he proposed eliminating CLSCs in urban centres, leaving them to the network of private clinics (Vaillancourt 1988, p. 157). The debate was also reflected in homecare services. A new program in 1986, Services intensifs de maintien à domicile (SIMAD), provided up to 35 hours a week of homecare, mostly of a non-medical sort. This program, administered by CLSCs, encouraged consumers to use their benefits to design their own mix of care, purchasing it from both non-public agencies and independent employees (including sometimes from the black market).

Nonetheless, after some hesitation, the Liberal government also continued its subsidies to the voluntary sector.

A major reform initiative began in 1988 when the Liberal government established its Commission d'enquête sur les services de la santé et les services sociaux (Rochon Commission). It was one of a series of efforts in these years to rethink the basic contours of the welfare state and the mix of responsibilities between state, economy, and community. Social assistance was being rethought and family policy was again on the agenda, just as employment policy was being restructured. These years were ones of intense political debate, which traversed the parties as well as other organized groups and which bridged the change in government in 1994. The two discourses of "privatization" confronted each other and opened some space for compromise.

The Rochon Commission described the existing system as having lost its way. Citizens' interests were not central because the whole system was supposedly hostage to the "special interests" of doctors, unionized workers and various institutions, all of which were protecting their turf. Implementation of the commission's recommendations began in 1990, led first by the Liberal minister of health and social services, Marc-Yvan Côté, and then by Jean Rochon, the chair of the commission who became minister of health in the Parti Québécois government elected in 1995.

Côté's reform spoke of the need to put the "citizen at the heart of the system" and to reduce central control by decentralizing authority to 16 Régies régionales de santé et de services sociaux, regional agencies which would be responsible for the development, coordination, and distribution of the budget in their area.[13] Thus, coordination remained a part of the health-care system but the process was decentralized to the regions. There was also an effort to develop market signals, in order to control costs. For example, higher payments were supposed to encourage doctors to relocate to underserved regions, while user-fees were supposed to induce patients to avoid non-essential use of emergency rooms. Some homecare clients received an allowance permitting them to purchase their own services.

This was not, however, a completely marketized system. Democratic institutions were built in, as were new links to the voluntary sector. "Consumers" of health-care services gained a majority of the seats on governing bodies,[14] and nonprofit community organizations were given new responsibilities. Those offering social or psycho-social services could count on receiving public funding. Again, the goal was to create an integrated system, at the same time as reducing both costs and the power of traditional health-care professionals by turning to the voluntary sector (White 1992, p. 243).

In all of all this, the CLSC was crucial and the emphasis on homecare remained front and centre. Coordination was the responsibility of the CLSC as well as regional bodies. To the extent that cost savings would be made, homecare was crucial, as well as the deployment of the voluntary and "informal" sector. Thus, for example, there was a slight shift in focus on the "who" of homecare needs. In particular, attention turned to the caregivers. Since somewhere between 70 and 80 percent of care is provided by family members, their needs had to be satisfied if "dumping in institutions" was to be avoided; as a result, programs for respite care were added to the basket. In 1992-93, CLSCs provided 87 percent of the public services in the regular programs for homecare.[15] The SIMAD aside, the CLSC also monopolized the medical dimensions of homecare. Other services were shared among the CLSC, the voluntary sector, and the private market.

These changes are sometimes termed a *virage milieu*, the idea being to keep people in the familiar situation of their home and community as much as possible. In 1995 a second and much more far-reaching *virage ambulatoire* was instituted by Minister Rochon. It brought a draconian reduction in spending, as hospitals were closed, beds eliminated, and staff induced into early retirement or let go. In Montreal alone, the cuts announced for 1995-98 were $200 million, and a further $55 million was scheduled for 1998-99. The region's budget fell by about 7 percent from 1995 to 1998, with a real reduction of perhaps 10 percent, given the increase in demand due to population change. Seven hospitals were closed in Montreal, emergency rooms went from 24 to 17, and an additional 441 beds were closed. At the same time, over 7,579 jobs were eliminated (RIOCM 1998, pp. 22-23, 49).

The pressure on the CLSCs and their voluntary sector partners was immense. They became responsible for providing homecare for patients sent home after surgery (several procedures became day surgery) as well as caring for patients who were no longer in long-term beds in the hospital. All this was added to existing responsibilities for homecare for the dependent elderly. Nor did the *virage* bring any corresponding increase in budget for the new responsibilities. While the pressure was intense, the model was not new. As Jean Rochon said when he presented his policy:

> il nous faut pouvoir compter sur nos services de première ligne, les CLSC, les cliniques médicales, et surtout le réseau des organismes communautaires ... Ce qu'on vise ultimement à faire, sur le plan de renforcement des communautés locales, c'est vraiment d'avoir les stratégies qui encouragent le developpement local et ce, en liaison et en complémentarité avec le réseau (MSSS 1997, pp. 151-52).

What has this meant for the relationship between the public and voluntary sector and the capacity of the latter?

The CLSC and the Voluntary Sector

In 1987 the General Assembly of the Fédération des CLSC stated its own vision of the role of the local institution in this way:

> Les CLSC réaffirment leur mission comme établissements locaux de santé, des services sociaux et d'action communautaire, orientés vers le développement de l'autonomie des personnes et des communautés, vers le maintein dans le milieu naturel et caractérisés spécifiquement par l'approche communautaire et la prévention (Favreau and Hurtubise 1993, p. 7).

The 1991 law setting down the mission of CSLCs incorporated much of this self-definition. The CLSCs were supposed:

> To offer at the primary level of care
>   a) basic health and social services of a preventive or curative nature;
>   b) rehabilitation and reintegration services;
> to the population of the territory it serves.
> *Persons requiring services for themselves or their family*
> . are contacted
> . needs are assessed
> . provided with the services they require
>   -at the CLSC
>   -in the person's own environment
>   -at school
>   -at work
>   -at home
> . are referred to agencies best suited to assist them (Kaufman 1998).

The CLSCs were meant to foster collaboration among doctors, social workers, nurses, and community organizers and to undertake community out-reach.[16] Members of the community sit on the boards of the CLSC. Moreover, health care and social work professionals must — according to the law — refer clients to support services.[17] This is very often to voluntary associations, which provide social services for free or at minimal costs.[18] Most typical of such services are friendly visits, meals-on-wheels, accompaniment of elderly persons to medical appointments, and help with the tasks of everyday living such as shopping. In addition, a typical CLSC employs a community animator to act as a coordinator at the interface between the centre as the representative of the public sector and the voluntary sector (see Favreau and Hurtubise 1993). As a result, the CLSC often supplies equipment or other program aids to the voluntary associations in its territory, either to support existing programs or to foster the creation of new volunteer programs. Representatives of the CLSC sometimes sit on the board of directors of voluntary associations, especially as they are getting started.

We see, then, that from the beginning the CLSC model structured a relationship between the public and voluntary sector with two major dimensions. First, the emphasis on coordination means that the CLSC and the Régie régionale have joint responsibility for assuring the presence of a healthy voluntary sector. While funding of groups is overwhelmingly the responsibility of the regional bodies, the CLSC are in charge of coordinating much of their work.[19] Guaranteeing the presence of adjunct services is part of its mission.[20] Second, the responsibility for referral means that the CLSC counts on the availability of services in the voluntary sector.

The CLSC Côte-des-Neiges and its Voluntary Sector since the Virages

The case of the CSLC in the Côte-des-Neiges area helps to provide answers to several key questions. What impact has the *virage ambulatoire* and associated reforms had on the voluntary sector on the ground? How have the changes affected volunteers and staff? What has been the effect on the voluntary sector and its relationship with the public sector, represented by the CLSC and the Régie régionale?

Interviews conducted for this project indicate that neither the professionals at the CLSC nor the representatives of voluntary associations used the *virage ambulatoire* to date their relationship. If they did evoke the idea of new pressures, new needs or shifts in the base of volunteers available, 1995 was not a moment of redefinition in the relationship. For one thing, the changes of the early 1990s formalizing their place in the system had been more important for their ties. Secondly, they were much more likely, as individual groups, to adopt a stance similar to that of their own association, the Regroupement intersectorielle des organismes communautaires de Montréal (RIOCM), and to blame the government in Quebec, Minister Rochon, and the Régie. Indeed, they tended to describe the current relationship to the CLSC as one of "cooperation," of mutual needs and benefits in the face of much tougher circumstances.

Two elements of the relationship deserve closer attention. The role of the CLSC in fostering voluntary action and the management of that relationship; and the pressures on the voluntary associations in the face of the *virage* and the CLSCs own increasing workload. With respect to the first of these elements, there are numerous examples of the CLSC actively helping to organize a new service, manage existing ones, and even create a voluntary association to carry out new services. Take, for example, the case of the Centre de bénévolat Côte-des-Neiges. It runs a number of programs, including outings, friendly visits, and a service (*Bonjour, ça va ?*) which makes daily telephone contact with 57 shut-ins living alone. The overwhelming majority of its clients come from CLSC referrals; indeed it far prefers CLSC referrals to self-referrals because the association does not have the expertise to determine whether a person really needs the service. The CLSC also negotiated a territorial division with the centre, one of whose major activities is to accompany elderly persons to medical appointments, and other groups so that it would be clear which group was responsible for which areas. The advantage for CLSC employees is that they knew exactly whom to call. This facilitated the CLSC's own referral processes. It also eliminated any competition among agencies for the same clients.[21]

Another example saw five voluntary associations, including the Centre de bénévolat, meet with the CLSC to organize a service called *épicerie en taxi*. It provides transportation and help to elderly persons for grocery shopping. The five organizations refer people to the CLSC office, which registers the names and passes them to the Centre de benévolat, which actually provides the volunteers to accompany the elderly persons. A similar cooperative initiative was being organized at the time of the interviews to set up a transportation network.This is a clear example of an institutionalized relationship between the public system and the voluntary sector turning on the provision of clients, a division of responsibilities, and a sharing of funding. The "other" is very present in the mind of each. Interviewees constantly mentioned the CLSC, while CLSC employees had a very clear idea of who "its" groups were, what their resources were, and who could be counted on to meet particular needs.

This is not to deny that the relationship can sometimes be difficult. For example, at least one voluntary agency reported being pressured by the CLSC — via the carrot of new funding and a CLSC person on the board — to mount a new service. The group did not really have the volunteers available and eventually backed out of the project. The interviewee then attributed the group's subsequent failure to receive sufficient referrals to sustain another project as the CLSC's revenge. Overall, however, our interviews revealed a general level of comfort with the relationship and with the role played by the CLSC.

This general satisfaction did not extend to the other parts of the public sector, particularly the minister of health and his *virage*. The voluntary agencies felt they were being squeezed between the needs of their clients and the resources they had.[22] Demand for their programs, particularly accompaniment and transportation, were rising much faster than their resources, especially in terms of volunteers. Whereas the meals-on-wheels (*popotte roulante*) providers were reasonably satisfied with the current situation, those who provided programs related to medical care felt stress. For example, they spoke of the problems of transportation. The concept of ambulatory services works only if the patient can get to and from the hospital. Transport has become a crying need since the *virage*. Frail and isolated old people often need help with this part of their care. Yet voluntary agencies are threatened by the legal implications for themselves and their volunteers of transporting people, where risks of falls and other accidents are high.

Several groups spoke of the problem of finding volunteers to match new needs. There is the problem of finding volunteers willing to take an elderly person for treatment or for an operation done on an out-patient basis. This demands a day-long, stressful but often boring commitment, and coordinators have difficulty finding volunteers who will accept the long waits at clinics. They also have trouble finding volunteers willing to assume responsibility for taking someone home to an empty apartment after day surgery, especially when the doctor indicates that the patient should not be left alone for the night. The volunteer faced the awful choice of leaving the elderly person alone or not being able to return to his or her own home and family. One agency coordinator described her dilemma each time she faced a cataract case. She needed to find a volunteer willing to pick up the "*petite dame*" at 7:00 in the morning, take her home about 4:00 in the afternoon, probably make her something to eat, and then try to deal with the doctor's instructions that she was not to be left alone for the night. Not surprisingly, the coordinator had few volunteers willing to undertake this kind of commitment, yet cataract operations were frequent among her clientiele. She experienced this situation as one full of stress, which threatened her own sense of being able to cope and deliver services.

The study thus reveals contradictory tendencies. In the case of certain ongoing activities, such as meals-on-wheels, the relationship between the public sector, represented by the CLSC, and the voluntary sector is relatively smooth and not much changed since 1995. Community workers can mount new services, associations find new volunteers, and the services continue. The major complaint relates to the uncertainty of funding from the Régie régionale, which runs on an annual basis and prevents long-term planning. Not surprisingly, several groups in our study advocated a longer financial commitment, and they do little independent fundraising, in contrast to the emerging situation in Ontario, as seen below. While the Régie régionale requires them to exhibit some effort to raising other money, most described this activity as both minimal and more likely to target creating group solidarity than to generate a major contribution to the budget. Representatives of the voluntary sector also felt the need for more training. As their clientele ages they find themselves facing frailer elderly. In particular, they feel unable to cope with Alzheimer patients or others who do not appropriately recognize the volunteer as a member of the community. In contrast, voluntary agencies touched by the shutdown in hospital beds and reduced staff are under stress. When the hospital previously kept cataract patients overnight, volunteers could be found to transport the frail and isolated. More reliance on day surgery has stressed the system immensely.

Overall and particularly since the PQ government's *virage ambulatoire*, the CLSCs find themselves pressed to provide more services to more people with fewer resources. The community groups in the voluntary sector, for their part, feel that they cannot cope with rising demands, new kinds of demands, and the uncertainties of the situation. They speak of burn-out and being asked to do more and more. As the report of the Montreal-wide grouping of community associations put it, the situation is as if community associations rather than public services "have become THE social security safety net" (RIOCM 1998, p. 75).

The Introduction of a New Institution

As Quebec's public services are restructured and reduced, a new type of institution has appeared, promoted by many of the same social forces that argued for the first style of privatization. This is the social economy corporation. While Quebec has long had a vibrant social economy (the *caisses* of the *mouvement Desjardins* is the best-known example), there has been a good deal of mobilization recently behind the idea that a developed social economy will address several ills simultaneously. The social economy corporation, a nonprofit, cooperative or community corporation with substantial volunteer participation, has been promoted at least since the vast mobilization by the Fédération des femmes du Québec (FFQ) in their March for Bread and Roses (*pain et roses*) in June 1995. It is an economic institution that provides needed services, at a reasonable cost, in a democratically managed way and employing individuals at risk of social exclusion.[23] In this way, the social economy is located at the intersection of employment policy and social policy. It responds to social policy needs in terms of the kinds and price of services provided and to employment policy needs when it moves individuals off social assistance and into continuing employment.

One area of targeted development for the social economy is the provision of housekeeping services and personal non-medical services for the dependent elderly and other persons. The need arises from the fact that commercial services are expensive and public ones are not available. Originally, employees of the CLSCs did do light housekeeping, but that was removed from the basket of services relatively early on. Faced with a client's need for housekeeping services, the CLSC had no recourse but to refer to the private sector, whether regular or black market.[24] In Côte-des-

Neiges a commercial firm, Geronto, was already providing housekeeping services in the early 1990s. More recently, however, a social economy company has developed in the area, and the CLSC now refers clients to the Grande Vadrouille. In other words, this new institution — itself at the intersection of the private and voluntary sectors — has been incorporated into the complicated mixture that is Quebec's pluralistic system for the provision of homecare for the dependent elderly.

ONTARIO: INSTITUTIONALIZING A NEW MODEL FOR SOCIAL RIGHTS AND CITIZENSHIP

Ontario has been similar to Quebec for the last few decades in its underlying philosophy about services for the dependent elderly. Both provinces have emphasized home over institutional care. Despite this, the debates have not been exactly the same, nor have the institutional arrangements that have developed generated the same division of labour among state, market, and community. Indeed, the policy reforms undertaken in the mid-1990s by the Conservative government of Mike Harris have moved Ontario even further from Quebec. Since 1995 the Conservatives have installed a system that would limit the state to an arm's-length coordinator and contractor of services in a competitive homecare "market." Under the Harris reforms, the historically privileged position of nonprofit organizations in service delivery has been replaced by an open, competitive bidding process in which large for-profit companies are increasingly successful.

Care for the Dependent Elderly in Ontario

The relationship between the state and community, between the public and voluntary sectors in Ontario has differed from the pattern in Quebec throughout the postwar years. Ontario has followed a step-by-step process in building its system, whereas Quebec followed — although did not always adhere to — a blueprint set out by the Rochon Commission.[25] In addition, in Quebec the welfare state put the emphasis on central direction, and coordination, and on citizen involvement in public institutions. In Ontario, the pattern was different. The central issue is not only the role of the private sector but also how to coordinate a "non-system."

Health and social services, including homecare, in Ontario are characterized by a separation of policy and service delivery, with privatization of delivery to both private firms and voluntary organizations. As Ramesh Mishra and his colleagues write about the growth of Ontario's social services from the 1940s until the 1980s:

> It is important to bear in mind ... that this spectacular growth in state welfare, far from superseding the nongovernmental organisations in fact helped in their proliferation. The secret of this relationship is that the government funded a variety of voluntary organisations, old and new, and entrusted many of them with the delivery of services. The growth of government did not mean a decline of the nongovernmental sector, indeed quite the opposite. Moreover, this post-war expansion of social welfare activities also helped the development of a commercial sector — profit-making organisations involved in the delivery of social welfare. Such, in brief, is the context of the more deliberate policy of privatization pursued by Ontario from the mid-seventies (Mishra, Laws and Harding 1988, p. 122).

Thus, exactly at the same time Quebec was being influenced by the Castonguay-Nepveu Commission to turn away from non-public provision, except in limited and special cases, Ontario was reinforcing the role of private agencies in service delivery. The Conservative governments that dominated postwar Ontario politics began a policy of privatization in the 1970s that continued until 1985. Government reports foresaw a coming fiscal crunch and proposed to avoid it by separating policy making and program delivery.[26] Governments and elected legislatures retained responsibility for the former. Democratic decision making in the legislature would guide governments on spending so as to ensure that services were forthcoming. The delivery, however, was best done in ways that would tap community skills and resources. Included among such skills were those found not only in municipal governments but also in "nonprofit organisations, in private, profit-oriented corporations, or in community corporations organized by special interest groups" (ibid. 1988, p. 122, quoting the Committee on Government Productivity report of 1971). Policy discourse made little distinction between community-based and nonprofit delivery on the one hand and commercial agencies on the other. Both were "the community."[27]

The Ontario government provided grants and subsidies to charitable organizations and municipal institutions to assist in delivery and to expand the availability of services. The period from the 1950s through the 1970s saw intensive involvement by the state in such assistance, particularly in promoting the construction of long-term care facilities (Government of Ontario Task Force on Aging 1981; Litwan and Lightman 1996; Williams 1996). The province mandated municipalities to provide and operate homes for the aged, subsidizing the capital and operating costs of both municipalities and nonprofit organizations. Provincial involvement in homecare formally began in 1958 with the introduction of the *Homemakers and Nurses Services Act*.[28] Municipalities had the choice of employing nurses and homemakers directly or contracting with nonprofit agencies, such as the Red Cross or Victorian Order of Nurses (VON).[29] During the 1960s, the Ministry of Health also established its own nursing and homecare programs, first directed at acute care for people with short-term needs during post-hospital convalescence, and extended by 1975 to those with chronic-care needs.[30] To add to the complexity, the Ministry of Community and Social Services was actively funding other non-medical services. Under the *Elderly Persons Social and Recreational Act*, passed in 1961, the ministry assisted nonprofit organizations with the costs of building and expanding social and recreational centres, known as Elderly Persons Centres (EPCs). Amendments to this legislation in 1966 provided for the use of provincial funds for home support services such as meals-on-wheels and assistance with shopping and cleaning, offered through the EPCs.[31]

This strategy resulted in a variety of services for the elderly, supported by various funding mechanisms and by different ministries operating under a patchwork of legislation and regulations. Access to services remained largely uncoordinated. In short, there were many services, but no *system* of services for the dependent elderly. Beginning in the 1970s, attention did go to the overall planning of the health-care system of which home and long-term care were increasingly important parts. In 1974, the Ministry of Health created District Health Councils (DHCs) as a means of planning and coordinating services at a regional level. But the DHCs, consisting of a mix of health-care professionals, government officials, and consumers, had a strictly advisory role with no control over budget allocations. In practice, their effectiveness in planning varied enormously (Kane and Kane 1985, pp. 95-96). They did contribute, however, to the growing debate over homecare. Many conducted extensive studies of the situation in their regions and consistently noted inadequate linkages between hospital and community facilities as well as the paucity of homecare and other community services.

During the course of the 1970s, limited coordination had also been introduced by the creation of Placement Co-ordination Services (PCS) in selected regions across the province. Their mandate was to assess and find placements for clients in long-term care facilities and to ensure that institutional care was used appropriately. Funded by the province, the PCSs were housed under different auspices, some under regional governments (as in Ottawa-Carleton), others under the VON or hospital boards, and still others incorporated separately (Kane and Kane 1985, pp. 98-99). Operating alongside, but distinct from the PCSs were Homecare Programs which purchased nursing, other professional services and homemaking from both nonprofit agencies and commercial firms. However, effective case management between the two local agencies was limited by their relative isolation,[32] and problems were simply exacerbated in areas of the province without a PCS. By this time, the inequity in services across the province, particularly between the large urban centres and rural communities, had become glaringly apparent while demand for services in all areas was rising steadily.

In response to these challenges, three successive governments (Liberal, New Democratic [NDP], and Conservative) grappled with reform. Each of the three put its distinctive stamp on reform proposals, consistent with its philosophy of the role of the state relative to the other two sectors. The central problems — the need for better access, improved coordination, the integration of homecare with the rest of the health-care system, and greater equity across the province — were identified in roughly similar ways, albeit with slightly different emphasis by the three successive governments. The main differences between them came in the details of management and delivery. But this detail proved vitally important. It was the detail, not the general policy direction, that would most affect the multitude of voluntary and nonprofit organizations engaged in service provision. Only the

Harris Conservatives have had the luxury of fully realizing their ideas, however, since electoral defeat intruded on the full implementation of the reform plans of both the Liberals and the NDP.

Under the Peterson Liberals, the emphasis in reform was on improving coordination. A lengthy discussion paper released by the Minister for Senior Citizens' Affairs in 1989, *A New Agenda: Health and Social Service Strategies for Ontario's Seniors*, put the key issue this way:

> [N]o single agency has either the mandate or the resources to conduct comprehensive functional assessments or to fully co-ordinate the delivery of a wide range of services for the elderly. Similarly, no agency has sole responsibility for monitoring changes in the individual's situation and arranging modifications in the range, type or intensity of services provided as the person's needs change. Consequently, some senior citizens never have the benefit of a comprehensive assessment and others, or their families, go from agency to agency in an effort to obtain appropriate services. There is a need not only to improve access but also to provide a more comprehensive approach to the delivery of community health and social services.

The proposed solution was to create or expand regional agencies to provide "one-stop shopping" for referrals, information, assessment, and coordination of community services. In keeping with the Liberal view of the state, it was intended that these agencies would *broker* services by community agencies, both nonprofit and for-profit, rather than provide them directly. The importance of volunteers was recognized and further initiatives were planned to support and expand their role.[33] Although defeated before fully implemented, the Liberals' efforts had measurable success. Services were expanded, all regions of the province were mandated to establish Placement Co-ordination Services (although they were not merged with Homecare Programs) and programs formalized eligibility rules and service levels. Long-Term Care Offices were opened in regions to promote more integrated planning, and a partial merger of funding envelopes between institutional and homecare made allocations between them somewhat simpler (Milne forthcoming).

Upon taking office in 1990, the NDP government moved quickly to imprint its own view of a larger role for the state in the management of services for the elderly through a set of ambitious proposals. Like its predecessor, the NDP government also stressed the need for improved access to and coordination of services by regional agencies, but it planned to move away from brokering services toward a more centralized administration and direct provision in some cases. Forty regional Multiple Service Agencies (MSA), each governed by a board representing both provider and consumer groups, would be mandatory points of access for homecare services as well as long-term care placement. Instead of brokering services provided by and existing in the community, these agencies would be more directive by determining the range of services community organizations would provide or by having MSA staff provide the services themselves. Where services were purchased, preference would be given to nonprofit agencies. In addition, there was to be greater uniformity of funding and greater equity in service levels across the province with a provincially mandated basket of services in each region, unified budgets between the two principal provincial ministries and integrated planning passing from Long-Term Care Offices to District Health Councils. In this vision, the Ontario agencies would have been more akin to Quebec's CLSCs than anything that has existed in Ontario before or since, although the difference in size remained an important distinction.[34] Attention was also focused for the first time on workers in care facilities and community-based organizations with proposals for regular employment, not hourly contracts, and for technical and cultural sensitivity training and worker involvement in planning.[35] Nonetheless, voluntary organizations, particularly community-based ones, were less than enthusiastic about the proposals because they feared they would be displaced by the MSAs and the strong volunteer component of their services lost. Although the Rae government passed the enabling legislation, Bill 173, its reforms were never implemented, curtailed by its defeat in the 1995 election.

The Conservative government of Mike Harris did not reverse all the reforms begun by the NDP. It continued to pursue increased coordination and in January 1997 created 43 Community Care Access Centres (CCACs) across the province. In implementing these reforms, however, the Harris government has differed significantly from its predecessors, including other Conservative governments, in its vision of the role to be played by the state and the desirable mix of public and private provision. For it, the key to efficiency in the system is the discipline of the market. The provincial government has two primary roles, both played at arm's length: it oversees the contracting process in a competitive market, and it dispenses information. Neither the provincial government, its own "wards" the municipalities nor the CCACs are direct providers of services to the dependent elderly.

In addition to institutional redesign, the Harris government has also cut health budgets and undertaken the long-term process of reallocation of money from acute care to long-term and community care. Significant cuts were made to the Ministry of Health's budget, $132 million in the first six months after the election. A complete overhaul of the health-care system was also in the works. An independent Health Services Restructuring Committee was given the authority to restructure the hospital sector and to recommend the reallocation of resources to community care and the integration of the acute and community care systems. It took two years, however, until money actually began to flow into the redesigned long-term and homecare services.

The Community Care Access Centres (CCACs)

The regionally-based Community Care Access Centre is intended to provide a single point of access for both placement in long-term care facilities and homecare services for the elderly and disabled adults and children. In contrast to Quebec's CSLC, the CCAC provides no services directly. Its job is to arrange contracts for the provision of specific services such as visiting nursing, shift nursing, occupational therapy, or homemaking through a competitive bidding process open to both nonprofit organizations and commercial firms. The CCAC is also to serve as an information and referral service for other community services, such as friendly visiting, transportation, and meals-on-wheels. Thus far, however, these activities remain outside the direct responsibility of the CCAC, again in contrast to the relationship between the CLSC and "its" voluntary organizations. CCAC employees serve as case workers, determining whether individual clients are eligible for homecare, or whether placement in a long-term care facility is warranted.[36] As part of the health-care system, there are no user-fees for the services contracted through the CCAC.[37]

Although the CCACs replace both the Placement Co-ordination Services and Homecare Programs, they are not government agencies. Rather, they are incorporated nonprofit organizations, run by a volunteer board of directors with membership available at minimal or no cost to the general public. While wholly funded by the provincial Ministry of Health, the CCACs are registered as charities under the federal *Income Tax Act*. This status leaves open the possibility that in the future they will be able to raise funds to meet some portion of their budgets from the public and corporations, using the incentive of income tax receipts.

The invention of the CCAC has radically restructured the voluntary sector's relationships with both the state and business. The nonprofits contracting for nursing and other homecare services with the CCAC must now compete not only with each other, but with commercial enterprises. Competitors must win all or a piece of a CCAC service contract in order to get referrals from it. Since the CCAC is the mandatory means of accessing publicly subsidized services for the elderly and disabled persons, winning a contract is vitally important to obtaining clients. One consequence is that nonprofits are called on to invest considerable administrative time and other resources in responding to a CCAC's Request for Proposals (RFP), a task that will become more sophisticated over time and may drive out smaller organizations, whether for-profit or nonprofit.

In the transition from a delivery system run exclusively by nonprofit organizations to an open market, the first two rounds of contracting reserved a certain "market share" of each service for the nonprofit agency that historically had been the provider of that service. In the 1999 round, however, there is no "special treatment" for nonprofits. In some specialized services, such as occupational therapy, the commercial competitors may be small firms or individual professionals. But, in the two largest service areas, nursing and homemaking, the for-profits are usually subsidiaries of very large companies.

Although many services, such as meals-on-wheels, friendly visiting, and transportation, remain outside the contracting regime of the CCAC and are still provided by geographically-based, community service associations, access to these services is largely mediated by the CCAC. Many community service organizations complain that the CCAC has not done a very good job of the referral process. It is accused of "protecting its turf" and being reluctant to provide information about or to refer clients to community service organizations.[38]

The CCAC Contracting Regime and the Voluntary Sector in Ottawa-Carleton

Our case study of the impact of Ontario's new contracting model in homecare focuses on the nonprofit organizations under contract with or affected by the largest CCAC in the province, the Ottawa-Carleton region.[39] In contrast to the evolutionary change described in Quebec, the institution of the CCAC in 1997 and implementation of its competitive bidding process marked a major shift in practice and government-nonprofit sector relations for homecare organizations in Ottawa-Carleton. The creation of the CCAC took place within a broader context of significant change in the health-care environment being experienced throughout Ontario. The closure of hospital beds presented increased demands: not only are there more clients, but there are many clients with complex needs who would probably have been hospitalized in previous years. As in Quebec, greater reliance on day surgery has made transportation, provided almost exclusively by volunteers, a critically important service. Funding pressures created by sustained fiscal restraint had meant several years of frozen or reduced provincial and municipal grants. In this context, the move to a new contracting regime presented its own set of special challenges. We address two specific questions in this case study, with particular attention to homecare. What impact has the new model had on the nonprofit organizations in Ottawa-Carleton *as* organizations? How have the changes affected volunteers and staff?

The most apt description of the experience of the full range of voluntary and nonprofit organizations in Ottawa-Carleton is heightened vulnerability. The issue is not simply one of competition because many have long competed with other nonprofits. Now, however, the CCAC contracting regime is the only game in town. Voluntary organizations are by nature particularistic, dedicated to serving specific constituencies, providing specialized services, in particular locales. If, for example, the Ottawa-Carleton Branch of the VON were to lose the CCAC contract to provide visiting nursing, it could not easily make up this lost revenue; the very existence of the organization might be in peril. The same is not true for its private sector competitors, such as Bradsons Inc., which might easily survive on income from its security or temporary office services or from its homecare contracts in other regions until the next round of CCAC bidding. The feeling of insecurity experienced by the nonprofits is exacerbated by a perception that the process is not sufficiently transparent and fair. In particular, the criteria upon which the RFPs are evaluated, and notably the relative weight accorded to price versus quality of service, remains unclear.[40]

The nonprofits respond to the vulnerability created by the contracting regime in several ways. First, they both specialize and diversify. By concentrating on providing high quality in their traditional core services, they hope to ensure contract success. At they same time, they are expanding the range of services they can provide and thus the number of contracts on which they can bid. For example, organizations once devoted only to nursing are beginning to offer homemaking services as well, and vice versa. In addition, nonprofit organizations are increasingly entering into business activities outside the CCAC contracting process. They are finding a variety of products that can be sold for additional income, such as contracting with individual companies to offer Employee Assistance Programs and selling their expertise in training and other education programs. Although both of these responses may promote financial stability, they create new organizational challenges related to the dangers of diffusing the mission, and they impose an increased administrative load.[41]

The community service and other voluntary organizations that do not contract with the CCAC are by no means immune from financial and organizational insecurity. They, too, feel the squeeze of both rising and changing demands for service *and* limited revenues.[42] Like the larger and professionally staffed nonprofits that are contracting under the CCAC, the community services organizations have had to cut costs and dramatically step up their fundraising activities. Since financial pressure is not new, most have already trimmed any administrative "fat" that might have existed. Thus substantial savings cannot be gained easily through cutting their core operations.[43] Some reductions in expenses have been obtained by moving to smaller, cheaper office space or by cutting service costs (for instance, by providing frozen meals so that the cost of daily trips could be reduced in meals-on-wheels programs).[44] Without exception, all the organizations we interviewed are doing more fundraising from individuals and corporations. And, without exception, all indicated that this is extremely difficult in today's competitive environment and a huge draw on their administrative capacity.[45]

Related to maintaining financial viability has come greater attention to issues of organizational governance. In particular, most organizations had recently restructured their boards of directors, reducing their size and shifting the role of the board from an administrative to a policy governance model in order to be more strategic. More attention has been given to recruiting board members for specific skills, especially fundraising and professional oversight. In short, most need their boards "to think more like business." A second dimension is the role of volunteers. It is important to note that there are two distinctive types of organizations in our case study, both of which could be said to be part of the "voluntary sector." Most of the nonprofit organizations that contract with the CCAC make little use of volunteers in their programs (although all have volunteer boards), whereas the meals-on-wheels and other community service associations rely heavily on volunteer labour to deliver their services. Volunteerism in the latter organizations has been influenced more by the general environment of health-care restructuring and other pressures facing all voluntary organizations than specifically by Ontario's new contracting regime.

The typical volunteer in the homecare organizations we studied is an older woman, 65-plus years or retired from the workforce, who has a family member in care and who gives on average 3.5 hours per week of voluntary service to the organization. Although there are fewer male volunteers, they have a distinctive niche as drivers and thus are in strong demand. In general, the number and recruitment of volunteers in homecare organizations is relatively stable. Since most volunteers are themselves seniors, the most significant reason for attrition is simply ageing. Younger, mid-career, volunteers differ from the seniors because they bring with them more sophisticated expectations of what they want out of volunteering and expect the experience to be not only challenging, but meaningful and rewarding (see Hall *et al.* 1998).

But the real issue of volunteerism in this case is not recruitment. It is the need for more training and supervision, as we saw in Quebec as well. As a result of health-care restructuring, volunteers in homecare have been asked to do more demanding tasks, many of which require specialized training and some of which are more appropriate roles for staff. For example, volunteers delivering meals-on-wheels increasingly must deal with psychiatric clients for whom they are the only daily contact and only source of information about how the client is doing. Even an apparently simple activity such as transporting an elderly person to a doctor's appointment may be demanding because the client is likely to be quite frail, requiring knowledge on the part of the driver as to how to assist in moving him or her. As in Quebec, long commitments of time may also be required by the driver/companion to assist a client undergoing day surgery.

Most executive directors whom we interviewed said that, while they recognize the need for training and are trying to use volunteers more efficiently and effectively, they are limited by financial and human resources. Since the state's role has been defined as a coordinating and contracting agent for services specified in RFPs, the CCAC does not have the mandate to build capacity within organizations and volunteer programs to ensure that adequate and appropriate services can be provided. This stands in marked contrast to the CSLC whose role is not only to access existing services, but to promote the health of the voluntary sector.

The new model in Ontario was specifically intended to reshape relationships between the state, business, and the voluntary sector by removing the historically privileged position of nonprofit organizations in the provision of homecare. There is no question that it has succeeded in introducing direct competition between the voluntary and corporate sectors. Inadvertently, it has also created some measure of competition between the voluntary sector and the state. Voluntary organizations fear that they will soon need to go head-to-head with the CCACs for fundraising dollars and that the CCACs are protective of their terrain in information referral.

Competition within the voluntary sector has also risen, although this has not been entirely negative. While voluntary organizations must compete with each other more than ever for contracts, grants, and fundraising revenues, the overarching sense of vulnerability has transformed some of this competition into collaboration. Many voluntary organizations recognize that the only way to continue to provide certain client services is to pool resources with other nonprofit homecare organizations or build partnerships with other kinds of organizations.

Increased collaboration has also been borne out of the need to become more vocal advocates. Given the amount and extent of change that has occurred in healthcare, even the more conservative voluntary organizations that formerly defined their roles solely in terms of service provision have come to feel that their responsibility to clients and constituencies includes public policy advocacy. Thus most homecare organizations have become more politically active in recent years, and in so doing, have formed coalitions with other community and intermediary organizations. The result appears to be an emerging cohesion within the sector. In the absence of strong regionally-based intermediary organizations with cross-sectoral membership, equivalent to Montreal's RIOCM, this cohesion has had to be invented, rather than emerging from an existing base. Restructuring has also produced increased suspicion of government and its professed commitment to the voluntary sector. Although the restructuring of the health-care system has been predicated on the assumption that home and community care to a large extent can replace institutional care, the change in the hospital system initially occurred without concomitant investment in the community system.[46] There is a lingering suspicion among community-based organizations that the provincial government does not appreciate the capacity and infrastructure required in the sector to fulfil its potential.

Not only has the ideology shifted from a preference for nonprofits to open competition. There has also been a shift from a community-service model to a health model. As part of the Harris government's restructuring, the funding and policy direction for nonprofit organizations has been consolidated in the Ministry of Health, rather than being shared by Community and Social Services. In contrast to Quebec where health and social services have long been closely integrated, the systems were divided in Ontario. For many community organizations, this new locus within the state spells a long-awaited integration of funding; for others, it implies the imposition of a medicalized model, bringing with it centralized control and standardization, resulting in a lack of creativity, loss of connection to community, and inability to solve problems locally. These concerns are heightened by the absence of a local agency like the CSLC to help build capacity and structure and animate a positive relationship with voluntary organizations in the community.

CONCLUDING REMARKS

By the end of these two stories the readers might feel that we are now comparing apples and oranges. The Ontario story focuses on the Ottawa-Carleton CCAC, a region-wide agency, and on voluntary agencies that are large nonprofits with many employees. While volunteers are important to the delivery of homecare in Ontario, their involvement occurs in community service associations that operate largely outside the official public system. In the Quebec story we touched much less on the Régie régionale, the regional health authority, and concentrated on one of over 20 CLSCs operating in Montreal, and its associated voluntary agencies which provide meals-on-wheels, friendly visits, transportation, and so on.

In fact, these two foci reflect the distinctive ways in which the two welfare states have restructured themselves to provide a basic social service. The policy legacies of choices made at each of the decision points of the last four decades about basic questions of the role of the state and relationships among the state, community, and economy have driven the neighbouring health-care systems further and further apart. A description of the relationship between state and voluntary sector in each province inevitably must focus on quite different institutions. Moreover, as we follow the trajectory of choices, we observe that the actors, institutions, and ideas in play are not the same.[47]

The crucial decisions taken in the early 1970s set out the first path. In Ontario, the decision to privatize was essentially a continuation of postwar practice, which had always relied on mixed public-private provision and a major role for nonprofit agencies with volunteer boards. In Quebec, the reforms of the early 1970s marked a break with the past. The mixed system was deliberately dismantled, to be replaced by almost exclusive public provision. Nonprofits and other voluntary sector agencies were even vilified by the Castonguay-Nepveu Commission, although the actual system left some place for them. So by the late 1970s, different institutions and actors were in place. Ontario had nothing like the CLSC, weak and discredited as it was at that time. Quebec did not have the large volunteer agencies providing health services that were being funded by the Ontario government as it moved through its first stage of privatization.

By the 1980s, the scene had shifted somewhat in Quebec, where the two discourses of privatization essentially competed. When the PQ government sought to "privatize," its electoral base led it to act at least in part in response to the discourse of progressives[48] calling for more local involvement, less centralization, more community development, and less institutionalization. At that time, funding was made available to community groups, but not to commercial agencies. Moreover, the CLSC's community development responsibilities were recognized and strengthened. That choice reinforced an existing public agency, heir to the popular struggles of the 1960s, with a mandate for community health and capable of materializing the goal of decentralization. Therefore, while the regional health authorities dispensed the bulk of the subventions, the coordination of community-based actors in the system depended on the CLSC. The other discourse on privatization, coming from business and the Liberals, gave birth to only one major reform, which is the direct allowance paid to those in need of care.

All of this meant that going into the last round of reform, Ontario was seeking to coordinate a patchwork of programs, a coordination that already existed in Quebec through the CLSC. But why coordinate by contracting rather than by using public sector employees? Here the answer can be found in two places. One is the ideology of the Harris Conservatives. They added to earlier Ontario preferences for little state involvement in service delivery a strong preference for service provision by market-signals, or at least market-mimicking behaviour. However, sheer ideological preference, while important, is not the full explanation. After all, neo-liberalism was not absent in Quebec; both the PQ and the Liberals had their share.[49] However, Quebec's neo-liberalism has focused more on cutting spending than on eliminating an active role for the state. Thus, Dr. Rochon could initiate his *virage* to cut wage bills as much as to reduce the use of costly services. Moreover, the CLSC already existed as an institution that seemed to fill a need; it is less costly to run and relies on real volunteer labour for a range of supplementary services that, when they work, facilitate ambulatory care. In Ontario, because of previous decisions about cost-saving which had moved service delivery into the community, the only way to save more money was to alter the cost structures of those voluntary agencies. Thus different policy legacies, interventions by social forces promoting different ideological packages, and different institutional structures all help to account for the diverging trajectories.

What, finally, can we say about the consequences of these differences for the relationship between public and voluntary sectors in the two cases? Two observations can be made here. The first relates to the "private." In Ontario, it is easy to identify the involvement of commercial agencies in homecare; they have to seek contracts with the CCAC too. It is difficult to do the same in Quebec. The commercial sector in homecare is virtually invisible because it rarely interfaces with the public or voluntary sectors. Commercial agencies provide nursing services, and the CLSCs do hire from them on an as-needed basis. However, individuals using private homecare do not appear "in the system."[50] The CLSC provides lists of care-providers, but it is up to the individual to make use of them as he or she sees fit. This makes the debate about "commercialization" difficult to engage in the public arena. It is an area of great invisibility in the pluralist welfare state under construction. Because we know that the public-voluntary interface is not the only one of importance and that the situation among users of commercial services will affect that interface, the silence is not necessarily positive.

The second observation follows from the differences in the two cases in the situation of volunteers and their agencies. In Ontario, volunteers providing "supplementary" services complained of a lack of successful connection with the CCAC-organized system. In Quebec, in contrast, the CLSC constantly monitored its volunteer resources and the volunteers were in a close relationship (good or bad, as the case may be) with the CLSC. The reason for this difference in the two systems, which speaks loudly of the advantages of "community involvement," is in large part an institutional one. The patient is not the CCAC's patient. No one from that agency actually provides care; the maximum involvement is evaluation. This is a very arm's-distance or hands-off relationship to the dependent elderly, not one that encourages problem solving in the face of new needs or creative combinations of service mixes. In the Quebec model, primary responsibility for the patient remains with the CLSC, which *needs* the voluntary agency to provide care for *its* patients. It needs meals-on-wheels to deliver food. It needs transportation services and friendly visits. Therefore, our study found numerous examples of cobbled-together caring arrangements with shared involvement from volunteers as well as CLSC workers. It is ironic, then, that the neo-conservative "common sense" revolution advanced in the name of more community responsibility may have designed a large institution which will actually undermine the service delivery which the volunteers want so much to give. However, the story is not over in either jurisdiction and it is far too early to draw more than tentative conclusions about the direction of change in the social rights of citizenship, as refracted through this crucial category of care.

Notes

The support of the Kahanoff Nonprofit Research Initiative for this research is gratefully acknowledged. We also thank André Picard for his collaboration, particularly in the early stages of this project, and Eric Desrosiers, Rachel Laforest and Lisa Seguin for their superb assistance with the research.

[1] André Picard (1999, pp. A1, A8-9) reports statistics from Health Canada showing that 59 percent of Canadians doing informal caring work are women, and in the prime earning ages of 45-64, women out-number men by almost 2 to 1. Over 65 the gender division is virtually equal. Almost half (46 percent) of informal caring work involves a parent, with 16 percent going to a spouse.

[2] The term "pluralism" is adopted from the work of Adalbert Evers and his colleagues. See, for example, Evers and Svetlik (1993).

[3] The classic example here is, of course, Gøsta Esping-Andersen (1990). He is not alone in stressing the wage relation as crucial to postwar welfare states and regulation.

[4] Feminists were obviously among the first to note the amount of caring, and unpaid, work being done in households and the effects of such kinds of work on women's labour force participation and equality. It is not surprising that much of the discussion of caring, which is now a mainstream term, originated with feminist scholars. See the special issue of *Social Politics: International Studies in Gender, State and Society*, 4(3), 1997, on Gender and Care Work in Welfare States.

[5] Theda Skocpol (1998) describes this pattern in the United States, where the right-wing seeks to displace the state by evoking the language of civil society. She quotes Newt Gingrich's call to replace the welfare state with "volunteerism and spiritual renewal," Arianna Huffington's advocacy group, the Center for Effective Compassion, and the Heritage Foundation's renamed journal, *Policy Review: The Journal of American Citizenship*, which describes its mission as "applied Tocqueville." As she also says, the Clinton Democrats and Tony Blair's New Labour were not far behind in seeking the roots of renewal in civil society. Similar shifts in Canada are described in Paul LeDuc Browne (1995).

[6] This section is based on our general analysis of the Quebec system via the literature, and a detailed study, including interviews, of a single case, the voluntary-public sector relationship in the territory of the CLSC Côte-des-Neiges in Montreal.

[7] White (1992, p. 234) calls it an "*approche fondamentale et visionaire.*"

[8] The mission was, from the beginning, a mixed one. The discourse of Castonguay-Nepveu as well as CLSC "enthusiasts" modelled this new institution on people's clinics set up in the 1960s in neighbourhoods without adequate health-

care services. They would be the core of democratic community development, and therefore citizens had to be represented within the institution. Indeed, as White says (1992, p. 240), in Quebec public health meant community health. However, for the Quiet Revolution technocrats, the CLSC was a way to deliver health care that would address prevention before the need to cure. This was a discourse of professional public health-care workers.

[9]Doctors, in particular, opposed the implantation of CLSCs, which they saw as competing with private practice. In the beginning they boycotted the CLSCs and established private clinics where they would be paid a fee for service rather than salaried, as CLSC doctors were (White 1992, p. 239). At the same time, the CLSCs were criticized by community activists and unionists for being too closely tied to the state, and therefore incapable of being real forces for change (Favreau and Hurtubise 1993, p. 4).

[10]See, for example, Bélanger and Lévesque (1990, p. 243) who describe a properly functioning CLSC as a "utopian" form for the post-Fordist future.

[11]No mention was made of the role of the for-profit sector, seemingly because the minister at the time, Péquiste Denis Lazure, was strongly opposed to its involvement in the homecare domain (see Vaillancourt 1997). For the funding details, see Vaillancourt (1988, pp. 159-60).

[12]He had become a prominent businessman after leaving the Health Ministry over which he presided in the early 1970s.

[13]These RRSSS (Régie régionale de santé et de services sociaux) are responsible, *inter alia*, for the distribution of grants to the voluntary sector.

[14]The goal here might have been less to democratize than to weaken the power of other interests, especially unionized workers and health-care professionals.

[15]In the case of the SIMAD, the CLSC provided only 43 percent of the services, while nonprofits and commercial services accounted for 28 percent.

[16]The CLSC itself provides services of various kinds for dependent elderly and their caregivers. Visiting nurses provide the out-patient or ambulatory care and supervision needed after discharge from the hospital or in the case of chronic illness. In earlier years it also provided housekeeping services, but these have been substantially reduced. Social work and respite services are also available.

[17]In the case of medical care, and in the face of rising costs, CLSCs have developed the practice of referring clients who can afford to pay to commercial services as well, while keeping the lowest income clients in the nonprofit sector.

[18]Depending on the preferences of the elderly and their personal situations, there are also referrals to commercial services, and even black-market workers. These tend to be for supplementary health care, *gardiennage*, and housekeeping.

[19]The Régie régionale de Montréal-Cente, within which Côte-des-Neiges is located, recognizes 553 community groups in the area of health and social services, of which 76 are engaged in programs for homecare and four in general services for the elderly. Fully 90 percent are funded by the Régie régionale, with the grants ranging from $1,749 to $1,187,574 (RIOCM 1998, pp. 49-50).

[20] It is interesting to note that the territories of the CLSCs, which have responsibility for community development in the health-care sector, frequently correspond to the territories of the agencies created to foster socio-economic development, the Corporations du développement économique communautaire (CDEC).

[21] Having clients is obviously crucial, since funding in part depends on demonstrated service delivery.

[22] This is the major theme that emerged not only in Côte-des-Neiges but also out of the consultations organized by the RIOCM and its report, *Leur équilibre, notre déséquilibre*, the title of which says it all.

[23] In the area of homecare, such corporations developed through the 1990s. For several examples, see Vaillancourt (1997, pp. 31-32).

[24] We heard several times of lists kept by the CLSC of people willing to do housecleaning. The list was then made available to potential employers. It seems to have been a sort of "don't ask, don't tell" arrangement with respect to the tax situation.

[25] For this comparison see White, (1992, pp. 234-35).

[26] While in Quebec in these years about 10 percent more of provincial spending went to health and social services, the rate of increase was higher in Ontario. Between 1970 and 1989, Quebec's expenditures rose by 8.7 percent and in Ontario by 10.5 percent (White 1992, p. 236).

[27] It is perhaps worth noting that in Quebec, as we quoted above, these actors were termed "private" by the Rochon Commission and others.

[28] It established programs for homemaking and home-nursing care to be cost-shared 50/50 by the province and municipalities, and to be operated under the discretion of the municipalities. In the late1960s, the provincial and federal governments' share of costs rose to 80 percent and the program was extended to permit the provision of preventative, respite, and emergency services, producing a substantial increase in demand.

[29] Charges for these services were levied according to ability to pay.

[30] These services were provided at no cost to the client if certified by a physician as medically necessary.

[31] By 1970, provincial grants for these services had more than tripled and other provincially funded home-support services, such as day programs and respite care, were being offered independently of the EPCs.

[32] The Homecare Coordinator, for example, had no authority to assess needs for institutional care and, although assessments often were shared with the PCS, information was not used in a systematic way to manage growing waiting lists for long-term care.

[33] Greater coordination of planning and management at both the provincial and local levels between the Ministries of Health and of Community and Social Services was also part of the package.

[34] Whereas Ontario would have had 40 MSA, Quebec has over 150 CLSCs, for a smaller population.

[35] The government at least tacitly realized that the costs of this centralized administration would increase (see Montigny 1997, p. 140).

[36] The homecare services provided by the CCAC are: nursing visits, shift nursing (longer than two hours), homemaking (e.g., cleaning, meal preparation, laundry), physiotherapy, occupational therapy, speech-language therapy, nutrition services, and social work.

[37] Of course, this does not mean that clients have no costs. For many, the allotted number of nursing visits or hours of homemaking services may be inadequate for their needs, forcing them to purchase additional services at cost from community-based or commercial providers. Private purchase of service is becoming more frequent because the demand for CCAC services is growing rapidly — by 17 percent in 1997-98 alone — with the result that 28,000 people are currently awaiting community services or placement in long-term care facilities and allocations of homecare services have been quite tightly rationed. Ontario Community Support Association, "OCSA Media Release," March 1998, Toronto. Available at http://www.ocsa.on.ca/whatsnew/body_media.htm. Of the 17,700 people waiting for long-term care beds, almost 20 percent (3,340) were in hospitals in September 1997 according to the Ministry of Health.

[38] In 1998, even the services and activities provided by the community service associations were to have been brought under the CCAC umbrella, so that referral to these services would flow through the CCAC. However, these plans have been indefinitely delayed.

[39] The Ottawa-Carleton CCAC has a staff of 300 and an annual budget of $62 million and provides homecare services to 9,000 clients a year. We conducted interviews not only with senior CCAC staff, but with the executive directors or senior staff of 17 voluntary organizations who either contract with the CCAC or broker community support services through it. They were agencies providing nursing (which in fact use very few, if any, volunteers in their programming), homemaking, meals-on-wheels (which rely for their service delivery on hundreds of volunteers) and other community services. The latter are mainly geographically-based multi-service organizations that provide community support services (such as transportation, adult day programs, friendly visits, and social activities) not contracted through the CCAC, as well as some homemaking service that clients may purchase to "top-up" the allocation provided by the CCAC. These organizations tend to be community-based and make extensive use of volunteers for most of their programming.

[40] There is enormous variation in the criteria used and the bidding process across the CCACs in the province. Thus it has been difficult for nonprofit organizations to share experiences and expertise across the province. A second aspect of unfairness derives from the status of the nonprofit organizations. As registered charities, they must file publicly accessible T3010 forms with Revenue Canada that provide information about salaries of senior staff, total budgets, and proportion of revenue spent on administrative costs, among other things. This degree of financial

transparency does not apply to their for-profit competitors and many fear that such information is being used to aid their competitors in producing lower cost proposals. A third inequity is that the nonprofit organizations are responsible for the costs of pay equity, whereas the for-profits are not, the costs of which can be substantial. Apart from issues surrounding pay equity, the representatives of nonprofit organizations whom we interviewed indicated that they have attempted to be model employers, recognizing that the vast majority of their employees are women, and especially in homemaking, are often marginalized women.

[41] For a discussion of the dangers of commercial activity, see Zimmerman and Dart (1998).

[42] Most of these voluntary organizations have had their funding from the provincial government frozen for several years. The relatively small grants, usually about 15 percent of their annual budgets, received from municipal governments were expected to be eliminated in 1998 as a response by municipal governments to provincial downloading of service responsibilities.

[43] The average number of staff in the community service organizations is five in programming and three in administration.

[44] Of the 17 organizations whom we interviewed, three had recently relocated; three had cut staff (and two had increased the number of staff due to increased demands); six had had discussions with other organizations about mergers and one had recently done so.

[45] Fundraising is particularly difficult for the small community service organizations that have no staff or experience to bring to this task. Here the intervention by the provincial umbrella association, the Ontario Community Support Association (OCSA), was critical. It used its more substantial resources to hire a fundraising consultant on contract whose services were provided free of charge to local organizations.

[46] There are many vital services that are falling between the cracks in the current system, including respite care, care for psychiatric and cognitively impaired persons, services in rural areas, and assistance to poorer seniors who are growing in number.

[47] These are three variables identified as central to historical-sociological comparative analysis in Thelen and Steinmo (1992).

[48] This is the term Vaillancourt uses in "Quebec."

[49] One of the first ministers to call for user-fees in health-care was Jacques Parizeau in 1981 when he was minister of finance (Vaillancourt 1988, p. 141).

[50] This is not the case quite as much in the regions outside Montreal where the direct allowances require the CLSC to know more about the commercially available services.

References

Bélanger, P. and B. Lévesque. 1990. "Les système de santé et les services sociaux au Québec: crise des relations de travail et du mode de consommation," *Sociologie du travail*, 2:132-45.

Browne, P. LeDuc. 1995. *Love in a Cold World? The Voluntary Sector in an Age of Cuts*. Ottawa: Canadian Centre for Policy Alternatives.

Esping-Andersen, G. 1990. *The Worlds of Welfare Capitalism*. Princeton: Princeton University Press.

Evers, A. and I. Svetlik, eds. 1993. *Balancing Pluralism: New Welfare Mixes in Care for the Elderly*. Aldershot: Avebury.

Favreau, L. and Y. Hurtubise. 1993. *CLSC et communautés locales. La contribution de l'organisation communautaire*. Quebec: PUQ.

Gidron, B., R. Kramer and L.M. Salamon. 1992. *Government and the Third Sector: Emerging Relationships in Welfare States*. San Francisco: Jossey-Bass.

Government of Ontario. Task Force on Aging. 1981. *The Elderly in Ontario: An Agenda for the '80s*. Toronto: Secretariat for Social Development.

Hall, M.H., T. Knighton, P. Reed, P. Bussière, D. McRae and P. Bowen. 1998. *Caring Canadians, Involved Canadians: Highlights from the 1997 National Survey of Giving, Volunteering and Participating*, Cat. No. 71-542-XPE. Ottawa: Statistics Canada.

Hansmann, H. 1980. "The Role of Nonprofit Enterprise," *Yale Law Journal*, 89:835-98.

Jenson, J. 1997. "Who Cares?" *Social Politics: International Studies in Gender, State and Society*, 4(2):182-88.

Kane, R.L. and R.A. Kane. 1985. *A Will and a Way: What the United States Can Learn from Canada about Caring for the Elderly*. New York: Columbia University Press.

Kaufman, T. 1998. "Integrated Community Services in Quebec: Strengths and Weaknesses." Paper presented at conference on "Canada in International Perspectives," Queen's Institute on Social Policy, Kingston, Ontario.

Lesemann, F. and D. Nahmiash. 1993. "Canada: Logiques hospitalières et pratiques familiales des soins (Québec)," in *Les personnes âgées. Dépendance, soins et solididarités familiales. Comparaisons internationales*, ed. F. Lesemann and C. Martin. Paris: Documentation Française, Notes et Études documentaires.

Litwan, H. and E. Lightman. 1996. "The Development of Community Care Policy for the Elderly: A Comparative Perspective," *International Journal of Health Services*, 26(4):691-708.

Mayer, R. and L. Groulx. 1987. *Synthèse critique de la littérature sur l'évolution des services sociaux au Québec depuis 1960*. Document prepared for the Commission d'enquête sur les services de santé et les services sociaux. Quebec: Publications du Québec.

Milne, T. Forthcoming. "Community Care in Ontario: Networks and Social Capital." Unpublished PhD Dissertation, School of Public Administration, Carleton University.

Mishra, R., G. Laws, and P. Harding. 1988. "Ontario," in *Privatization and Provincial Social Services in Canada*, ed. J.S. Ismael and Y. Vaillancourt. Edmonton: University of Alberta Press.

Montigny, E.-A. 1997. *Foisted Upon the Government? State Responsibilities, Family Obligations, and the Care of the Dependent Aged in Late Nineteenth-Century Ontario*. Montreal and Kingston: McGill-Queen's University Press.

MSSS. 1997. *Discours officiels 1995*. Quebec: Publications du Québec.

O'Connor, J. 1997. "From Women in the Welfare State to Gendering Welfare State Regimes," *Current Sociology*, 44(2):4-123.

Organization for Economic Cooperation and Development (OECD). 1996. *Caring for Frail Elderly People*, Social Policy Studies No. 19, Paris: OECD.

Picard, A. 1998. *A Call to Alms: The New Face of Charities in Canada*. Toronto: The Atkinson Foundation.

_____ 1999. "Conscripted by Love," *The Globe and Mail*, 20 March, pp. A1, A8-9.

Regroupement intersectoriel des organismes communautaires de Montréal (RIOCM). 1998. *Leur équilibre, notre déséquilibre*. Montreal: RIOCM.

Roy, M. 1987. *Les CLSC. Ce qu'il faut savoir*. Montreal: Éds. Saint-Martin.

Salamon, L.M. 1995. *Partners in Public Service*. Baltimore: Johns Hopkins University Press.

Skocpol, T. 1998. "Unravelling from Above," *The American Prospect*, March-April, pp. 20-25.

Thelen, K. and S. Steinmo. 1992. "Historical Institutionalism in Comparative Politics," in *Structuring Politics: Historical Institutionalism in Comparative Analysis*, ed. S. Steinmo et al. New York: Cambridge University Press.

Vaillancourt, Y. 1988. "Quebec," in *Privatization and Provincial Social Services in Canada*, ed. J.S. Ismael and Y. Vaillancourt. Edmonton: University of Alberta Press.

_____ 1997. *Vers un nouveau partage des responsabilités dans les services sociaux et de santé: rôle de l'État, du marché, de l'économie sociale et du secteur informel.* Montreal: Cahiers du laboratoire de recherche sur les pratiques et les politiques sociales.

Ware, A. 1989. *Between Profit and State: Intermediate Organisations in Britain and the United States.* Princeton: Princeton University Press.

Weisbrod, B.A. 1988. *The Nonprofit Economy.* Cambridge, MA: Harvard University Press.

White, D. 1992. "La santé et les services sociaux: réforme et remises en question," in *Le Québec en jeu. Comprendre les grands défis,* ed. G. Daigle. Montreal: Presses de l'Université de Montréal.

Williams, A.M. 1996. "The Development of Ontario's Home Care Program: A Critical Geographical Analysis," *Social Science and Medicine,* 42(6):937-48.

Zimmerman, B. and R. Dart. 1998. *Charities Doing Commercial Ventures: Societal and Organizational Implications.* Toronto: Trillium Foundation and CPRN.

3

Religious Nonprofits: Social Service Provision by Congregations in Ontario

Femida Handy and Ram A. Cnaan

In 1994, there were 71,413 charities registered in Canada, of which 36 percent are classified as "places of worship," making them the single largest category of charities. Places of worship include the mix of congregations related to Christian, Jewish, Islamic, and other denominations.[1] They number 25,458 in Canada, of which 9,253 (37 percent) are registered in Ontario, where they also represent by far the single largest category of charities. However, congregations account for only 6 percent of the $90.5 billion revenues received by all registered charities. A sizable portion (60 percent) of charitable organizations' revenues comes from government; congregations receive fewer government dollars than any other charitable type including private foundations. Only 1 percent of congregational revenues come from the government. The bulk of these revenues come from private giving (81 percent), the rest from earned income (18 percent). Congregations receive the highest percentage of their budget from private giving compared to any other type of registered charity (Hall and Macpherson 1997).

Congregations emerge as ubiquitous, almost wholly privately funded charities. They are best known as local churches, temples, mosques, synagogues, and other places of worship, and are often viewed as member organizations where individuals go to fulfil spiritual and religious needs. Yet, there is another important role congregations play in society that is rarely documented.[2] It is their commitment to the provision of social services to their communities. From the earliest days of the nation to the present time, religious congregations in Canada have been providing for both the spiritual and social welfare of their congregants and communities (Marks 1995; Martin 1985). Indeed, involvement of congregations in local social services in North America is a legacy from English colonial rule (Coll 1969).

In *An Essential Grace*, Martin (1985) documents the role of churches in the provision of social services in Canada. As early as the eighteenth century, the church played an important role in dispensing and financing many social services, providing relief for the poor and educational services in the communities. However, churches relied largely on government for financial support for these initiatives. For example, in Lower Canada government grants to help the poor were only given to religious communities organized for such philanthropic work. In Upper Canada such work was also financed by government grants, given to both churches and private organizations.

By the mid-nineteenth century almost every church had a charitable organization connected to it and was involved in providing some social services including health and education (Martin 1985). Although the state and secular private organizations started assuming a larger role in education, health, aid to the poor, and other philanthropic work by the late nineteenth century, churches continued to provide similar services. Records from the 1890s in Ontario show that congregations in large and small towns provided assistance to the poor; and most congregations had a fund for the poor of some sort with much of their funding coming from municipal grants (Marks 1995). Only at the beginning of the twentieth century did the balance tip decisively, with religious-based social services in North America giving way to secular services and churches receiving less state funding to assist in the provision of social services (Martin 1985). By the mid-twentieth century, the secularization of society and evolution of the welfare state led to the assumption that religious congregations, no longer financed by the government, did not play a critical role in social service delivery (Cnaan 1997).

Nevertheless, recent studies have shown that, despite dramatic growth in public welfare this century, local religious congregations have not forfeited their social responsibilities. These studies are exclusively done in the United States. Cnaan's studies (1996, 1997) of Philadelphia-based congregations and of six cities in the US, a Chicago-based study by the Community Workshop on Economic Development (1991), and a national survey by Hodgkinson *et al.* (1993) all report extensive involvement of congregations in local social service provision.[3]

For many decades, community involvement by congregations has been targeted to a variety of causes. Congregations are hubs for a range of neighbourhood services, from daycare centres and Boy/Girl Scout programs to senior citizen centres and shelters for the homeless. Churches have done all this while remaining centres of worship. The facilities that congregations use to house their religious and community activities range from store fronts to historic structures, often of architectural grandeur and importance. These buildings may be found in thriving downtown areas and suburbs, ethnic neighbourhoods, and small rural communities. Historically, congregations of all denominations have served not only as religious centres but also as community centres and as innovators in the provision of social services.[4]

Little is known in Canada about the extent of social and community involvement of religious congregations, and that which is known is not well-documented.[5] While anecdotal evidence indicates extensive involvement in social service activities, a systematic and multi-city study is needed to determine the extent to which religious congregations use their resources to benefit the greater community.

With increasing devolution, both at the federal and provincial level, and cutbacks in social service provision, many politicians and community leaders have urged private nonprofit agencies to fill the gaps.[6] For example, in Ontario the *Social Assistance Reform Act* (Bill 142) reduced many of the social services provided by the government, and thus needs such as homelessness have dramatically increased (Ontario Social Safety Network 1996). If private nonprofit organizations, including congregations, are expected to help shoulder the burden of meeting society's needs, it is necessary to document their capacity to do so.[7]

This study documents and analyzes the current involvement of religious congregations in social service provision. In addition, it addresses important related policy issues. There has been some discussion of religious congregations as essentially membership organizations that provide benefits to their own members only. This has led some commentators to question whether they deserve to retain their charitable status (Brooks 1999). This is an important policy question, and it is therefore necessary to document whether congregational activities are oriented to their own members only. Thus, the main questions addressed by this research are: To what extent are congregations involved in the provision of social services? What are the nature of the services offered? Who benefits from the services? And what is the financial value of social and community programs provided by congregations?

STUDY DESIGN

Although a national study would be ideal to document the role of congregations in Canada, due to the limited resources we concentrate on urban congregations in southern Ontario. This will give us a preliminary indication of the role of congregations and form a stepping stone to a larger more comprehensive national study which must include suburban and rural congregations. We chose three cities for our study: Kingston, London, and Toronto, which represent small, medium, and large urban centres respectively in southern Ontario.

The study is an in-depth survey of local religious congregations in these three urban areas. For each city, we obtained lists of congregations from the telephone directory and the local Council of Churches. From the combined lists, we generated a random list of congregations to be studied in each city. We telephoned the clergy, described our research project and asked them if they would consent to be interviewed. This was followed by a letter and information on the project and research team. The sample includes 15 congregations in Kingston, 15 congregations in London, and 16 congregations in Toronto for which we were successful in completing interviews. All 46 congregations were generous with their time as the interviews often lasted well over the allocated time of two hours. The interview was conducted at the congregation premises with the clergy, lay leaders, and members who were most involved in service provision. Where necessary, subsequent telephone calls were made to complete data collection and for triangulation of data.

In carrying out this study, we used a comprehensive range of research instruments or questionnaires to determine the congregation's role in the provision of social services.[8] The first instrument asks for general descriptors of the congregation such as denomination, geographical stability, membership, ethnicity of members, governance, history, future plans, staff, budgets, etc. The second instrument elicits the breadth of the community and social services provided by the congregation. The third instrument asks for details for up to five programs offered by each congregation. This instrument asks for data on service provision including the specific hours of volunteer and paid time, who and how many benefited from the program, who initiated the program, the reasons for initiating the program, space provision, etc. We limited our data collection to a maximum of five services to reduce the burden on our interviewees.

FINDINGS

Sample Characteristics

The first instrument provided a portrait of the congregations including membership size, ethnicity, age, and income. Membership size varied widely among the congregations. The mean membership for the sample was 433 members. The number of members ranged from a low of 39 to a high of 5,500 (SD = 818). Although the sample included a large majority of Christian congregations, as seen in Table 1, it was not exclusively so, and was fairly representative of the population.[9] The ethnic composition of congregations in the sample revealed considerable homogeneity, as indicated in Table 2. Many of the congregations were composed solely or primarily of one ethnic group: 38 congregations (83 percent) reported that three-quarters or more of their members belonged to one ethnic group and 16 of those congregations (35 percent) reported that all of their members belonged to one ethnic group. Not surprisingly, given the Ontario

Table 1: Congregations by Denomination

	Kingston N=15 (%)	London N=15 (%)	Toronto N=16 (%)	Ontario Total N=46 (%)
Presbyterian	1 (6.7)	1 (6.7)	2 (12.5)	4 (8.7)
Baptist	-	1 (6.7)	1 (6.3)	2 (4.3)
Methodist	1 (6.7)	-	-	1 (2.2)
Catholic	3 (20)	1 (6.7)	-	4 (8.7)
Lutheran	1 (6.7)	1 (6.7)	-	2 (2.2)
Anglican	1 (6.7)	3 (20)	6 (37.5)	10 (21.7)
Christian Missionary Alliance	3 (20)	-	-	3 (6.5)
United Church of Canada (UCC)	1 (6.7)	3 (20)	2 (12.5)	6 (13)
Other*	4 (26.7)	5 (33.3)	5 (31.3)	14 (30.4)

Notes: * Includes Independent churches, Synagogues, Islamic, Salvation Army, Mennonite, Nazarene, and other non-denominational congregations.
Numbers appearing in brackets denote the congregations in cell as a percentage of N in that column.

Table 2: Ethnic Composition of Congregations by City

	Kingston N=15 (%)	London N=15 (%)	Toronto N=16 (%)	Ontario Total N=46 (%)
A. Percent of congregations with 100% membership				
Asian	1 (6.7)	-	1 (6.3)	2 (4.3)
Caucasian	7 (46.7)	4 (26.7)	2 (12.5)	13 (28.3)
Hispanic	-	-	1 (6.3)	1 (2.2)
Total	8 (53.4)	4 (26.7)	4 (25)	16 (34.8)
B. Percent of congregations with 75% or more membership				
African-American	-	-	1 (6.3)	1 (2.2)
Asian	2 (13.3)	-	1 (6.3)	3 (6.5)
Caucasian	11 (73.3)	13 (86.7)	9 (56.3)	33 (71.7)
Hispanic	-	-	1 (6.3)	1 (2.2)
Total	13 (86.6)	13 (86.7)	12 (75)	38 (82.6)

Note: Numbers appearing in brackets denote the congregations in cell as a percentage of N in that column.

population, the most dominant group was Caucasian. However, it is also striking the extent to which minority communities established their "own" congregations.

The mean age of the congregations in our sample was 73 years. The oldest congregation in the sample was founded in 1797, the newest in 1994 (SD= 60). Many congregations reported that they have been at the same location for many years. The number of years a congregation has been housed in the same property averaged 50 years, with a range from one to 145 years (SD = 43). Although congregations are often housed in buildings that are costly to maintain, only a few in the sample considered relocating. When asked "Are/were there plans for a relocation of the congregation from its current building?" only 3 of 46 (6.5 percent) congregations answered positively. The low percentages is a strong indication that congregations consider themselves a permanent fixture of their community. In an era of high geographical mobility, congregations are stable community institutions and are often viewed as a permanent fixture of the neighbourhood. Individuals who do not belong to a congregation can often identify the local congregation as part of their personal landscape in their own communities.

To determine the strength of the congregations, we asked about their operating budgets. An overwhelming majority of congregations reported operating budgets that ranged between $50,000 and $500,000 (Table 3). These budgets are exclusive of building funds and school budgets. Another indicator of congregational strength is the existence of a full-time paid clergy. In Table 4, we report the results regarding the number of paid clergy. Only 15 percent of the congregations reported not having any full-time staff, and approximately 20 percent have two or more staff members.

Since many of the social services delivered by the congregation are done on-site, we asked who was responsible for making decisions regarding the use of the buildings. With the exception of one congregation whose decisions were made by the denominational office, all decisions were made in-house, the majority by an executive committee of the congregation (board, vestry, deacons). In other cases, decisions were made by the clergy (pastor or lay leader) or special committees. This suggests that local decision making is often fine-tuned to the resources of the congregation and the needs of the community.

Table 3: Operating Budgets of Congregations by City

	Kingston N=15 (%)	London N=15 (%)	Toronto N=16 (%)	Ontario Total N=46 (%)
Under $50,000	-	-	1	1 (2.2)
$50,001-$100,000	6 (40)	3 (20)	4 (25)	13 (28.3)
$100,001-$200,000	8 (53.3)	10 (66.7)	3 (18.8)	21 (45.7)
$200,001-$500,000	-	2 (13.3)	7 (13.8)	9 (19.6)
$500,001-$1,000,000	-	-	-	-
$1,000,000+	1 (6.3)	-	1 (6.3)	2 (4.3)

Note: Numbers appearing in brackets denote the congregations in cell as a percentage of N in that column.

Table 4: Number of Paid Clergy

No. of Clergy	Kingston N=15 (%)	London N=15 (%)	Toronto N=16 (%)	Ontario Total N=46 (%)
None	2 (19.3)	2 (19.3)	3 (18.8)	7 (15.2)
One	11 (53.3)	10 (66.7)	9 (56.3)	30 (65.2)
Two or more	2 (19.3)	3 (20)	4 (25)	9 (19.6)

Note: Numbers appearing in brackets denote the congregations in cell as a percentage of N in that column.

Social Service Delivery

We used the second instrument to determine the scope of social and community services provided by the congregation. Interviewees were asked whether their congregation had provided, within the past 12 months, any of the services listed in our instrument. The list consisted of some 200 services that had been identified from congregational literature, previous work of the research team, and consultation with experts in the field. We included *only* non-religious services and excluded those services that were integral to the faith traditions such as communal prayers, Bible classes, or religious worship services. Details of the survey are provided in Appendix One.

Table 5: Most Commonly Offered Programs

Program	Ontario N=46 (%)
Food pantries	38 (82.6)
International relief	37 (80.4)
Clothing closets	36 (78.3)
Choral groups	29 (63)
Recreational program (for teens)	31 (67.4)
Soup kitchen	28 (60.9)
Shelter for men	26 (56.5)
Shelter for women/children	25 (54.3)
Summer day camp	25 (54.3)
Hospital visitation	25 (54.3)
Community bazaars/fairs	25 (54.3)
Interfaith collaboration	25 (52.2)
Music performances	23 (50)
Recreational programs for children	22 (47.8)
Recreational programs for the elderly	21 (45.7)
Visitation—buddy programs	21 (45.7)
Cubs/Boys/Girls/Brownies—Scouts	21 (45.7)
Holiday celebrations	21 (45.7)
Financial assistance (poor and homeless)	20 (43.5)
Summer programs (teens)	20 (43.5)
Intergenerational programs	20 (43.5)
Alliance with neighbourhood associations	14 (30.4)
AA	14 (30.4)

Note: Numbers appearing in brackets denote the congregations in cell as a percentage of N.

The results indicate that 41 different services are carried out by more than a quarter of the congregations in the sample. The range of services is impressive: counselling programs for families; programs for the elderly; programs for children and youth; programs for the homeless, poor and other needy persons; health programs; educational programs for adults; community security programs; arts and cultural programs; community organizations and development; and a diverse set of social concerns. Table 5 presents the 24 most frequent services. More than 75 percent of congregations dispense food, clothing, and international relief. Soup kitchens, services for the homeless, shelters for men, shelters for women and children, and hospital visitation are offered by over 50 percent of the congregations. Cultural activities such as choral groups and music performances were also supported by over half of the congregations as were special programs such as summer day camps, recreational programs for teenagers, community bazaars, and fairs. More than 45 percent of the congregations provided space for Scouts/Guides/Cubs/ Brownies and over 30 percent provided space for Alcoholic Anonymous meetings. These findings illustrate the wide variety of social services supported by many congregations, and the ways in which their services, with the exception of international relief, are linked to the needs of the local community.

Comparing Cities in Ontario

In Ontario, as noted earlier, there has been a continued downloading of responsibilities in social services from the federal to provincial government and from the provincial to municipal level. Provincial governments, unable to meet demands on shrinking federal grants, have responded by cutting back in their funding for services (Shields and Evans 1998). All three cities have suffered from these cuts. Additionally, there has been an emphasis on privatization of public service programs with an additional emphasis on voluntarism (Day and Devlin 1997). Although all three cities are affected, it is of interest to see if there are any differences in the kinds of services provided and whether these differences reflect the size of the city and its particular characteristics. This would give additional weight to the hypothesis that congregations respond uniquely to the needs of their communities.[10] *Kingston* is the smallest city in our sample, with a population of 56,597 (1991), and has experienced an annual growth rate in population of 7.6 percent between 1981 and 1991 (KAEDC Business Development 1997). Congregations in this city provided more programs per congregation than those in Toronto and London. More than 86 percent of the congregations in Kingston provided *five or more* programs, whereas the corresponding number for London and Toronto were 60 percent and 25 percent respectively. Congregations in Kingston were involved in more services pertaining to counselling and other programs for families, especially in the area of parenting skills, abortion and pro-life counselling, and teen pregnancy. In programs for the homeless and the poor, there were no outreach programs in Kingston, in stark contrast to a 50 percent participation rates in London and Toronto. Kingston congregations had greater participation in programs dealing with prisoners than London or Toronto, reflecting the concentration of prisons in Kingston. Congregations were heavily involved in programs for the homeless and the poor, such as "housing for the needy." In light of the recent report by the Social Planning Council of Kingston and Area that the housing and hunger crises were among the top human service priorities (Kingston. Social Planning Council 1996), as congregations appear to be responding to the most pressing needs in society.

Congregations in Kingston were most active in "educational opportunities" programs. Their participation in this category was particularly striking: 16 programs were offered in Kingston in contrast to only two in London and three in Toronto. This may be related to the presence of two universities and a community college. In programs related to the local environmental action and voter registration, Kingston also had the highest participation.

The 1991 Census reported the population of *London* as over 381,000, making it the second largest city in our sample. The average family income is 20 percent less than Toronto in 1991. London congregations participated more in programs for immigrants and refugee resettlement than did congregations in the other two cities, reflecting the large refugee population in the city. In 1991, immigrants comprised 19 percent of the population as compared to the provincial average of 16 percent, and 38 percent of them came as refugees compared to the provincial average of 15 percent (United Way of London and Middlesex 1994). In programs related to seniors, London offered 25 percent fewer programs than Toronto, and in this respect it was similar to Kingston. In programs related to children and youth, London congregations were more heavily involved but they had very low participation in daycare and tutoring programs. London congregations were heavily invested in services for the homeless and poor people and "housing for the needy." They were unique in their heavy (60 percent) involvement with "transitional living programs" in stark contrast to congregations in the other cities which sponsored almost no such programs. This commitment, however, manifested itself primarily as support for services provided by other organizations. Programs related to "community security" were found more in London than compared with Toronto. In the arts and culture programs, with the exception of music-related programs (where congregations in all the cities actively participated), congregations in London participated the least.

Toronto is a large metropolis of 2.4 million people, the largest city in our sample. It is relatively slow growing as compared to the surrounding Greater Toronto area (GTA). Congregations in Toronto were more active in seniors' programs than London and Kingston. This comes as no surprise as Toronto has a large number of seniors and, in general, seniors are more likely to be involved with their congregations.[11] There were no striking differences in the type or number of programs offered for counselling and family, and programs for children and youth. In programs for the homeless and the poor, Toronto congregations offered no programs for transitional living and had the greatest number of health-care programs for the homeless. Very few programs for refugee resettlement and immigrants were offered. This is surprising given that Toronto attracts many immigrants: 42 percent of all new arrivals to Canada settle in Toronto. It is likely that services for immigrants and refugees in a large city such as Toronto are being provided by other secular private or public organizations.

Toronto's congregations, unlike those in Kingston and London, were involved in neighbourhood cleanup and civic beautification, but were not involved in programs dealing with abortion and pro-life advocacy or environmental action. This again may reflect the large number of secular organizations that exist in Toronto which deal with such issues. Only one Toronto congregation participated in the Habitat for Humanity program in contrast to a 40-percent participation rate for Kingston and London, but they were more likely to collaborate with housing corporations and other groups to assist in providing housing for the needy.

These findings point to interesting inter-city variations in the types of social programs supported by congregations. This backs the hypothesis that congregations do respond to local issues and community needs and differences in the strengths of other organizations in their city.

Beneficiaries and Costs

In the third instrument we asked each congregation to identify *up to* five programs that were most representative of their social and community involvement. For each of these programs, respondents were asked to provide details: the nature of the program, funding levels, the beneficiaries, where it was carried out, whether the congregation derived any income from the program, etc. Since we limited our data collection to no more than five programs from each congregation, the findings that follow come from a total of 190 programs reported by the 46 congregations, a mean of 4.13 programs per congregation.[12] The following categories of services are most frequently provided programs for children/teens (41 programs); food servicing/distribution (30 programs); programs for the poor (21 programs); programs for the elderly (18 programs); programs for men and women (16 programs); programs for families and parents (12 programs); programs for the homeless (12 programs); programs for refugees and immigrants (11 programs); space provision to others (11 programs); and others (52 programs).

As noted earlier, some commentators have suggested that congregations are membership organizations that primarily look after their own members (Brooks 1999). While this is true when members meet for religious and spiritual purposes, it is not a comprehensive picture of what congregations do. To determine who benefits from the social programs, we asked the respondents to indicate for each program: (i) the total number of individuals served monthly and (ii) the total number of non-members served monthly. We also asked for the numbers of members and non-members involved in providing each service. The mean number of participants *per program* provided by or housed in a local religious congregation was 142.92.[13] Of these beneficiaries, 27.12 were members and 115.80 were non-members. Beneficiaries were thus four times more likely (4.27 :1) to be non-members than members. Toronto reported the highest ratio in favour of serving others (6.86 :1); those in London and Kingston were lower (3.52 :1 and 3.75 :1 respectively). This may suggest that in larger cities, congregations are able to attract greater numbers of participants and have access to resources that allow them to reach out to serve more members in the communities.[14]

An interesting complement to the issue of "who benefits" is "who provides" the services. Non-members provide some services in full (such as AA or Boy Scout meetings), and assisted members in other cases. Members were slightly outnumbered by non-members in the provision of service by a ratio of 0.88 :1. This ratio suggests that non-members played an active role in providing services, either participating with congregation members or using congregations' buildings for their own programs.

Overall, these findings strongly indicate that local religious congregations should be viewed, not as member-serving organizations only, but as charitable organizations concerned with the welfare of others. Although members and non-members were likely to provide services that congregations offered, the recipients were more likely to be non-members by a ratio of more than four to one. The focus of most services provided by congregations was the amelioration of community life. They not only provide services to others directly and in partnership with other organizations, but they also make their facilities available for a wide range of community activities.

We asked the respondents to assess their program costs, to the best of their ability. We focused on the following types of costs: monetary support provided by the congregation, type of space used and its assessed value, in-kind support, utilities cost, and amount of time (total hours worked by clergy, staff, and volunteers). We asked the respondents to assess the *monthly* cost of the program, regardless of whether the program was offered daily, weekly, or annually. We then placed an economic value on all of the in-kind contributions. In order to measure the net costs incurred by congregations, we asked our respondents to report any revenues generated by their programs, such as rental fees and in-kind support. With these data, we were then able to calculate the net costs of the social services provided by our congregations. Details of the calculations are provided in Appendix Two.

The costs of these programs are clearly significant. The annual average total costs of a single program is over $36,000, and the net costs are over $35,000. Since congregations provide an average of 4.13 programs, the overall cost is almost $145,000 per congregation. By any standard, this is a notable contribution to the well-being of their local communities.

Another way to assess the contribution of congregations to their community is the percentage of their annual operating budget allocated to social ministry (also known as social action, social outreach, and community outreach). The mean percentage of the operating budget allocated to social ministry was 22.35 percent. In all three cities, the mean percentage allocated to social ministry was higher than that of tithing (10 percent). Although collectives such as congregations are not theologically expected to tithe, many of our interviewees — clergy and lay leaders alike — expressed a collective desire to tithe by allocating a certain amount of the congregational budget and staff work time to support the needs of others locally or globally. The exception to this pattern was some congregations that are struggling financially, and reported social spending below the 10-percent level. In general, however, congregations intentionally and directly support their community. Moreover, in-kind support (volunteer hours, utilities, rent, and the like) should be considered in addition to the percentage of the operating budget in order to get a broader picture of congregational giving.

How and Why Do Congregations Get Involved?

A congregational decision to assist the needy is not a random one. Social ministry requires that a need be identified and that someone propose a response. As seen in Table 6, social programs provided by religious congregations are initiated by many actors. Those most influential in initiating social services were individual members and the clergy. Other champions included congregational committees and human service organizations. Kingston was unique in the number of programs initiated by human service organizations; government agencies and staff members had influence in Kingston but almost no impact in London and Toronto. In general, external organizations such as diocese or judicatory organizations, neighbourhood community coalitions, government agencies, other congregations, and human-service organizations had little influence in initiating programs. Thus, it is the internal participants and those directly affiliated with the congregation that influence the decision to embark upon a new social program.

When respondents were asked why their congregation had initiated new programs, other than responding to an evident need, an interesting finding emerged. Of the 190 programs, 18 percent had been initiated due to a change in the community. Cutbacks in government spending accounted for 14 percent at the provincial level and 8 percent at both the local and federal level. Congregations did not see themselves as directly responding to government cutbacks by stepping in to fill the gaps created, but were responding to the social needs resulting in their communities due to the cutbacks.

Table 6: Persons/Groups as Initiators of Programs by City*

Initiator	Kingston N=15 (%)	London N=15 (%)	Toronto N=16 (%)	Ontario Total N=46 (%)
Clergy	33 (45.8)	24 (37.5)	24 (44.4)	81 (42.6)
Staff member(s)	6 (8.3)	-	1 (1.9)	7 (3.7)
Member(s)/groups	43 (59.7)	30 (46.9)	21 (38.9)	94 (49.5)
Congregational committee	11 (15.3)	6 (9.4)	5 (9.3)	22 (11.6)
Diocese/judicatory	6 (8.3)	1 (1.6)	5 (9.3)	12 (6.3)
Other congregation	1 (1.4)	1 (1.6)	-	2 (1.1)
Human service organization	10 (13.9)	-	1 (1.9)	11 (5.8)
Neighbourhood com. coalition	4 (5.6)	1 (1.6)	3 (5.6)	8 (4.2)
Government agency	6 (8.3)	-	2 (3.7)	8 (4.2)

Notes: *Totals for each city yield more than 100 as the answers to each question were not mutually exclusive.
Numbers appearing in brackets denote the congregations in cell as a percentage of N in that column.

Table 7: Reasons for Initiating a Program by City

Reason*	Kingston N=15 (%)	London N=15 (%)	Toronto N=16 (%)	Ontario Total N=46 (%)
Local public spending	11 (15.3)	1 (1.6)	3 (5.6)	15 (7.9)
Province/state spending	18 (25)	3 (4.7)	6 (11.1)	27 (14.2)
Federal spending	11 (15.3)	-	4 (7.4)	15 (7.9)
Redlining of existing program	1 (1.4)	-	2 (3.7)	3 (1.6)
Community change	24 (33.3)	3 (4.7)	8 (14.8)	35 (18.4)

Notes: *In addition to responding to an evident need.
Numbers appearing in brackets denote the congregations in cell as a percentage of N in that column.

CONCLUSION

We find that congregations in urban centres in southern Ontario are well established in their relative communities, having operated in the same location for an average of over 70 years. Most of the congregations are relatively homogenous and composed primarily of one ethnic group; an overwhelming majority report operating budgets that ranged between $50,000 and $500,000. All congregations are providing at least one social service in their community, with an average of 4.13 programs per congregation. We find considerable variety in the types of programs offered by congregations in different cities, suggesting that congregations meet unique and specific needs within their communities. Over half the congregations provide programs that meet the following societal needs: food pantries, international relief, clothing closets, choral groups, recreational programs for teens, soup kitchens, shelters for men, shelters for women/children, summer day camp, hospital visitation, community bazaars/fairs, interfaith collaboration, and music performances. These and other programs cover a wide range of human needs and collectively form an impressive network of social and community services.

Congregations provide their social services overwhelmingly for non-members, with a ratio among beneficiaries of over 4:1 in favour of non-members to members. Religious congregations clearly channel their energies into the delivery of important social and community services to the public good. Thus, we do not consider congregations to be membership organizations in their social ministry, and find them legitimately registered as charities by the definition used by Revenue Canada in administering the *Income Tax Act*.

Although all congregations assisted services financially and with in-kind resources, the major contributions were volunteer hours donated and the provision of space. Of all programs, 87 percent reported the use of volunteers and 70 percent provided space. Accounting for volunteer labour and other such resources, we estimated the average gross value of a program to be over $36,000 per year. When we deduct all cash and in-kind support that congregations receive as revenue or resources for their programs, we find the *net contribution* to be over $35,000 per program per year. The value of congregational support is estimated to be almost $145,00 per congregation per year. With an estimated 25,458 congregations registered in Canada and 9,253 in Ontario (Hall and Macpherson 1997, p. 4), the total contribution to social services by congregations is clearly significant.

The initiative for these programs comes largely from individual members or groups of members and the clergy. Although 30 percent of the programs reported were initiated due to changes resulting from spending cutbacks by all levels of government, respondents emphatically reported that the initiative to offer the service came from within the congregations and clergy and not as a direct response to public cuts. Congregations do *not* see themselves as substitutes to government in providing social services, but they do respond to some of the immediate needs in their local communities regardless of why the needs arise.

This is the first study of Ontario congregations to present evidence on the involvement of congregations in the provision of social services.[15] The findings, preliminary as they are, suggest that congregations are actively involved in the provision of social services based on the needs of their local communities. Although congregations provide an array of social services which are not explicitly coordinated, one can find congregational-based services to meet almost any human need. Although the congregations' primary goal is religious worship, they are also an important part of our nation's social safety net. In part because of the separation of church and state in North American societies, many community leaders are uncomfortable with the notion that religious congregations consider the provision of social services to be part of their ministry. The role of congregations in the provision of social services is therefore often overlooked in public debate.

It should also be stressed, however, that no matter how much congregations attempt to provide in terms of social services, they cannot come close to filling the gaps created by the state devolution (Salamon 1995; Steinberg 1996). Although congregations provide an impressive net of services that are important locally, they can merely complement services provided by the public sector. Social and community service provision is a secondary goal of religious congregations and the nature and magnitude of services depend upon the congregation's ability to mobilize sufficient resources and human capital to that end.

Congregations fulfil an important role in our society, not simply in the provision of social services. Verba, Schlozman and Brady (1995) found local religious congregations to be the most important source of civic competence in contemporary America. In an era in which mutual aid societies are practically vanishing, traditional lodges and fraternal orders are rapidly declining (Hall 1996; Putnam 1995), and large corporations downsize and relocate, there is one community institution — the congregation — that is still active and visible in most communities. Religious congregations use their internal social and human capital to generate other activities unrelated to worship. As noted by Coleman (1988), social organizations formed for one purpose that then expand to serve other purposes not only realize the social capital inherent in the organization but expand it, creating a multiplier effect. As many of the activities undertaken by congregations are extended to non-members in their communities or involve coalitions with local organizations, congregations contribute to a sense of community and enlarge the social capital of their neighbourhoods. Rooted in their communities, congregations clearly enhance the local quality of life and contribute to the formation of social capital in contemporary society.

Notes

First and foremost, to the many clergy and lay-leaders who participated in our study, we are grateful for their cooperation and goodwill. The data collection, computer assistance and data entry required the work of many research assistants: Lynn Graham, Rob Mound, Tasmin Rajott, Laurie Uytterlinde Flood, Mat Greenwood, Karin Prochazka, Huaquing Zhao, Ami Dalal and Stephanie Boddie. We appreciate their commitment and enthusiasm. We thank Michael Hall for helpful comments and for providing us with valuable references. We remain solely responsible for any mistakes and omissions. Financial support for this study was provided by the Kahanoff Foundation's Nonprofit Sector Research Initiative through the School of Policy Studies, Queen's University. Research support was also received from the Faculty of Environmental Studies, York University. Additional support for Dr. Cnaan's work came from the Lilly Endowment.

[1] Places of worship do not include convents, monasteries, religious foundations and trusts, missionary organizations or corporations. They are classified under "religion" and account for 7.3 percent of registered charities (Hall and Macpherson 1997).

[2] The 12 April 1993 issue of *MacLean's*, Canada's weekly news magazine contained a 16-page cover story on religion in Canada. However, the congregations' role in the provision of social services or community involvement is not alluded to even once.

[3] Similar findings are reported by La Barbera (1991); Ammerman and Roof (1995); and Wineburg (1994) for other cities in the United States.

[4] Several scholars have commented on the role of congregations. Bellah (1991); and McDougall (1993) have stated that congregations are more than places of worship; they are places where people can come together and can organize to attend to the needs in their communities. The theology and teachings of major religions emphasize mutual responsibility to the weak and poor, which legitimates their involvement in providing for the indigent in the community (Cnaan with Wineburg and Boddie 1999; Queen 1996).

[5] Congregations are excluded from a recent study of religious nonprofit organizations in Alberta (Hiemstra 1999).

[6] A trend started by the Canadian federal government to reduce the federal deficit of $22 billion in 1995 resulted in downloading health and welfare responsibilities to provinces. Provincial governments responded by cutting back on many services hitherto provided (*The Economist* 1998, p. 37).

[7] In an open letter to the Premier of Ontario, the leaders of multi-faith religious congregations urged Premier Harris to revise Bill 142. Changes and cutbacks in provincial funding have increased dependence on religious and secular nonprofit agencies that were not equipped to respond (Dr. Brice Balmer, *Toronto Star*, 2 November 1996). Similar trends exist in the US. Under section 104 of the *Personal Responsibility and Work Opportunity Reconciliation Act* of 1996 signed by President Clinton, religious organizations are encouraged to apply for state and local grants to provide social services. These services might maintain the religious character and integrity of the organization (Esbeck 1997).

[8] We used instruments by Cnaan (1997) modified for the Canadian context.

[9] The "other" category included Synagogues and Islamic mosques, and non-denominational Christian congregations. This group represented 30 percent of the sample which compares to the 35 percent population "other" category (Sharpe 1994). Catholic congregations are highly underrepresented in the sample as compared to the national population, this is due to the large number of Catholic congregations outside Ontario in Quebec.

[10] It is of interest that international relief, not a local concern, was favoured as a program by congregations in all three cities with a mean participation rate of over 80 percent.

[11] Toronto's residents include a greater proportion of people 65 years and older living in the GTA. It is projected that by the year 2001, 10.9 percent of all metropolitan residents will be 70 years and older.

[12] One hundred percent of the congregations provided at least one program and 56 percent provided five or more programs. Our limit of five programs underestimates the social service provision of congregations. These numbers are similar to those found in the US (Hodgkinson *et al.* 1993; Cnaan 1997).

[13] The analysis in this section is per program and not per congregation. As noted above, each congregation in our sample, on average, carried 4.13 programs, Thus,

in order to transform the numbers reported below (per program) to numbers relevant per congregation, they should be multiplied by 4.13.

[14]We exclude from our analysis figures such as those for a cultural series that attracted more than 10,000 people. Congregational involvement in many of these programs consisted of providing space or sponsorship rather than providing service. These figures can bias the results and hence, we limit the number of beneficiaries to a ceiling of 3,000 members. This provides a more modest picture, but one that we believe is more accurate.

[15]Research by Marks (1995) and Valverde (1995) showed the extensive role of congregations in social service provision in rural Ontario in the late nineteenth century. However, they find that the resources for these services came from municipal and property taxes and not from the congregations.

References

Ammerman, N.T. and W.C. Roof. 1995. *Work, Family, and Religion in Contemporary Society*. New York: Routledge.

Bellah, R. 1991. *The Good Society: Individualism and Commitment in American Life*. New York: Alfred A. Knopf.

Brooks, N. 1999. "The Role and Financing of the Voluntary Sector in a Modern Welfare State." Paper presented at the "Charities: Between State and Market" conference at the Faculty of Law, University of Toronto, January.

Brown, E. 1997. "Assessing the Value of Volunteer Activity," *Nonprofit and Voluntary Sector Quarterly*, 28(1):1-17.

Clemens, J. and J. Francis. 1998. "Estimating the Value of Volunteering," *Fraser Forum*. 19-26 June.

Cnaan, R.A. 1996. *Social and Community Involvement of Philadelphia Religious Congregations Housed in Historic Religious Properties: Data Analyses of Mailed Questionnaires*. Report submitted to Historic Religious Properties Program of the Philadelphia Historic Preservation Corporation.

_____ 1997. *Social and Community Involvement of Religious Congregations: Finding from Six American Cities*. Philadelphia: The Program for the Study of Organized Religion and Social Work, University of Pennsylvania.

Cnaan, R.A. with R.J. Wineburg and S.C. Boddie. 1999. *The Newer Deal: Social Work and Religion in Partnership*. New York: Columbia University Press.

Coll, B.D. 1969. *Perspectives in Public Welfare*. Washington, DC: US Social and Rehabilitation Services.

Coleman, J.S. 1988. "Social Capital in the Creation of Human Capital,"*American Journal of Sociology*, 94:S95-S120.

Community Workshop on Economic Development. 1991. *Good Space and Good Work: Research and Analysis of the Extent and Nature of the Use of Religious Properties in Kingston Neighborhoods.* Kingston: Inspired Partnerships Program of the National Trust for Historic Preservation in the United States.

Day, K.M. and R.A. Devlin. 1997. *The Canadian Nonprofit Sector.* Ottawa: Canadian Policy Research Networks Inc.

The Economist. 1998. "Ottawa Against the Provinces," 17 October, p. 37.

Esbeck, C.H. 1997. *A Guide to Charitable Choice.* Washington, DC: Center for Public Justice and Christian Legal Society.

Hall, M.H. and L.G. Macpherson. 1997. "A Provincial Portrait of Canada's Charities," *Canadian Centre of Philanthropy Research Bulletin,* 4(2/3):1-12.

Hall, M.H., T. Knighton, P. Reed, P. Bussière, D. McRae and P. Bowen. 1998. *Caring Canadians, Involved Canadians: Highlights from the 1997 National Survey of Giving, Volunteering and Participating.* Cat. No. 71-542-XIE. Ottawa: Statistics Canada.

Hall, P.D. 1996. "Founded on the Rock, Built upon Shifting Sands: Churches, Voluntary Associations, and Nonprofit Organizations in Public Life: 1850-1990." Unpublished manuscript, PONPO, Yale University.

Handy, F., R.A. Cnaan, J. Brudney, L. Meijs, U. Ascoli and S. Ranade. 1998. "Defining Who is a Volunteer: Cross-Cultural Comparisons." Paper presented at the Annual ARNOVA conference, Seattle.

Hiemstra, J.L. 1999. *Government Relations with Religious Non-Profit Social Agencies in Alberta: Public Accountability in a Pluralist Society.* Alberta: Canada West Foundation.

Hodgkinson, V.A. and M.A. Weitzman. 1994. *Giving and Volunteering in the United States.* Washington, DC: Independent Sector.

Hodgkinson, V.A., M.S. Weitzman, A.D. Kirsch, S.M. Noga and H.A. Gorski. 1993. *From Belief to Commitment.* Washington, DC: Independent Sector.

Kingston. Social Planning Council of Kingston and Area. 1996. *Planning for Today and Tomorrow: A Social Planning Council Report on the Kingston and Area Community.* Kingston: Planning Council.

_____ KAEDC Business Development. Human Resources 11/5/97 [on - line] http://www.kingstonarea.on.business/humanres.html.

La Barbera, P.A. 1991. "Commercial Ventures of Religious Organizations," *Nonprofit Management & Leadership,* 1:217-34.

Marks, L. 1995. "Indigent Committees and Ladies' Benevolent Societies: Intersections of Public and Private Poor Relief in Late 19th Century Small Town Ontario," *Studies in Political Economy,* 47:61-87.

Martin, S.A. 1985. *An Essential Grace.* Toronto: McClelland & Stewart.

McDougall, H.A. 1993. *Black Baltimore: A New Theory of Community.* Philadelphia: Temple University Press.

Ontario Social Safety Network. 1996. "Ontario's Welfare Rate Cuts: An Anniversary Report," Toronto.

Putnam, R.D. 1995. "Bowling Alone: America's Declining Social Capital," *Journal of Democracy,* 6(1):65-78.

Queen, E.L. 1996. "The Religious Roots of Philanthropy in the West: Judaism, Christianity, and Islam," Working Paper No. 96-4. Indiana: Indiana University Center on Philanthropy.

Salamon, L.M. 1995. *Partners in Public Service: Government-Nonprofit Relations in the Modern Welfare State.* Baltimore, MD: The Johns Hopkins University Press.

Sharpe, D. 1994. *A Portrait of Canada's Charities: The Size, Scope and Financing of Registered Charities.* Toronto: Canadian Centre for Philanthropy.

Shields J. and M.B. Evans. 1998. *Shrinking the State.* Halifax: Fernwood Publishing.

Steinberg, R. 1996. "Can Individual Donations Replace Cutbacks in Federal Social-Welfare Spending?" in *Capacity or Change? The Nonprofit World in the Age of Devolution,* ed. D. Burlingame, W.A. Diaz, W.F. Ilchman and Associates. Indianapolis: Indiana University Center on Philanthropy.

United Way of London and Middlesex. 1994. *Listening to London.* London.

Valverde, M. 1995. "The Mixed Social Economy as a Canadian Tradition," *Studies in Political Economy,* 47(Summer):91-123.

Verba, S., K.L. Schlozman and H.E. Brady. 1995. *Voice and Equality: Civic Voluntarism in American Politics.* Cambridge, MA: Harvard University Press.

Wineburg, R.J. 1994. "A Longitudinal Case Study of Religious Congregations in Local Human Service Delivery," *Nonprofit and Voluntary Sector Quarterly,* 23:159-69.

Appendix One

SOCIAL AND COMMUNITY SERVICES: DETAILED FINDINGS

Interviews sought to identify the services that congregations provided through the programs they ran on the premises, elsewhere, or by the programs run by others on the congregation's property. Respondents were asked to review the list of some 200 services and to indicate whether or not their congregation provided a program that included the service. Responses were categorized as follows:

0 = No (In the past 12 months nothing was offered anywhere in this area).

1 = Upon request or when needed (sporadically offered).

2 = Program run on the congregation's property (A formal program offered on-location).

3 = Program run by the congregation elsewhere (A formal program offered off-location).

4 = Program run by someone else on the congregation's property (Congregation provides space).

5 = Support for a program carried out elsewhere (A formal program not offered by the congregation, but in which the congregation actively invests — such programs are often offered by a local coalition of congregations or by the denominational office).

We report in Table A1 findings for services with answers corresponding to categories 2 to 5 above. The data do not reflect congregational response to "Upon request or when needed." For example, if in the past 12 months one or more families approached the clergy for family counselling, but no formal program was established to that end, family counselling was *not* included as a service provided by the congregation. Some of the programs were carried out jointly with other agencies or involved supporting local coalitions. The findings in Table A1 represent those services in which there is a significant degree of commitment in providing the services through an ongoing and organized program.

It should be noted that the number of *services* listed in Table A1 does not total the actual number of *programs* provided by local religious congregations. In some cases, a program was broken down into several components (services) for this instrument. For example, a congregation may have as a program "Help for the Homeless," and it may include services such as providing shelter or a soup kitchen, and providing financial assistance. For some congregations, these are distinct programs; for others, it is a single program. The instrument required that they be identified as separate services.

Table 5 in the text does not include frequencies of all 200 services listed in the instrument. For the sake of brevity we include only those services reported by at least four congregations (25 percent) in any one city. For example "health screening" was offered by only one congregation in Toronto and "health education" by two congregations in Kingston. These services do not appear in Table A1. Finally, it should be noted that the names of programs and their order of appearance in the table only reflect the format of our instrument.

Table A1: Programs Reported by at Least 25 Percent of Congregations in at Least One City

Programs	Kingston N=15 (%)	London N=15 (%)	Toronto N=16 (%)	Ontario Total N=46 (%)
A. Counselling/Programs for Families				
Couple counselling	**4 (26.7)**	-	**4 (25)**	8 (17.4)
Marriage encounters (retreats)	**6 (40)**	**5 (33.4)**	**5 (31.3)**	**16 (34.8)**
Family counselling	**4 (26.7)**	1 (6.7)	3 (18.8)	8 (17.4)
Spouse abuse/domestic violence	-	**5 (33.4)**	3 (18.8)	8 (17.2)
Programs for widows/widowers	2 (13.3)	2 (13.3)	**5 (31.3)**	9 (19.6)
Parenting skills	**7 (46.7)**	3 (20)	**5 (31.3)**	**15 (32.6)**
Abortion/pro-life counselling	**7 (46.7)**	3 (20)	1 (6.3)	11 (23.9)
Teen pregnancy	**5 (33.3)**	3 (20)	**4 (25)**	**12 (26.1)**
Intergenerational programs	**8 (53.3)**	**6 (40)**	**6 (37.5)**	**20 (43.5)**
Loss of spouse — support group	**6 (40)**	**5 (33)**	3 (18.8)	**14 (30.4)**

... continued

Table A1 (cont'd.)

	Kingston N=15 (%)	London N=15 (%)	Toronto N=16 (%)	Ontario Total N=46 (%)
B. Programs for Seniors				
Communal (on-site) meals	2 (13.3)	1 (6.7)	**6 (37.5)**	9 (19.6)
Meals-on-wheels	3 (20)	2 (13.3)	**6 (37.5)**	11 (23.9)
Recreational programs	**7 (46.7)**	**8 (53.3)**	**6 (37.5)**	**21 (45.7)**
Visitation — buddy programs	**6 (40)**	**9 (60)**	**6 (37.5)**	**21 (45.7)**
Organized tours	1 (6.7	2 (13.3)	**5 (31.3)**	8 (17.4)
Transportation	**6 (40)**	1 (6.7)	**4 (25)**	11 (23.9)
Health care (physical and mental)	2 (13.3)	1 (6.7)	**4 (25)**	7 (15.2)
Exercise	**4 (26.7)**	3 (20)	**4 (25)**	11 (23.9)
C. Programs for Children and Youth				
Day care (preschool)	**4 (26.7)**	1 (6.7)	5 (31.3)	10 (21.7)
Mother's morning out/Mothers of preschoolers	**6 (40)**	**5 (33.3)**	**4 (25)**	**15 (32.6)**
Summer day camp	**7 (46.7)**	**11 (73.3)**	**7 (43.8)**	**25 (54.3)**
After school care (recreational)	1 (6.7)	-	1 (6.3)	2 (4..3)
Tutoring	**4 (26.7)**	1 (6.7)	4 (25)	9 (19.6)
Cubs/Boy Scouts/Brownies/Girl Scouts	**8 (53.3)**	**9 (60)**	**4 (25)**	**21 (45.7)**
Recreational programs (children)	**9 (60)**	**6 (40)**	**7 (43.8)**	**22 (47.8)**
Recreational programs (teens)	**12 (80)**	**11 (73.3)**	**8 (50)**	**31 (67.4)**
Summer programs (teens)	**9 (60)**	**6 (40)**	**5 (31.3)**	**20 (43.5)**
Scholarships for students	**6 (40)**	**6 (40)**	**4 (25)**	**16 (34.8)**

... continued

Table A1 (cont'd.)

	Kingston N=15 (%)	London N=15 (%)	Toronto N=16 (%)	Ontario Total N=46 (%)
D. Homeless and Services for the Poor				
Shelter for men	7 (46.7)	13 (86.7)	6 (37.5)	26 (56.5)
Shelter for women/children	7 (46.7)	12 (80)	6 (37.5)	25 (54.3)
Day mission/program	3 (20)	11 (73.3)	3 (18.8)	17 (37)
Transitional living program	1 (6.7)	9 (60)	-	10 (21.7)
Clothing closets	10 (66.7)	13 (86.7)	13 (81.3)	36 (78.3)
Food pantries	15 (100)	13 (86.7)	10 (62.5)	38 (82.6)
Soup kitchen	7 (46.7)	11 (73.3)	10 (62.5)	28 (60.9)
Health care for the homeless	1 (6.7)	2 (13.3)	7 (43.8)	10 (21.7)
Financial assistance	11 (77.3)	5 (33.3)	4 (25)	20 (43.5)
Mental health care	4 (26.7)	4 (26.7)	3 (18.8)	11 (23.9)
Street outreach	-	8 (53.3)	8 (50)	16 (34.8)
Job placement	2 (13.3)	4 (26.7)	3 (18.8)	9 (19.6)
Vocational training	2 (13.3)	4 (26.7)	3 (18.8)	9 (19.6)
E. Other Programs Serving People in Need				
Programs for refugees (in community)	2 (13.3)	5 (33.3)	6 (37.5)	13 (28.3)
Refugee resettlement	3 (20)	6 (40)	1 (6.3)	10 (21.7)
Programs for immigrants	1 (6.7)	5 (33.3)	2 (12.5)	8 (17.4)
International relief	15 (100)	12 (80)	10 (62.5)	37 (80.4)
Prison ministry	9 (60)	2 (13.3)	3 (18.8)	14 (30.4)
Prisoners' families	7 (46.7)	2 (13.3)	1 (6.3)	10 (21.7)

... continued

Table A1 (cont'd.)

	Kingston N=15 (%)	London N=15 (%)	Toronto N=16 (%)	Ontario Total N=46 (%)
F. Health Programs				
Hospice	2 (13.3)	2 (13.3)	**4 (25)**	8 (17.4)
Sick/homebound	**5 (33.3)**	**6 (40)**	**4 (25)**	**15 (32.6)**
People with physical disabilities	**4 (26.7)**	3 (20)	-	7 (15.2)
Health screening	-	-	1 (6.3)	1 (2.2)
Health education	2 (13.3)	-	-	2 (4.3)
Drug and alcohol prevention	**4 (26.7)**	2 (13.3)	2 (12.5)	8 (17.4)
HIV/AIDS programs	1 (6.7)	**4 (26.7)**	2 (12.5)	7 (15.2)
AA	3 (20)	**5 (33.3)**	**6 (37.5)**	**14 (30.4)**
NA	1 (6.7)	3 (20)	3 (18.8)	7 (15.2)
Blood drive	1 (6.7)	-	-	1 (2.2)
Hospital visitation	**10 (66.7)**	**10 (66.7)**	**5 (31.3)**	**25 (54.3)**
G. Educational Opportunities (Adults)				
Scholarships for students in need	**6 (40)**	3 (20)	**4 (25)**	**13 (28.3)**
Adult literacy program	**4 (26.7)**	3 (20)	2 (12.5)	9 (19.6)
H. Community Security				
Crime watch	2 (13.3)	1 (6.7)	-	3 (6.5)
Cooperation with police	-	**6 (40)**	1 (6.3)	7 (15.2)
Space for police/community meeting	-	**4 (26.7)**	1 (6.3)	5 (10.9)
Paying for security of the property	-	**5 (33.3)**	1 (6.3)	6 (13)

... *continued*

Table A1 (cont'd.)

	Kingston N=15 (%)	London N=15 (%)	Toronto N=16 (%)	Ontario Total N=46 (%)
I. Art and Culture				
Art exhibits	**5 (33.5)**	1 (6.7)	3 (18.8)	9 (19.6)
Music classes	**4 (26.7)**	**6 (40)**	2 (12.5)	**12 (26.1)**
Community theatre	2 (13.3)	2 (13.3)	**4 (25)**	8 (17.4)
Music performances	**7 (46.7)**	**9 (60)**	7 (43.8)	**23 (50)**
Lecture series	**4 (26.7)**	1 (6.7)	**4 (25)**	9 (19.6)
Architectural and historic tours	-	-	3 (18.8)	3 (6.5)
Choral groups	**13 (86.7)**	**11 (73.3)**	**5 (31.3)**	**29 (63)**
J. Community Organizing / Providing Space for Other Organizations				
Neighbourhood associations	**5 (33.3)**	**5 (33.3)**	**4 (25)**	**14 (30.4)**
Protests	3 (20)	1 (6.7)	**4 (25)**	8 (17.4)
Interracial collaboration	3 (20)	-	3 (18.8)	6 (13)
Interfaith collaboration	**10 (66.7)**	**8 (53.3)**	**6 (37.5)**	**24 (52.2)**
Neighbourhood cleanup	-	-	**4 (25)**	4 (8.7)
Community bazaars/fairs	**9 (60)**	**9 (60)**	7 (43.8)	**25 (54.3)**
Historic preservation	1 (6.7)	3 (20)	3 (18.8)	7 (15.2)
Sport activities	**4 (26.7)**	3 (20)	3 (18.8)	10 (21.7)
Holiday celebrations	**9 (60)**	**4 (26.7)**	**8 (50)**	**21 (45.7)**
K. Community Economic Development				
Job counselling and placement	2 (13.3)	1 (6.7)	**4 (25)**	7 (15.2)
Disaster relief	**7 (46.7)**	**6 (40)**	**5 (31.3)**	**18 (39.1)**
Civic beautification/improvement	-	-	**4 (25)**	4 (8.7)

... continued

Table A1 (cont'd.)

	Kingston N=15 (%)	London N=15 (%)	Toronto N=16 (%)	Ontario Total N=46 (%)
L. Social Issues				
Civil rights	2 (13.3)	2 (13.3)	2 (12.5)	6 (13)
Social justice	4 (26.7)	8 (53.3)	6 (37.5)	18 (39.1)
Racism	3 (20)	4 (26.7)	1 (6.3)	8 (17.4)
Interfaith relations	8 (53.3)	6 (40)	4 (25)	18 (39.1)
Pro-choice/pro-life advocacy	5 (33.3)	7 (46.7)	-	12 (26.1)
Gay and lesbian issues	-	1 (6.7)	4 (25)	5 (10.9)
Women's issues	3 (20)	9 (60)	3 (18.8)	15 (32.6)
Family values	4 (26.7)	6 (40)	2 (12.5)	12 (26.1)
Peace	2 (13.3)	5 (33.3)	1 (6.3)	8 (17.4)
Poverty/welfare rights/advocacy	5 (33.3)	5 (33.3)	6 (37.5)	16 (34.8)
Voter registration	4 (26.7)	-	2 (12.5)	6 (13)
Environmental action	4 (26.7)	2 (13.3)	-	6 (13)
M. Housing for the Needy				
New building initiatives	1 (6.7)	-	2 (12.5)	3 (6.5)
Housing rehabilitation	2 (13.3)	-	3 (18.8)	5 (10.9)
Habitat for Humanity	6 (40)	6 (40)	1 (6.3)	13 (28.3)
Collaboration with housing corporations (CDC, etc.)	3 (20)	1 (6.7)	4 (25)	8 (17.4)
Collaboration w/groups to provide housing	2 (13.3)	3 (20)	4 (25)	9 (19.6)
Advocacy for housing	3 (20)	1 (6.7)	2 (12.5)	6 (13)

Notes:
1. Numbers appearing in brackets denote the congregations in cell as a percentage of N in that column. For example, in the first cell of section A, 4 out of 15 congregations in Kingston offer couple counselling. This implies that 26.7 percent of all Kingston congregations offer couple counselling.
2. Bolded cells denote the cases in which the program was provided by 25 percent or more of the congregations.

Appendix Two

DETAILED CALCULATIONS OF PROGRAM COSTS

Monetary Support by Congregations. Congregations financially support their programs in modest amounts, 137 out of 190 programs (72.1 percent) received direct financial support from the congregations. In a few cases, extremely high support was reported for programs; these often reflected start-up costs or one-time purchases of equipment and furniture and are excluded from our calculations.[1] The total monthly sum allocated directly to the 133 programs was $61,029, with a mean of $459.53 per program.

Market Value of Space Provision. A major form of support offered by congregations is the use of their facilities, including places to meet, kitchen facilities, storage facilities, etc. Congregations reported that in-house programs used a variety of locations on their property and many use more than one room/area of the property. The room most commonly used for programs is the parish/fellowship hall, followed by classrooms, basements, and sanctuaries.[2]

To determine the monetary value of the space provided by congregations for social and community service, we asked the respondents to assess the market value of the space that they provide for the programs. We asked them how much comparable space would cost to rent in their neighbourhood on a *monthly* basis. Although some found it difficult to assess the value, many were familiar with property values in their community (and some even studied the market value of their properties in the process of planning to offer the space for rent). The latter were usually congregations that provide space to larger and more formal programs such as summer camps. These programs often required the use of several rooms including the kitchen.

We received 122 (64 percent) responses regarding the market value for the space provided for programs. The rest either did not provide spaces for the programs or were not able to respond to the market value of the space. The average monthly value of the space provided per program, for the reported 122 programs, was $745.00.[3]

Space provision by a congregation also involves indirect costs in terms of cleanup, security, etc. Although we have attempted to capture these costs, we strongly believe that program costs were largely underestimated by the congregations in our sample. This was due to the low response rate regarding the market value of the space, and many respondents noted that comparable space was not available in the community and thus were reticent to give values. They offered conservative estimates based on local property values that were often not comparable.

Volunteer Work. Our findings also show that volunteers are an important resource in the provision of social services by congregations, 165 of the 190 programs (87 percent) reported the use of volunteers. Local congregations have an important advantage in recruiting volunteers within the congregation to help with the social services they initiate and provide. Congregation members generally know one another quite well, share a commitment to similar values, and are regularly requested by their clergy to lend a helping hand to the needy in the community.

The number of volunteer hours per program per month ranged from half an hour to 5,710 hours. The mean number of hours of volunteer work per program per month was 170 hours for 165 programs. Thus, the total number of volunteer hours contributed in the sample for the 165 programs that reported the use of volunteers is 28,037.20 hours per month.[4]

These findings indicate a high rate of volunteer hours, considering each congregation has on average more than four programs. The average number of hours per program volunteered (approximately 170 hours per month) is equivalent to the time worked by a full-time employee. These high numbers are not surprising as there appears to be a positive connection between religiosity and volunteering. Volunteer participation rates and volunteer hours for individuals with strong religious ties were higher than national averages (Hall *et al.* 1998).

Several authors have tried to assess the financial contribution of volunteer hours (Brown 1997; Hodgkinson and Weitzman 1992; Clemens and Francis 1998). Suggestions of a single hourly rate at the industrial average, differential hourly rates reflecting sectoral wages, and minimum wage rates have been suggested singly or in varying combinations. We chose to use a single hourly wage rate based on findings by a study that established that volunteers were perceived to incur equal opportunity costs regardless of the significant variability in their real opportunity costs (Handy *et al.* 1998). We use an hourly rate of $11.46, the average of sectoral wages in Canada, to estimate the value of volunteer time.[5] For our sample, the estimated monetary value of the 28, 037.20 volunteer hours per month by the 165 programs reporting the use of volunteers was $324,670.72. This is a mean of $1,708.79 per program per month. Clearly, our congregations contributed a significant value in volunteer service to their communities.

Clergy and Staff Hours. Clergy and staff time was often required, directly and indirectly, in the provision of social services. In some congregations, the clergy and staff invested considerable time in community service programs. Clergy were involved in 117 of the 190 programs (62 percent) and staff in 71 programs (37 percent). To estimate the value of this resource, we asked how many hours per program per month were contributed by clergy and staff. Hours worked per program per month averaged eoght by clergy and 63 by staff.[6] We estimated the financial value of this time using an estimate of average of wages paid by congregations : $20 per hour for clergy and $15 per hour for staff. Clergy support for the 117 reported programs was, thus, at a mean cost of $167.62 per month, while staff support for the 71 reported programs was at a mean cost of $626.14 per month.

In-Kind Support. In addition to monetary support, provision of space, and volunteer, staff and clergy support, congregations in the sample assisted the numerous programs by in-kind support. This kind of support is often taken for granted, but the real costs are borne by the congregation. These costs include materials for classes, photocopying, transportation, telephone, publicity, and often may include food provided by the congregation at no charge. This in-kind support is an important contribution of congregations to their communities. We asked respondents to assess the cost of the in-kind support they provided to the programs. In-kind support was reported for half of the 190 programs at a mean cost of $133.59 per month.

Cost of Utilities. Religious congregations are housed in properties that are often centrally located and perceived as non-threatening. They are attractive to a variety of community groups and organizations to use for their meetings and programs. These groups usually pay little or no rent or sometimes a small user fee. However, congregations incur costs in keeping their buildings open for programs such as heating, water, security, insurance, cleaning, supervising, and depreciation. We asked respondents to assess utility costs; 95 (50 percent) of all 190 programs reported the cost of their utilities with the mean cost per month being $152.91.

Average Monetary Value of a Congregational Program per Month. In determining the average monetary value of a program provided by a congregation per month, we used traditional economic methods for imputed values, which are detailed in the notes at the foot of Table A2.1.

We carried out calculations for all dimensions of costs incurred by the congregations in service provision. The results presented in Table A2.1 provided an overall assessment of the average monetary value of a congregational program per month. The average monetary value of a program was $3,001.48 per month.

Table A2.1: Assessed Averaged Monetary Value per Month per Program for all Programs*

	Kingston	London	Toronto	Ontario Total
In-kind support	$68.15	$99.83	$70.37	$79.45
Utilities	$30.14	$25.16	$199.00	$76.46
Financial support	$280.96	$361.83	$326.22	$321.21
Clergy hours (@ $20 hr.)	$99.33	$78.34	$140.42	$103.22
Staff hours (@ $15 hr.)	$465.38	$23.43	$182.00	$233.98
Volunteer hours (@ $11.58 hr.)	$936.24	$2,462.38	$1,819.35	$1,708.79
Value of space	$370.89	$302.00	$820.07	$478.37
Total	**$2,251.09**	**$3,352.97**	**$3,557.43**	**$3,001.48**

Note: *We calculated the *average monetary value in each cell* by adding the total reported costs for programs and dividing the result by the number of all programs whether or not they reported such costs. For example, for the Ontario sample, 95 (50 percent) of all 190 programs reported the cost of their utilities. Among these programs, the mean cost per month was $152.91. Thus, the total mean utility cost per month was $14,526.45 ($152.91x95 programs). In order to obtain a *conservative* cost estimate that will be applicable for all programs we assume that the programs which reported no costs for utilities had zero utility costs. Thus, we calculate the average monthly cost of utilities by dividing the total average cost per month ($14,526.45) by the total number of programs (190). That gave us an average monthly utilities cost of $76.46 per month per program.

Average Monetary Income of a Congregational Program per Month. To assess the net costs to congregations, we need to consider any revenues generated by services. Our findings indicate that few programs, in fact, do generate income for the congregation beyond some rental fees and in-kind support given to the congregation as a token of appreciation for hosting the program. In one congregation, for example, an AA group who paid $50-a-month rent laid a carpet in the church basement at their own cost. Only seven of 190 programs reported a monthly total of $8,359.40 in cash support, with a mean of $1,144.20 per reported program; and five programs reported in-kind support valued as a total of $6,731, or a mean of $1,346.20 per reporting program. To assess the average monetary value of compensation received per program, we used the method described above and divided the totals for cash support and in-kind support by the total (190) programs. The monthly means per program were $43.97 from rent or cash support and $35.43 from in-kind support. Thus, the assessed average monetary value of the compensation received per month per program is $79.40.

Assessment of Net Contribution of a Congregational Program per Month. To estimate the net contribution of a congregational program per month, we deduct the total monthly income figure ($79.40) from the total monetary value reported for the entire sample ($3,001.48) in Table A2.2, we derive an overall estimated contribution of $2,922.08 per program per month.

Assessment of Net Contribution per Congregation. As indicated above, the analysis in this section was based on social programs as the unit of analysis. To assess the mean contribution of congregations, we need to remember that, on average, each congregation in Ontario reported 4.13 programs. Thus, we multiplied the financial values reported above by 4.13 in Ontario to obtain the imputed values of the monthly congregational contribution to society. The value of congregational support is estimated to be $12,068.19 per congregation per month, or $144,818.28 per congregation per year. In order to assess the monetary contribution of each congregation in each city, we multiplied the city's net congregational contribution per program per month with the average number of programs in that city. See Table A2.2 for details.

Table A2.2: Assessed Net Contribution

	Kingston	London	Toronto	Ontario Total
Gross contribution by congregation /per program/per month	$2,251.09	$3,352.97	$3,557.43	$3,001.48
Compensation received by congregation for services/per program/per month	$91.67	$0	$157.22	$79.40
Net contributions by congregation /per program/per month	$2,159.42	$3,352.97	$3,400.21	$2,692.10
Net contributions by congregation /per month	$10,365.22	$14,317.18	$11,475.71	$12,068.19
Yearly net contribution per congregation	$124,382.59	$171,806.14	$137,708.48	$144,818.28

Notes

[1] We omitted from our analysis any program whose monthly monetary cost exceeded $5,000 so as not to bias the findings. These funds were generally supported from external grants for start-up costs. Four programs out of 137 in the sample met this criterion and were excluded.

[2] It should be noted that some programs are offered off-site. Our analysis of contributions includes only in-house programs that use congregational property as it represents an indirect contribution to the programs. For the sample, 129 of the 190 reported programs (67.9 percent) were based solely in-house. Another nine programs (4.7 percent) were based both in-house and off-site for a total of 72.6 percent.

[3] This average monthly value per program in Toronto was $1,107.10 which was significantly higher than Kingston ($651.32) and London ($471.41). These values are not out of line given the differences in market value for space in these cities.

[4] Kingston (93.89 hours) reported far lower hours than Toronto (209.93 hours) and London (219.50 hours). In Kingston non-members were more likely to provide services than members, unlike London and Toronto where the reverse was true. Thus it is not surprising that programs offered in Kingston did not use many volunteer congregation members as London and Toronto.

[5] Using the average sectoral wage rate derived from Canadian data used by Clemens and Francis (1998) infers that the types of services offered by congregations reflects the mix of all services. We think it a reasonable estimate that lies between the high-end estimate using an average industrial wage and the low-end estimate using minimum wages.

[6] London exhibited significantly lower contributions by staff and clergy but had the highest contribution by volunteers. In a more careful reading of the programs offered by congregations in London, it is clear that many of the programs involved other nonprofit and public organizations, unlike Toronto and Kingston. It is likely that the programs in London also used personnel from other organizations and required less involvement of clergy and staff.

4

After Government Cuts: Insights from Two Ontario "Enterprising Nonprofits"

Raymond Dart and Brenda Zimmerman

Most Canadian nonprofit organizations derive a large portion of their overall revenue from governmental sources, and this source of revenue has declined significantly at almost all levels across the country for several years (Day and Devlin 1996). The impacts from this resource shock have often been exacerbated by significant increases in demand for the programs or service of many of the same organizations that have had their governmental funding cut. Responses to this situation are almost as varied as Canadian nonprofit organizations themselves. However, one significant and relatively novel response to the revenue shortfall has been the initiation of "business ventures" or "business-like ventures" by nonprofit organizations. These ventures are typically intended to generate revenues that the organization can use to fund other forms of charitable or mission-related work.

This paper is centred on the emerging issue of Canadian nonprofits undertaking business activities. The idea of "nonprofits going into business" rings a variety of alarm bells to a great many people and is a highly-charged issue. The concern of critics centres on the extent to which commercial activities will affect the integrity, ethos and "public good" orientation of organizations in the nonprofit sector. In a more positive vein, researchers also wonder whether commercial ventures might improve the productivity and client focus of nonprofit organizations. Important normative and policy questions such as these need to be answered. However, it is impossible to evaluate the "value" of nonprofits undertaking business initiatives until we have a clearer understanding of the effects of these activities on the *raison d'être* of nonprofits.

The primary research question posed here has two parts: How do business activities "work" in Canadian nonprofit organizations, and what effects do these activities have, particularly on the mission-related service provision of these organizations? The study is intended to contribute to discussions of nonprofit organizations in Canada by providing the first detailed empirical examination of this controversial and emerging phenomenon. The analysis reported here is based on in-depth qualitative case studies of two nonprofit organizations located in Ontario. The qualitative case study method has been chosen over a more representative cross-sectional survey because of the need for detailed data on a phenomenon that remains undocumented and poorly understood. However, analysis of the case study data will hopefully help to refine the categories and questions necessary for a broader survey at a later date.

THE ANALYTICAL FRAMEWORK, RESEARCH METHOD AND DATA

There has been relatively sparse treatment of the nonprofit enterprise phenomenon in the research literature.[1] Overall, the literature that does focus on nonprofit commercial enterprise is American in origin, normative in orientation, and "how-to" in focus. The literature works from the premise that commercial enterprise can be appropriate for nonprofits and provides "some ways it can be made to work." Most of the examples cited in this literature (cf. Brinckerhoff 1990, 1994 *a,b,c*; Budd 1996; Dees 1998; Emerson and Twersky 1996) are "community economic development" or vocational training organizations (rather than more typical social-service nonprofits) where the synthesis of mission-fulfillment and business development objectives are likely most readily achieved. Crimmins and Keil

(1983) provide the earliest study of nonprofit commercial enterprise and offer some tentative and anecdotal treatment of potential effects of commercial development on other aspects of the nonprofit organization. For the purposes of this study, the gaps in the existing literature are as important as the issues that it has covered. Specifically, none of the previous work gives the policy community a sense of the way business ventures are used in the nonprofit sector, or the kinds of effects these activities have on individual organizations.

This paper is intended to extend the framework and thinking developed in the preliminary analytical examination of *Charities Doing Commercial Ventures* (Zimmerman and Dart 1998). The wide-ranging interviews and literature review undertaken for that study suggested that the central issue at the nonprofit-business interface was not whether these commercial activities could succeed. Rather, executive directors of organizations, researchers, and academics alike mused that the most important issues were likely to be the myriad unintended internal and external consequences of the development of commercial activities. These unintended consequences or effects, they suggested, were central to an evaluation of commercial ventures for nonprofits.

These effects have dimensions which are multiple, complex, and largely unmapped. Our previous work suggested that the effects of commercial activities on nonprofit organizations could be organized into four dimensions: responsiveness, resources, relationships, and reputation. This framework is reproduced in Table 1. We have chosen this framework to structure our analysis of the two cases studied here. We do not intend to answer all of these questions or to confirm the utility of all of the categories discussed in Zimmerman and Dart (1998). Rather, we see the primary goal as more clearly framing the most relevant dimensions of emergent effects and therefore the most important questions to pose.

The paper is best described as an exploratory study, as its primary purpose is to characterize or map poorly understood and/or relatively new phenomena (Neuman 1994). To uncover the depth and detail of data that is the primary goal of this research, two in-depth qualitative case studies have been developed as the basis for thematic qualitative data analysis. Yin (1994) and Jorgensen (1989) recommend the use of such case studies over other qualitative and quantitative methodologies when the phenomenon to be

Table 1: Emergent Outcomes

Resources	Relationships	Reputation	Responsiveness
• cannibalization	• board of directors	• community perception	• increased productivity
• shifts away from intentional giving	• recipients/ beneficiaries/clients	• market perception – unfair competition	• change to less hierarchical, more adaptable structure
• synergies/ decreased financial risk	• donors/funders	• shifting definition of success	• "low-hanging fruit"
• increased financial risk	• volunteers		• customer focus
• using more energy to get fewer dollars	• organized labour		• mission and values of charity are undermined by business venture
• burning charitable dollars	• professional staff		
• volunteers			
• cost of hiring business managers			
• reward structures would have to be changed			
• commercial activities can be undermined by the mission and values of a charity			

Source: Zimmerman and Dart (1998).

studied is contemporary and *in situ* and when the phenomenon and its contexts are neither clearly evident nor fully understood.

The organization of data collection was as follows. A search and screening process was undertaken to find relevant sites, and each site was visited several times over an eight-month period[2] to collect documentation and to organize and undertake interviews. Within each case study setting, interviewing and observation was multi-level and multi-functional. Since the organizational effects of commercial activities are seldom documented, interviews were conducted with staff ranging from front-line service providers, volunteers, middle and senior managers, and board members. In total, more than 20 one-to-two hour interviews were conducted. These interviews were supplemented by a variety of less formal follow-up conversations. Both case study sites were registered charities in southern Ontario. The sites were chosen based on access opportunities and on indications that these organizations had initiated significant commercial activities. While researchers of nonprofit commercial enterprise note that such enterprises can be characterized as either "fee-for-service," "related diversification" or "unrelated diversification" (e.g., Skloot 1987), only fee-for-service and "related diversification" activities were considered for study here.[3] Issues of organizational and staff/stakeholder confidentiality were important in the data collection phase of this research. In order to get beyond the "rhetoric" of nonprofit commercial venturing, confidentiality was assured for interviewees and their organizations. Thus, both the organizations and individuals documented below have been given pseudonyms and identifying data has been either edited out or disguised. Quotations have also been partially edited for readability and grammar, but overall content has been affected in the most minimal manner possible.

THE CASE STUDIES

Counselling Organization

A Counselling Organization (CO) is a medium-sized, social-service nonprofit organization located in a southern Ontario city. It has an annual budget of approximately $1 million, which supports relatively stable ongoing programs. It has 14 full-time staff and uses a relatively small number of volunteers. Most of its activity is focused on the city within which it is located, but particular elements of programs and services can be accessed in smaller communities within a radius of approximately 80 km. The organization provides various forms of counselling and interpersonal social support, and while these programs are open to all, the clientele of the CO tend to be low-income individuals and families.

The CO has experienced a great deal of organizational and environmental change in the past four years. In 1996, as a result of the restructuring of Ontario's approach to Community Care Access Centre (CCAC) model, the CO lost almost $500,000 of funding for programs and infrastructure. These programs and their administration were essentially taken over by the CCAC as it consolidated service to senior citizens regionally. A year earlier, the Financial Counselling Program which the CO operated lost all of its provincial government funding (at the time, 60 percent of the program's budget) when the provincial government made a decision to discontinue funding this kind of program right across the province. Paralleling these major financial shocks, the CO experienced a major shift in management. A long-serving executive director described by several as a "traditional agency manager" was replaced by a new executive director, who is a self-described "entrepreneurial social worker."

CO offers three types of services: clinical services, financial counselling, and employee assistance programs. The clinical services range from traditional one-on-one counselling with a social worker to discussion and therapy groups. The issues dealt with in clinical services are quite serious, ranging from marital problems to depression, sexual abuse, and family violence. Clinical services is the largest program area at CO, with a manager (who also maintains a sizable caseload), three full-time clinician-counsellors, and some part-time and contract staff.

Clinical services provides an interesting example of a program that is quite "commercialized," in that it is organized according to business or managerial principles, yet retains traditional grant-based funding. Prior to the arrival of the new executive director and the cuts in funding, the clinical model at CO was characterized by long waiting lists, clients "in therapy" for protracted periods of time, and a counselling style focused on psychotherapeutic traditions. Soon after the arrival the new executive director, the clinical model changed to a "brief therapy" model. This is characterized by rapid intake, a three-session contract with clients (which can be extended if necessary or relevant), and a counselling style described as "cognitive" therapy which focuses on particular skills and/or disciplines. In the "brief therapy" model, clients are in and out more quickly, and the counselling is more focused on readily applicable tools. This shift in the program delivery model did not occur in isolation. In fact, counselling staff at CO speculated that they might have been among the last organizations to leave the traditional "long-term therapy" model behind.

Funding for clinical services remained quite traditional as of mid-1998. The bulk of funding came from a variety of provincial government agencies, primarily from the Ministries of Health and of Community and Social Services, and from the United Way. Minor revenue for this program area came from user-fees that were structured on a sliding scale from $5 per hour to $75 per hour depending on the client's personal and family income. In practice, however, the average hourly fee-for-service charge was the lowest charge, $5 per hour. As the executive director put it, "the sliding scale seems to always slide to the bottom here."

Another major program area is financial counselling, which provides counselling and a debt-management program for individuals and families that are experiencing significant financial problems, typically from excessive credit-card debt. Staff report that the client group has a large demographic overlap with that of clinical services because financial and familial problems are often closely related. The financial counselling program has two full-time counselling staff, one of whom is also the overall program manager. Additional support is provided by administrative staff.

Counselling in this context includes the provision of information about budgeting, managing debt, coping with collection agencies, and overall household finance. This kind of service has recently been eclipsed in importance by the Debt Management Plan (DMP). The DMP is a relatively unique service and has become the financial mainstay of the Financial Counselling Program (FCP). It comes from the special ability of the financial counselling program to negotiate the suspension of credit-card interest payments for individuals or families where the debt-to-income situation has become unworkable but where bankruptcy is unnecessary. In the DMP, staff negotiate the suspension of interest payments for their clients in exchange for the clients undertaking a strict debt management plan. These plans consist of monthly payments to the financial counselling program which are placed in a trust account and disbursed to creditors to cover the principal owed. Interest charges are forgiven. Thus, through this program, individuals or families can work themselves out of their debt situation without declaring bankruptcy and creditors can recoup the principal of the money owed.

This program has an unconventional financing structure as well. Funding for the financial counselling program from the provincial government was eliminated in 1996 when the government withdrew financial support for all organizations of this type. At present, the financial counselling program retains a small United Way grant. The remainder of the program's revenue is earned. More than half of the program revenue comes from creditor organizations. They provide charitable donations based on a fixed percentage of the money that the DMP disburses to them. In addition to this downstream fee-for-service, clients are also charged a fixed percentage service fee. This fee is rationalized by staff on the basis of overall revenue needs of the program and because of the money that clients save when their interest payments are suspended. At present, overall program revenue based on service fees is experiencing a significant upswing.

The Employee Assistance Program (EAP) is taken by many to be a clear illustration of the potential for nonprofit organizations to initiate commercial ventures, which in turn benefit the core of the organization. This is the most overtly commercial program at CO since it is based upon competitive bidding with other, primarily for-profit, organizations and is intended to produce a financial surplus or profit. CO has been in the EAP business for more than ten years, and as such, these activities pre-date the provincial funding cuts of the mid-1990s.

The EAP is in certain respects a for-profit mirror image of the clinical services program. It consists of a variety of kinds of personal support, ranging from one-on-one therapy to group crisis counselling. The program is provided by the manager and staffing of the clinical service program, and is undertaken as supplemental work during and around regular work hours. Moreover, EAP is delivered using the same brief therapy model as clinical services, with only a few differences as specified by the contracts tendered to provide these services. One difference is that EAP clients are guaranteed that requests for counselling will be met within 48 hours. Another is that CO must produce a newsletter and various publicity items for all of the employees of the organizations for which it retains EAP contracts.

The revenue for EAP work is based on contracts awarded by organizations for the benefit of their employees. All of this revenue is on an earned revenue fee-for-service basis where CO is paid a set amount per hour by the contracting organization for counselling provided to its employees.

For example, CO has contracts with a hospital, a large local industry, and a local department of a federal government ministry. When one of their employees has a work or personal issue requiring counselling, CO provides the counselling at the employer's expense. The amount of profit that this program produces has been declining steadily over the past four years as competition for contracts depresses the hourly fee that will be paid by employers and increases the number of other unpaid activities (such as newsletter production) that is required.

Environmental Organization

The Environmental Organization (EO) is a small environmental nonprofit organization located in southern Ontario. It has an annual budget of around $300,000 supporting a nearly full-time manager, who is paid for four days per week, several part-time positions, and some project-based and seasonal contract positions. Particular EO programs make extensive use of volunteers, while others are delivered by paid staff only. The organization's services are intentionally targeted widely in the community in which it is located to appeal to members of the public who would not necessarily identify themselves as "environmental." In contrast to the typical environmental organization that focuses on education, research, advocacy, and policy intervention, the EO focuses on the design and delivery of tangible services and activities.

EO's past four years have also been quite turbulent, particularly in terms of funding. Before the change of provincial government in 1995, EO had a multi-year funding commitment from the provincial Ministry of Environment and Energy for a variety of its core programs. The total annual budget peaked in 1994 at slightly more than $500,000, half of which came from provincial funding. Shortly following the change of government, EO's provincial funding was eliminated completely. At present the organization has no core grant funding and its program areas subsist on an amalgam of third-party service fees, earned revenue, volunteers, and small staff grants.

EO offers three distinct programs: household visits, used clothing collection, and an ecological garden. The household visit (HV) has existed as EO's core program for approximately five years. The HV basically involves one or two EO staff going to a client's residence and doing an energy, water, and waste assessment with the client. The assessment is practical in nature; the client is shown what kinds of energy-use problems may exist and the types of materials needed to improve energy use. Clients are also shown how energy-saving materials can be properly installed. As well as assessment, the HV includes the installation of a variety of energy and water-conserving technologies (for example, a water-conserving toilet dam and a shower faucet aerator).

At present, funding for this program consists of a mixture of user-fees, third-party beneficiary fees, and the organization's "endowment." Direct user-fees are variable: a basic HV installation visit has no service charge, but a longer and more comprehensive assessment, complete with computer diagnostic, customized check-list and product samples costs $49. In addition, several third parties provide service fees, reflecting the socially beneficial nature of this program in residential energy, water, and waste conservation. These third parties include: the local municipality, which directly benefits from reduced waste volumes and reduced water consumption; the local utility commission, which, as a public utility, engages its mission of minimizing its clients' energy bills; and the local gas utility, which has elements of energy-demand management as part of its corporate plan registered with the Ontario Energy Board.

The Used Clothing Collection (UCC) program was initiated in 1997 as a commercial revenue-generating venture that was consonant with the mission of EO. It consists of twice-yearly clothing drives where interested local residents can leave used clothing in Blue Bags on the sidewalk. EO contracts people to drive around the city to pick up these donated clothes and fabrics. Clothing is then aggregated in a large truck and shipped to a reseller. The UCC is ad hoc and project-based rather than ongoing. The present plan is for three to four UCC campaigns per year. Both the planning/management staff and the pick-up/delivery staff are on short-term project contracts.

The UCC program is funded on the basis of earned revenue, although the organization's small financial endowment funded the initial planning and start-up costs for the venture. As an ongoing program, the UCC program's single source of revenue comes from the sale of the textiles shipped. An average UCC nets approximately $12,000, although this figure includes only the project's direct costs.

The Ecological Garden (EG) is a program pre-dating both the HV and the UCC. Unlike the HV, the garden has never had a significant funding base and has always had a number of highly dedicated volunteers. The EG is focused on developing and maintaining a site for the demonstration of ecological gardening, horticulture, and landscaping techniques. It has a permanent site in the city, and maintains a variety of gardens (e.g., children's garden, low-water garden, butterfly garden, perennial garden) for use in educational contexts. While it has taken several years to get fully established, many community members now drop in for a visit and walk around to see the many sights. Workshop registration and participation is variable.

The EG is more volunteer-based than other programs at EO, and is led by a dedicated staff-person whose employment status varies from nearly full-time to part-time seasonal depending on the funds available. EG revenue consists of user-fees, donations, revenue from the sales of vegetables, perennials and seeds, government staffing grants and funding from the endowment base of the EO. During the spring, the EG hosts several school groups which pay user-fees for the visit. In terms of sales, the EG sells vegetables and cut flowers at a local market as well as on-site. Compost provided free by the municipality is also sold on-site. Grants for summer garden staff who both maintain the gardens and deliver educational programs are received from the provincial government as part of a Summer Employment program.

FINDINGS

From the broadest perspective, the two case studies provide a wealth of insights that add considerable detail, clarification, and nuance to the framework developed in Zimmerman and Dart (1998). Table 2 summarizes the extent to which the findings relate to the themes developed in the framework. The cases also add several surprises that were not anticipated in the framework and form the basis of a reframing of themes. Because of the limited number of cases, there is no information at all for several of the themes. For example, neither organization illustrated "shifts away from charitable giving" because neither organization had an appreciable

Table 2: Overall Results Summary

Resources	Relationships	Reputation	Responsiveness
• **cannibalization**	• *****board of directors**	• *community perception*	• **increased productivity**
• *shifts away from intentional giving*	• *recipients, beneficiaries, clients*	• *****market perception – unfair competition**	• *change to less hierarchical, more adaptable structure*
• *****synergies and decreased financial risk**	• *donors and funders*	• **shifting definition of success**	• *****"low-hanging fruit"**
• *****increased financial risk**	• *volunteers*		• **customer focus**
• *using more energy to get fewer dollars*	• *organized labour*		• **mission and values of charity are undermined by business venture**
• *****burning charitable dollars**	• *professional staff*		
• *volunteers*			
• *****cost of hiring business managers**			
• *****reward structures would have to be changed**			
• **commercial activities can be undermined by the mission and values of a charity**			

Notes:
- *Italics* = minor or no insight from this study.
- **Bold** = illustration, clarification or refinement of theme in this study.
- *****Bold** = significant new insight or reframing of theme in this study.

charitable giving program before the initiation of commercial ventures. Both organizations are relatively small and strongly community-based. The intimate relationships with both stakeholders and community members provide a nexus of opportunity and constraint that is distinct from organizations less complexly networked into their community.

The Resources Dimension

The following table briefly summarizes the findings on the critical issue of the impact of commercial activity in the resources of the two organizations.

Table 3: Emergent Outcomes: The Resources Dimension

Resources	Summary Notes
• **cannibalization** • *shifts away from intentional giving*	• revenue streams other than donations can be both cannibalized and supported by commercial ventures
• ***synergies and decreased financial risk** • ***increased financial risk** • *using more energy to get fewer dollars*	• a commercial activity can simultaneously increase the revenue stability and the financial risk for the nonprofit, also the risks and benefits of commercial activities may be felt asymmetrically within the host organization
• ***burning charitable dollars** • *volunteers*	• revenues other than donated ones can be "burned" developing commercial ventures, but one-time expenditures from the organization's financial base may be necessary to fund restructuring
• ***cost of hiring business managers**	• organizations may deal with the somewhat different issue of "how to manage a business venture" without a business manager, particularly when costs preclude hiring someone outside the existing staff complement
• ***reward structures would have to be changed**	• performance-based rewards may be unnecessary when program survival depends on productivity; in addition, the motivation for a commercial venture need not be *productivity* and *profit* and thus may not need different reward structures
• **commercial activities can be undermined by the mission and values of a charity**	• a nonprofit's culture and goals place strong limits on the degree to which it can be oriented toward "maximizing financial return"

Notes:
  • *Italics* = minor or no insight from this study.
  • **Bold** = illustration, clarification or refinement of theme in this study.
  • ***Bold** = significant new insight or reframing of theme in this study.

Cannibalization. Cannibalization refers to the possibility that commercial ventures will detract from donation and/or fundraising opportunities. It should not be surprising that little evidence was found that commercial venturing by these two organizations had a cannibalizing effect on donations and non-transaction-based exchanges. After all, the whole donation/fundraising revenue stream was minimal for both organizations. Also, while both CO and EO had a few donors in the community, these were people quite distinct from the communities to which either organization sold services.

However, the situations at CO and EO provide examples of how to refine and clarify the meaning of *cannibalization.* The comments of the executive director of the United Way in the community where CO operates highlighted a way that commercial ventures might negatively impact *grants* rather than donations: the United Way's allocations are based at least partially on "demonstration of financial need," and "at least hypothetically if someone had a business that was successful, we might see that as showing they have less financial need than an organization that couldn't do it." These concerns did not apply to CO's grant evaluations, but they highlight two important additions to our understanding of the way that nonprofit commercial ventures might affect the organization's overall resource situation. First, they highlight a mediating variable — perceived financial need — that is part of the decision metric of grants that a commercial venture could affect. Second, they broaden the scope of the kinds of revenue streams that could be affected by increases in commercial revenue.

The ecological garden at EO also shows a distinct way of framing the cannibalization concern. At the garden, attempts at fundraising have been largely unsuccessful. However, sales of cut flowers and fresh vegetables to supporters and associates of the organization have been comparatively successful. The coordinator of the ecological garden said that, for some people, purchasing products from the garden "was a way to ... support what we are doing." This highlights a positive way of framing issues of cannibalization. Rather than viewing product sales as something that might interfere with donations, product sales can be seen as an opportunity for people to apply their "donative" or supportive impulse. This suggests that commercial ventures may sometimes provide contexts for community members to contribute to an organization when donation or fundraising opportunities are not tenable. This question needs additional exploration, particularly for the large population of smaller organizations in the nonprofit sector which do not have the public visibility or the organizational resources to mount sophisticated fundraising campaigns.

Financial Synergies and Risk. "Synergies" refers to the possibility that commercial ventures can strengthen both the charitable mission of the organization as well as improve, stabilize, and diversify its finances. However, it is also possible that commercial ventures increase the financial risk experienced by the organization.

The only intentionally commercial program of the EO was the used clothing collection program. Despite the fact that the UCC coordinator was reluctant to call this excess, "profit," surplus funds from this program were used to subsidize other programs and the administrative core of the organization. From one perspective, this program could be seen to enhance the financial stability of the organization. The last clothing drive produced a net profit of approximately $12,000, although considerable organizational costs were not factored into this amount. From this angle, it did contribute to the overall financial viability of the organization. However, as a bottom-line endeavour, the UCC program also exposes EO to significant financial risk. The coordinator outlined the way that the UCC is necessarily risky because of the need for costs to precede revenues, unlike the traditional nonprofit funding model.[4]

> That's the funny thing about the clothing drive because you go into it not knowing every time whether you are going to make a cent or not ... or is it going to actually cost you? So in that sense I guess it's like a lot of business things, you might get a product that doesn't sell. From the minute we start the clothing drive practically, the costs are going to be there whether people put up product or not. And we had a textile drive where it rained every day and the volume went down tremendously. It still cost us the same hard costs to run that drive so we can accomplish our objective of getting the material out of the landfill and feel good about that ... But clothing drives are a hell of a lot of work. They are an incredible amount of work and we may end up with nothing.

This initiative illustrates the way that a new source of commercial revenue can diversify the finances of its host organization and yet also expose the organization to considerable financial risk. In effect, financial "risk" can be paradoxically increased and decreased by a single commercial venture. A commercial venture might pose a greater financial risk or uncertainty in cash flows than any of the organization's other activities. Hence, financial risk is increased. However, the diversification of revenue sources has the capacity to reduce the financial risk of the entire portfolio or activities. At the level of each individual activity, risk is increased; but for the overall organization, risk may be decreased.

In contrast to the relatively new and small venture of EO, CO has managed a relatively large, overtly "commercial" program for several years. Their employee assistance program is designed explicitly to be a for-profit venture of the kind highlighted by Skloot (1987). In the early 1990s, it was highly profitable for CO, producing sufficient profit to pay for a portion of the building that CO bought to house itself. However, at present, EAP contracts produce a surplus or profit when direct out-of-pocket costs only are factored in. When such "indirect" costs as management, marketing, administration, and client service other than counselling are factored in, the clinical service manager at CO actually believes that they *lose* money on their for-profit EAP contracts. On a full cost accounting basis, the contracts lose money.[5] Further, given the deregulation and restructuring of the EAP market nationally,[6] CO expects major difficulties in retaining EAP contracts when the next round of competitive bidding takes place. This latter observation, made without hesitation by the executive director at CO, highlights some of the possible intrinsic competitive limitations of a relatively small community-based organization in markets that are restructured to be dominated by economies of scale.

The story at CO, however, also illustrates another possible meaning of increased and decreased financial stability and risk. The motivation for CO to gain or retain EAP contracts is not quite the for-profit cross-subsidization strategy outlined in Zimmerman and Dart (1998). The EAP contracts have been used to facilitate *human resources* stability rather than financial stability. CO has been quite conscious that it is unable to pay its dedicated counselling and social work staff as much as they might earn in a larger institutional setting such as a hospital or in private practice. EAP revenue was structured to provide counselling staff an opportunity to earn extra revenue above the amount that can be derived from the organization's grants. Thus, this for-profit initiative is primarily organized to benefit the professional staff rather than the organization. There is evidence that the EAP contracts do improve the financial situation of its staff considerably more than the organization. This disjuncture in commercial enterprise benefits and risks was not anticipated in Zimmerman and Dart (1998).

The used clothing collection program and the employee assistance program thus provide clear examples of the way that for-profit ventures simultaneously enhance and undermine the financial stability of their host nonprofit organization. Two additional themes emerged when the perspective is broadened. First, in neither organization was there any evidence of steady, long-term, for-profit revenue stream from any of the so-called commercial or for-profit ventures. Second, programs based on a diverse blending of fees, such as EO's household visit and ecological park and CO's financial counselling program, demonstrated much more financial stability than the so-called for-profit ventures themselves. There was evidence from both cases that revenue diversification *within* programs is a much more significant source of financial stability than is cross-subsidization from a for-profit venture to a more mission-based program.

Burning Charitable Dollars? There was no evidence from either organization that donated funds were either used or lost in the development of for-profit ventures. However, the manner in which other analogous funds were both risked, lost, and recouped in a variety of programs at CO and EO suggest that this theme of "burning" revenue should be reframed and broadened.

Although EO has only a nominal fundraising and donations program, it does have a nest egg of money left over from the period in which the provincial government withdrew funding from the organization. The EO was funded to the year-end, but cut staff and office costs before that time and saved the money to fund future necessities. This nest egg of capital subsidized the organization's administration, the household visit program and the ecological garden on a limited basis and more than 50 percent of this capital has now been used.[7] This represents a kind of burning of funds, because the organization itself is still not financially self-sustaining and the funds go directly to an ongoing program subsidy rather than to program redevelopment or redesign costs.[8]

In contrast to EO's use of a financial nest egg for ongoing program funding, the financial counselling program at CO used its nest egg for program redevelopment. After its provincial funding was cut, the financial counselling staff-person went to the board of directors with a plan to use its nest egg for a risky plan to restructure the program in a financially sustainable manner. He told the board:

> We've got a little bit of a reserve left that we haven't used up. We need that money for seed money so that I can hire a really good individual and we can use the money for a period of a year ... This year will be a make or break situation because it is basically one chance to generate enough new Debt Management plans, to get our numbers way up so that by the time this provincial money is used up in the reserve we will have replaced it with enough donations[9] so that we can put this new person on full time.

The financial counselling program provides an example of the use of unallocated funds as part of a process to redesign the program rather than simply to keep a financially unviable program afloat. Funds were used here as a kind of start-up capital, and therefore they were put at risk. However, this risk should be compared with the certain dissolution of the program if it had continued in its earlier form.

This is another aspect to reframing the concept of burning charitable dollars. The pockets of unallocated funds available to EO and the financial counselling program represented an anomalous situation resulting from massive public sector funding cuts. There is no such capital available for a program like clinical services at CO and its for-profit analogue, the employee assistance program. The manager of these programs at CO complained that part of the reason that they were unable to compete with large health management organizations (HMOs) on EAP contract bidding was that CO had no financial resources to fund the marketing and contracting phase of the venture.

> They [for-profit competitors] have full marketing departments, they have budgets that you can take people out to lunch with.... A woman I know who does this full time for an American health management organization that now works in Canada, they give her a clothing allowance. It's like a true capitalist expenditure thing. We don't have that here. We don't have those resources. If I took $10,000 to market our E.A.P., I would have to lay off one of my counsellors.

For the clinical service program at CO, there are no unallocated funds to use for investment and start-up costs for commercial ventures. This raises serious questions about the long-term viability and profitability of nonprofit commercial ventures, especially in areas of competition with commercial firms.

Cost of Hiring Business Managers. Since managers in for-profit organizations typically earn more than their nonprofit counterparts, how can a nonprofit afford the kind of manager needed to make a commercial venture work? And how can this avoid sending "two-tiered" messages back to the rest of the organization?

The experience of both EO and CO suggest that the business manager issue is framed quite differently in smaller, more community-based organizational settings. Both EO and CO have managers or executive directors with private sector experience. But in both organizations, they are the general managers of the organization rather than the managers of the commercial ventures. EO's commercial venture was managed by a person with a long-term connection to the organization, and with primarily public sector and nonprofit sector experience. Despite its considerable size, CO's EAP was managed by the clinical services manager whose background and training is in nonprofit social work. For both organizations, the issue was not how much to pay a business manager and how to avoid a conflict between business and nonprofit pay scales, but rather how to manage a commercial venture using in-house personnel resources. This reframes the way that the business manager issue is likely to be considered in such organizations.

The choice of in-house staff as venture managers is an interesting one and adds a great deal of complexity to the business manager issue. For the EAP, there was no opportunity to recruit a business manager because in order to tender a competitive bid, CO had to remove its 3 percent administrative overhead fee. The clinical services manager explains:

> Now we won these contracts, I hate to tell you, by undercutting other people. Other people were trying to get a 3 percent administration charge put on every billing every month. Our clients which fund a huge E.A.P. wouldn't pay it, so I said I would do fee-for-service. It was a big mistake. But nonetheless I won it. Because we undercut [our competitors], now I hear they are dropping their administration fee to be competitive when the contract comes up in three months.

The lack of an expected entrepreneurial business manager to manage the ventures is surprising at first, but makes sense in the context of the cash-poor situation in which both organizations find themselves.

Reward Structures. Would commercial ventures mean the use of performance-based compensation systems for the host nonprofit organization? Reward structures are part of a broader issue of motivation and control of staff, and the experience of CO and EO provides evidence on this larger issue. Neither organization has changed to any kind of performance-based compensation for front-line staff or management. However, the concept of reward structures has been reframed in a very interesting manner in both cases.

The financial counselling program at CO has a reward structure that is premised on staff performance, but the reward is not so much pay increments as continued employment. In the FCP, more than 80 percent of the overall revenue from which salaries are drawn is now derived from service fees rather than block grants or contracts. If services are not provided, then the program has no revenue and staff do not get paid. The origin of this reward structure was the cut in provincial government funding. The financial counselling manager described the need to increase their debt management plan account load substantially through aggressive promotion and client recruitment.

> After losing our provincial grants, we just worked our butts off and we're still doing it now, and we've never looked back since then. Before the cuts, we were disbursing [amount] per year to creditors, right now we are disbursing [amount] per month, so that's around [2.5 times the earlier figure] a year. That's [amount] of client deposits into our trust account, and creditors return approximately 25 percent of this to us in donations. After we lost our funding, we brought our numbers of clients way up and we had no choice. The days of basically laying back and saying 'we are funded here, we're a Social Services Agency and we don't have to worry about our funds' ... those days are over.

The EAP program at CO is structured based on somewhat different priorities. As noted earlier, CO organizes this program to allow their relatively poorly paid staff to top-up their income working as private practitioners *within* rather than *for* CO. The clinical services manager described it as follows:

> With staff so poorly paid in this kind of nonprofit agency, it was the only way my staff had of making some extra bucks a year. If my staff were adequately paid, I'd chuck the EAP out the window in a second. The staff here do the nonprofit work but they can also choose, on their free time, to do EAP clients. So it is almost like they get two chunks of money from the agency, one in their regular job and one as private practitioners I've hired. So it is like overtime. Some choose to do it and some don't. In organizations like ours across Ontario, counselling staff make about $15-20,000 less than their equivalent in hospitals. So there is a huge push for us to make some money for our staff to keep them here.

This is another example where commercial ventures relate to employee compensation, but not in the manner suggested in Zimmerman and Dart (1998). Here the issue is not the managerially-oriented concept of productivity but rather a more staff-oriented perspective of fair compensation and staff retention.

Commercial Activities Can Be Undermined by the Charity. Does the mission and culture of nonprofit organizations reduce the viability and vitality of for-profit initiatives?

There was ample evidence that the nonprofit basis of both CO and EO posed significant constraints on the for-profit or commercial initiatives that they began. For example, the used clothing collection program at EO consciously made several choices which are consonant with its mission-focus but potentially limiting for its financial success. They chose a textile buyer that was a mission-focused charity rather than a for-profit commodities broker, and they chose to sell textiles unsorted rather than risk having product remaining that would end up in the landfill. The coordinator explained their choices:

> We are selling clothes unsorted at [number] cents a pounds right now. I can get probably up to [1.25 times more] cents a pound unsorted from other companies. You would wonder immediately why we haven't gone to the higher amount because it is an appreciable difference. One of the reasons is that we got burned in the past. We sold to a private broker and the textiles went there and the money never came back. We know that the [charity buyer] pays and they pay quickly. With a nonprofit, there is also that sense of people supporting us because we doing good work. We are keeping textiles out of the landfill and other people are going to have a chance to use them. As we get deeper and deeper into the brokerage area of textiles as a commodity,

it becomes more pure profit and less of a good feeling thing to do for people. We don't honestly know how dependent our support is on people's perception of donating to charity and helping others. That's always a problem in the charitable world when you are trying to make money.

Once you are into textile brokerage, it's a very big field of commodities and a very rough and tumble world. When you see something like shoes that will sell for forty-two cents a pound, you think maybe we should sort but what do you do with what you have got left over? ... Our primary objective is to get that waste out of the landfill.[10] If we start picking the plums out of the textiles, then what we are left with is a product that nobody will want and probably will have to be landfilled. We could make a lot more money, but not reach our environmental objective. That's the horns of the dilemma that we increasingly are on at EO.

The financial counselling program at CO constrains its revenue base in a similar manner, based on their nonprofit mission. Given their position in the financial counselling and bankruptcy markets, they have opportunities to get finder's fees from bankruptcy trustees as well as financial counselling contracts with individuals going through the bankruptcy process. The FCP decided that they were unable to accept finder's fees, despite their role as a referring organization, because the FCP does not want to be perceived as benefiting from referring individuals into bankruptcy. As well, a potentially lucrative financial counselling opportunity was regarded negatively because of its association with the bankruptcy trustee industry. The FCP manager described the situation as follows:

I have a real ethical problem. If I take a finder's fee, then we are going to appear to be 'for-profit only' in the eyes of the community. We will lose our credibility with the United Way. If we take a finder's fee, I think we would lose our credibility because we would send a message out that we are prepared to exploit people. We may send people down to the bankruptcy trustee. Maybe they shouldn't have gone there but we sent them down because we got $100 for doing it. I can't do that.

I know that someone from a large bankruptcy trustee organization is going to be coming here with a very lucrative offer. They are going to have a traveling trustee who is going to come into the community. He is going to want us to do counselling and bankruptcy services out of this building. In return, he will give us contracts for the first and second session of bankruptcy counselling, not just on our clients I refer but on every client that he would deal through their advertising. So this could be maybe $50-60,000 a year for us. I will be recommending to the Executive Director when that offer comes up that the agency reject it because, again, it's not why we are here. We lose our credibility and objective if we do that ... and that is not why we are here. Definitely it will be hard to turn down.

Despite the relatively commercial nature of the used clothing collection program and the financial counselling program, revenues or profits were deliberately limited and curtailed in both cases. In both cases, the organization's nonprofit mission and staff's concerns about the community's perception of the mission provide significant constraints on commercial ventures and contribute to a strong sense that commercial activities are, indeed, undermined by the mission and values of the charity.

The Relationships Dimension

The following table briefly summarizes the findings discussed in greater detail in the following section.

Table 4: Relationships

Relationships	*Summary Notes*
• ***board of directors**	• Boards recognize the need to access new revenue sources, but there is mixed opinion concerning whose responsibility it is to actually organize and initiate the ventures.
• *recipients, beneficiaries, clients*	
• *donors and funders*	
• *volunteers*	
• *organized labour*	
• *professional staff*	

Notes:
- *Italics* = minor or no insight from this study.
- **Bold** = illustration, clarification or refinement of theme in this study.
- ***Bold** = significant new insight or reframing of theme in this study.

Boards of Directors. Do the boards of directors play a significantly different role in nonprofits that undertake commercial ventures? The initiation of "commercial ventures" and more broadly a "commercial orientation" had no effect on the composition of the board of either organization studied here. Moreover, although the boards of both organizations were beginning to reconsider, there was a sense that they were not thinking differently enough.

At EO, the board of directors remains a mix of representatives from key stakeholder organizations such as the government and utilities commission as well as the local business and environmental communities. This composition has not changed appreciably since the loss of provincial government funding. What has changed is the board's emphasis on revenue generation. The board has become quite keen for the staff to initiate money-earning activities. As a long-time board member explained:

> As a board member, we will be discussing making more money from the used clothing collection program.... I don't know that there is a consensus between the staff and board about this. [Not being profit-oriented] is one of the reasons staff remain here. If we as a board told them to choose the profit motive over the environmental objective, many of the staff wouldn't be here. I don't know if the organization would exist. The sense you get at the board is that things have got to be sustainable, and the only way it can become sustainable is to earn enough money to pay the staff.

The EO board member discussed a possibility for EO staff to pursue a large utility service contract in the community that could be a revenue-generator used to subsidize core EO functions.

> So there is a job there. A huge job there, to be done which could keep EO viable. That could be the cash cow that keeps EO viable and pays for all the other EO projects for a number of years. [A board member] talks about it all the time but I never hear it mentioned at EO by staff. It's talked about at the board all the time.

There are other examples as well. The general pattern is that the board of directors senses a variety of revenue-generating possibilities, but the staff are not particularly enthusiastic about the idea of doing them. It is extra work, and it is not why they work at EO.

A similar tension is visible at CO. Its board of directors also suggests revenue-generating ideas to staff, but the staff is reluctant to undertake the extra work necessary to initiate new activities. A staff-person at CO explains:

> Most of the people who sit on boards are lovely people but do they know how to grind money out of other places? No. First of all, boards of organizations like this are not entrepreneurial. You might get a business man or business woman on your board, but that's the luck of the draw. It's usually because their mother needed services and we dealt with them. It is not because they say 'CO as an agency needs to stay alive.' It is because they have a personal thing.
>
> So you get this nice board of directors. You get lovely staff, all of whom are trained to be counsellors but not trained to raise money. I'm one of these people who went to school forever. I never took a single course in how you make any money.
>
> [The ED] has not been able to get our board to look at fund raising, period. The only fund raising that has occurred here was a book sale the staff put together and I can tell you I am totally against the staff of agencies doing the fund raising. Already you work five days a week and then come in all day Saturday to do a book sale ... You have the same six or seven amazingly dedicated people on, like, eight boards. To ask them to do another fundraiser, I think it is almost cruelty and they honestly don't know how to do them.
>
> ... so there has been some discussion about our board trying to do a gala, and one of the staff said, 'I'm not going anymore' ... The board's expectation was the staff were going to do this because it directly benefited the staff by keeping them employed and the staff were thinking their job was to work here, not to do the fund raising.

The close parallels in the board-staff tension at both CO and EO reframes issues that were not explicit in Zimmerman and Dart (1998). When staff are overworked as a result of funding and staff cuts, and when board members are spread thin through involvement in other activities, where does the extra person-power come from to initiate a new venture? In addition to the particular skill set of board members, their activity level may also be a crucial element in the scope for new ventures. Further, the situations at both organizations reveals the potential for board-staff conflict on their respective roles and responsibility to undertake work that had previously been seen as the responsibility of neither.

The Reputation Dimension

The following table briefly summarizes the findings concerning the reputational dimension of the framework.

Table 5: Reputation Outcomes

Reputation	Summary Notes
• *community perception* • ***market perception – unfair competition**	• Nonprofits compete in both for-profit and mission-based program areas, with both for-profits and other nonprofits. Some for-profit ventures are constrained by ethical concerns about competition. While some program areas do have intrinsic competitive advantages based on their nonprofit status, others see their competitive abilities as fundamentally tenuous and limited.
• **Shifting definition of success**	• Most nonprofit program areas already emphasize the short-term, tangible and individual benefits that commercial ventures were suggested to encourage.

Notes: • *Italics* = minor or no insight from this study.
  • **Bold** = illustration, clarification or refinement of theme in this study.
  • ***Bold** = significant new insight or reframing of theme in this study.

Market Perception of Unfair Competition. Nonprofits are alleged to have advantages such as tax-free status, extensive volunteer networks, and grant revenue that allow them to compete unfairly with businesses in their communities.

This study did not include interviews with private sector competitors of the commercial and quasi-commercial initiatives of CO and EO. However, interviews within the organizations themselves help clarify and reframe the issue of unfair competition. Most importantly, the issue of competition with private sector organizations was relevant not only to the commercial programs of the nonprofits, but to their core mission programs as well. This finding itself has many implications for our understanding of the nonprofit/for-profit interface.

The overtly commercial employee assistance program of CO had competitors ranging from large HMOs to small associations of private practitioners. However, its clinical services program also served the same market as a variety of for-profit organizations, and some of its clientele had the financial means to go elsewhere. Similarly, while the relatively commercial used clothing collection program of EO competed with several charitable organizations for donations of textiles, the household visit program provided some services that were also available from private sector firms. This broad perspective suggests that perhaps the issue of unfair competition is not limited to nonprofit commercial ventures.

Perceptions of *competition* and *fairness* varied from one program to another. EO's concern with perceptions of the local business community leads to a kind of self-restraint in planning new initiatives. Plans for a construction material re-use business were cancelled at the last minute because a similar small business was being set up and there were fears that EO's venture would make the small business unviable. This kind of concern about competing with business limits the number of potential commercial opportunities that EO has been able to pursue. The director of EO indicated:

> It's hard to think of an area where we can be revenue generating that somebody else hasn't already heard about or doesn't hear about by virtue of us looking at it. So at what point should you back down? You set something up and then somebody else sets one up ... well you're competing with it ... While we were funded by [the provincial government], that was a concern. But right now we are not government funded. We are an independent nonprofit and I think we should go out and compete in the market the same way as anybody else on those things that satisfy our mandate.

Clearly, perceptions of the relevance of *unfair competition* change according to the funding status of the organization.

In contrast, CO's concerns with competition reflected traditional discussions of comparative advantage and market segmentation. Its most commercial program, the EAP, harboured no illusions about unfair competition. CO's competitors are organizations that have marketing departments, dedicated proposal writers and front-line staff who are paid approximately half as much per hour as CO pays their staff.[11] Rather than viewing CO as having unfair competitive abilities, they view their competitive situation as extremely difficult and tenuous. The clinical service manager describes the situation:

> A couple of things happened in the last five years. One was, once someone identified this EAP market locally, other people noticed and said, 'we can

take it on too.' [When we began], I think we lived in a dream world. We thought this was going to be a little paradise of counselling and we were such nice people [the contractors] would go for our proposal. But these health management organizations who compete with us are business. They are very clear about it. Well, we can't compete the same way.

In the same organization, the financial counselling program has a fundamentally different unfair competition issue. Its niche (i.e., serving people in failing personal financial situations) is also served by a variety of for-profit organizations including banks, bankruptcy trustees, paralegals, and financial advisors. FCP has several competitive assets which seem to give it significant competitive advantages over other competitors. For example, when the provincial government cut the funding for such programs across the province, it made legal provisions for such nonprofit programs to operate trust accounts to collect money and distribute it to creditors. Paralegals who offer similar debt management services have no such ability. Further, because FCP is part of a charitable organization, it is able to issue charitable donation receipts, which for-profit agencies are unable to do. The manager of the FCP views these unique abilities as commensurate with their mission-based focus on the interests of their clients rather than the interests of creditors.

Shifting Definitions of Success. It is proposed that the experience of commercial venturing and its necessary market orientation will affect the kinds of services that are offered by the nonprofit organization and that the nonprofit will drift toward programs with immediate benefits for individuals (i.e., Quadrant A below) and away from perhaps more important programs which are long term and societally focused. In this way, ideas of success will change.

The two case studies highlight the complex distinction between the increase in the commercialization of the nonprofit sector and particular examples of commercial ventures or programs. Most broadly, we found that almost all program areas in both organizations were *already* oriented toward activities that benefited individuals rather than society and that promised results more quickly rather than more fundamentally. Programs in both organizations that were framed as more commercial, such as EO's used clothing collection and CO's employee assistance program, were no more oriented toward Quadrant A than were the programs that were

Figure 1: Typology Framework for Charities

	Goods and Services	
	Private	*Collective*
Short **Cause and Effect Lag**	**A** *Examples:* • Cultural interpretation • Food Banks • Training adults for future employability	**B** *Examples:* • Environmental group focused on recycling • Creating parks in low income neighbourhoods
Long	**C** *Examples:* • Educating children to prevent welfare status • Family counseling	**D** *Examples:* • Advocacy for literacy • Environmental group focused on prevention/diversification • Disease prevention

Source: Zimmerman and Dart (1998).

supposedly *core* and *mission-based*. In CO's clinical services area, the shift in the organization parallels broader changes within the social work profession. The social work field has changed in the past decade from forms of therapy focused on fairly fundamental psycho-therapeutic changes in clients over a fairly long period of time to a "consult clinic" model focused on cognitively-oriented sessions of brief therapy. This model fit beautifully said the executive director, "with the kinds of changes we were trying to do here":

> We went to a 'consult clinic' model. People were seen faster. Clients had to be very motivated. Years ago seeing people for five years of therapy was basically creating a dependency and it was really about pathology ... These people were always going to be pathologically unsound. Now our approach is: you're well enough to survive this long, you are having some trouble now, we are going to give you some tools to deal with that, some cognitive therapy and then you are out of the system or you can come back if you need to but you are not coming here forever. Very clear. So it is a huge shift in styles.

Counselling, then, has been reorganized around basic conceptual and behavioural tools which can be learned and applied relatively quickly, often within the initial three sessions of counselling. While this shift at CO has certainly had an impact on its definitions of success, it did not have its origin directly in cost minimization.[12]

The financial counselling program at CO has also shifted into Quadrant A activities — although for reasons that were more financial — and intimately connected with the loss of core grant funding. Prior to the loss of public funding, the FCP provided a considerable amount of direct assistance to individuals (often with mental disabilities) who were unable to manage personal budgets. The manager of the FCP described their move toward program activities which provide more earned revenue:

> When funding was always there for us from the government and United Way, we could spend a lot of time sitting down with people working out budgets. I used to have clients who would walk in here, who wanted budgeting help. They needed help paying monthly expenses, from their disability cheques.... They have the money paid to them in twos, fives, and have it put into a paper bag and brought it in here. Put it right there on my desk. We worked out a monthly expense sheet for them and we have an envelope for every expense. Groceries for the month of May, clothing for the month of May, rent, heat, hydro and I take that money and I divvy it up into each envelope and I send them away and say, there you go. That's it for the month. You do not touch that envelope unless you are paying the expense that envelope is for. We can't do that any more. It is just not possible.

> I know that sometimes there are people who come in here who would want budgeting help. I can't give them as much straight budgeting help as I would have been prepared to give 10 years ago. It doesn't help knowing that the United Way is reducing [CO's] funding to us as well because we always felt that the United Way funding represented that portion of what we gave to the community in general.

> How do we justify that [focusing on services that generate earned revenue] morally here? Well, the only way that we could provide community services to those people whom we don't charge fees to, is to make sure that we stabilize our Debt Management Program. We have to put a lot of effort into getting Debt Management plans in order to have enough funds so that we can provide free services to the community.

Budget counselling is not the only activity that the FCP has curtailed as it pursues revenue generation. Before their provincial grants were cut, FCP staff would represent the interests of clients directly to collection agencies that were harassing individuals. Their approach has since shifted:

> I would have been prepared in the past to call the collector directly and argue with them but I don't do that anymore. Now I say [to clients]: If you are being harassed, read this booklet. If you are still being harassed then you ask the collector, this, this and this. If they refuse to answer these questions for you, call that number and make a formal complaint to the government.

The programs examined have not redefined *success* in an explicit way. But some programs have redefined what could and should be done and therefore what constitutes success. This shift has important implications for the responsiveness of these organizations.

The Responsiveness Dimension

The following table briefly summarizes the findings on responsiveness.

Table 6: Emergent Outcomes: The Responsiveness Dimension

Responsiveness	*Summary Notes*
• **increased productivity** • *change to less hierarchical, more adaptable structure*	• Examples of "business-like" productivity are common, but do not necessarily originate in actual business venturing.
• *****"low-hanging fruit"** • *customer focus* • **mission and values of charity are undermined by business venture**	• Programs may exclude difficult-to-service clientele for more ethically defensible reasons of overall program effectiveness rather than simply due to financial concerns. • Nonprofit mission and values are challenged but not undermined by business ventures.

Notes: • *Italics* = minor or no insight from this study.
 • **Bold** = illustration, clarification or refinement of theme in this study.
 • ***Bold** = significant new insight or reframing of theme in this study.

Increase Productivity. Commercial ventures may add a rigour and discipline to nonprofit organizations which allows programs and services to be delivered in a more productive manner.

The CO provides strong examples of increased productivity. However, these productivity innovations seem to have their origin, not in commercial activity, but in other factors: in coping with public sector funding cuts, the transformation of social work practice, and the conscious application of a kind of generic commercial mindset. As noted earlier, the clinical services program has been transformed dramatically in recent years to a cognitively-based brief therapy model. This has had several clear productivity effects. The executive director sums up the way in which a generic commercial mindset and the brief therapy model significantly increased the productivity of clinical services:

> If you were running a franchise in selling hamburgers right now, and you always had lineups and only the first twelve people were served within the first 15 minutes, and the rest of the lineup disappeared, you would wonder where the ones who leave are getting their hamburgers. When I came to the Agency we had a waiting list and sometimes it was 6-8 weeks and sometimes it was months before people could get into counselling. So we looked at this from a business point of view and said: 'okay, we have a clientele, how are we going to serve them?' From a business point of view, we can't afford to have a waiting list.

In CO's financial counselling program, productivity improvements can be directly correlated with their loss of government funding. Their manager explains the program's transformation from one in which two staff members managed fewer than 30 debt management plans and waited for clients to come to them to its present form where two staff manage more than 210 debt management plans and actively market, network, and recruit across the region in which they operate:

> All of a sudden, we advertised heavily, very heavily, which is something we never had to do before ... the funding was there so why did we need to advertise? We got paid whether the clients come through our door or not. Now, we are doing many many workshops and newspaper articles. We have expanded our service to [other places in the region]. We now have a regular office in [another town].

Thus these quasi-commercial improvements in productivity have come from a variety of unanticipated sources: the business backgrounds of the executive director and the manager of the FCP, institutional and professional norms such as the brief therapy model; and from the loss of core provincial funding.

Low-Hanging Fruit. One implication of commercial thinking is that organizations should focus on clientele that are more readily and efficiently serviceable (i.e., the "low-hanging fruit"). Hard to service, difficult to access or intractably-complex or problematic clientele are anathema to commercial ventures and commercial thinking because of their limited potential for efficient processing and therefore financial return.

The low-hanging fruit issue recurred throughout the course of this research, and the evidence is sufficient to fundamentally reframe the concept. In the case of the household visit program at EO, there is no evidence that suggested EO deliberately chose their clientele. Demand for their core household visit service has fallen off in recent years to the extent that there is no real waiting list for service. Clearly, low-hanging fruit may be an issue of relevance only to those programs where demand exceeds service availability. In contrast, CO clinical services recently made decisions that seem to illustrate, in a complex manner, some aspects of the low-hanging fruit issue. One of the major achievements of the new executive director has been the elimination of the long waiting list. In addition to the productivity improvements facilitated by brief therapy, choices were made to focus the clientele of CO and to limit service to the medicated psychiatric population. The executive director explains the decision as follows:

> One of the most interesting things that has come up so far is that the Clinical Services Manager, who seems to feel we need more staff, suddenly finds we're dealing with an inappropriate group of clients. We shouldn't be dealing with people who are psychiatric clients, who are depressed and who are medicated. We shouldn't be dealing with those. They should be referred to [hospital with psychiatric facilities]. So we have now come to the point, which everybody accepts, that we have some clients here who shouldn't be here. We don't need two extra staff. Instead we can look at what our mandate is and to some extent cut out according to the funding that we have got, but also the mandate that we have.

> There are ethical issues in there. Should we be taking people who won't take their medication? To me, that is an irresponsible use of resources. A medicated psychiatric client can sit in counselling until the cows come home.... In fact, if they are not taking their medication, we will never resolve that problem ... their behaviour is beyond counselling. So we draw the line in the sand and say: 'okay you are a medicated psychiatric patient and there are counselling resources for you in the hospital. They should give you the medication and they should give you counselling.' It is not our responsibility and it's not part of our mandate anyway.

On the surface, this issue could be framed as a relatively clear and obvious illustration of the low-hanging fruit principle, since CO has consciously decided to focus program access to a more readily served segment of clientele. By excluding medicated psychiatric clients, CO avoids a group of clients that is in need of long-term intensive service for which few positive results may be seen. However, there is nuance and complexity to CO's situation which may add to our understanding of the low-hanging fruit issue. The executive director never frames the choice in terms of *convenience*, but rather in terms of *function* (medicated psychiatric patients cannot be properly served at CO), *mandate* (this client segment is supposed to be served by another organization) and *core competence* (we need to focus on what we do best). This managerial attitude is perhaps commercial in origin, but not premised on financial efficiency so much as program effectiveness. The executive director reframes the low-hanging fruit issue in positive managerial terms:

> In a lot of organizations, managers come in to manage what they are told and what they are given to manage. In this organization, what we say to people all the time is: 'create what it is you're going to manage.' This emphasizes the positive stuff of delivery of service because you ask what the service should be. This involves creating mandates and extending mandates and pulling back in mandates to get the best out of what we are.

The concept of low-hanging fruit described in Zimmerman and Dart (1998) was premised on the idea that pulling back from difficult to more readily served clientele would be a result of a quasi-commercial decision-metric based on financial efficiency criteria. The clinical services case demonstrates that the same activity can be undertaken for reasons with more positive implications for service delivery and clientele. This situation also highlights a positive reframing of the "meeting needs and filling niches" distinction made in Zimmerman and Dart (1998). Rather than seeing niches as a commercial tool used to frame nonprofit clientele in financial terms, niche can also be a more generic managerial tool used to specify which client segments an organization can most effectively and productively serve.

The financial counselling program at CO provides a similar example. As noted earlier, the FCP has changed its emphasis from providing budget counselling to focusing more on the revenue-generating possibilities of debt management plans. With this change comes an implicit change in clientele, since most of the budget counselling clientele were extremely poor and/or mentally disabled individuals who were unable to even incur debt. The manager of the FCP illuminated the low-hanging fruit issue:

> We never turn a person away. We see anybody who wants to come in .... I think we are more efficient in our budgeting help, whereas before ... they came in here month after month after month.... Now I would be more prepared to say, 'I am sorry, I can't do that for you. I can show you how to do a budget but if you are having problems with it, if there is another area in your life there is a void, something that is preventing you from following the budget or something that is making you basically work against yourself, perhaps you need a professional in another field to deal with that.' So I would be more likely to pass them on to a therapist than what I would before.

The logical structure of this argument is that FCP implicitly focuses on clients who can more readily be served and reduces service to those with more difficult and/or intractable problems. This pattern is similar to that described in clinical services. Once again, the low-hanging fruit issue is perhaps more accurately framed as a generic program effectiveness issue.

These examples reframe the low-hanging fruit issue into something much more complex and nuanced. Clientele can be narrowed and focused for positive reasons of program effectiveness as well as more financial or efficiency criteria. The discussion, however, should not end here. In both cases, program effectiveness was perhaps improved at the expense of excluding members of marginal and vulnerable social groups. While it is perhaps true that they could not be effectively served at CO, it is also important to ensure that they are being referred to institutions or programs that are specifically organized to serve them and that they do not slip between the cracks.[13] Part of the analysis, then, moves to the societal level: Which organizations or institutions will see those with intractable problems as part of their effectively served niche?

Mission and Values Undermined by Business Venture. "The business venture can undermine the effectiveness of a charity achieving its mission because of the focus on efficiency" (Zimmerman and Dart 1998, p. 38).

Evidence from both organizations suggests that business ventures, and more broadly, the business thinking implicit in these ventures, challenge but do not necessarily undermine nonprofit values. As mentioned previously, the used clothing collection program at EO had a dilemma of to whom to sell their textiles. They could maximize their revenue by selling textiles to a for-profit commodities trader, but there would be no guarantee that the textiles would be used in socially beneficial ways or that some significant portion of them would not be landfilled. On the other hand, using their charitable textile buyer preserved social and environmental values, but generated less revenue. However, the unresolved status of this issue and the fact that even the choice of a for-profit buyer *could* benefit EO's mission indirectly (by providing more revenue) means that we are unable to conclude that any charitable values have been undermined in this process.

At CO, where the commercialization of programs is perhaps more developed, there was some overt resentment of the influence of business on programs. Some staff noted that the EAP creates a kind of two-tier counselling service where EAP clients get precedence over non-funded CO clients.

> [Y]ou know the E.A.P. people are guaranteed that someone will see them within 48 hours. We can't guarantee that for anybody else... So [staff] resent the two tieredness of it when I come in and say, 'you have to cancel this [clinical service client] because we have an emergency at [an EAP client]' ...
> If the staff were adequately paid, I suspect no one here would be doing that.

Here again we see the challenge that the practice of the commercial venture provides to the values of those staff who work in both nonprofit and commercial spheres.

In the financial counselling program we see a similar example of commercial logic challenging nonprofit logic. The FCP is in the odd position of being funded by creditor organizations such as banks and finance companies on the basis of its work on behalf of debtors who have defaulted on

AFTER GOVERNMENT CUTS / 143

payments. Staff in the FCP see their role as working for the best interests of the debtors, despite possible financial gains if they behaved with the interests of the creditor feepayers in mind. A staff member clearly frames the distinction:

> It is a love-hate relationship with the creditors. To be quite frank, I fully believe that most companies, chartered banks, wish that we didn't exist ... They are not there for the customers, they are there for the shareholders. They would ... send [overdue accounts] off to collection and let the customers be harassed and trampled on by collectors. When we say to these banks, 'we are trying to help these people, can you give them a break because they have got a family and if you don't do this they are probably going to have to file for bankruptcy.' The banks' attitude, is ... 'if they want to go bankrupt we don't have to care.'
>
> If we maintain our rocky relationship with our funders, then I feel we are doing our job. Because if everything were just hunky dorry and friendly with the banks, then I think we would lose touch with why we are here and I don't think the banks understand that. They think that because they're funding it [the FCP], we should be toeing the line.

Evidence from both organizations suggests that commercial values challenge, but do not — at least not yet — significantly undermine the mission-based values of the nonprofit organization.

SOME TENTATIVE GENERALIZATIONS

The primary goal of this study was to elaborate the findings from the two case studies in terms of the themes and categories discussed in Zimmerman and Dart (1998). In addition, we have examined the nonprofit enterprise in the context of relatively small and community-based nonprofit organizations, an understudied population in the nonprofit sector (Horton Smith 1997). While exploratory qualitative case studies do not warrant extensive generalization, five themes that have emerged during the course of our research illuminate our understanding of nonprofit commercial ventures.

First, the case studies highlight the challenges faced by nonprofits that initiate commercial activities. While both organizations had commercial activities that were considered relatively successful, the activities were actually quite challenging to the organizations. Rather than being a panacea as suggested by some (Emerson and Twersky 1996; Dees 1998), the commercial activities undertaken by both organizations were financially challenging and organizationally difficult. This should not be surprising. These ventures occur in the rough and tumble world of the commercial marketplace where competing organizations with different structures and value sets are also working to generate profits. We should question any assumption that commercial ventures by nonprofits are likely to be easy or that they are lucrative and significant revenue sources. In particular, our research highlights the particular difficulties of cash-poor, small-to-medium-sized nonprofit organizations. Without significant funds and/or economies of scale, they are unlikely to be able to make the kinds of business development investments that would allow them to generate significant longer term returns.

Second, the case studies broaden our understanding of the purpose(s) of nonprofit enterprise. The working premise of previous literature (e.g., Zimmerman and Dart 1998; Brinckerhoff 1990, 1994; Skloot 1987; Dees 1998; Crimmins and Keil 1983) was that nonprofit commercial enterprise exists either to generate revenue for use in the organization's mission-fulfilling programs or to help to engage the nonprofit mission itself. Our findings suggest that this list should be expanded, or viewed quite differently. Even in this very small sample of organizations and programs, we found commercial and quasi-commercial activities which existed to generate revenue to fund the administration of the organization, to retain professional staff by providing a salary top-up, and to provide would-be donors with an opportunity to give to the organization.

These examples illustrate ways that nonprofit commercial enterprise can *indirectly* support the mission of a nonprofit organization without directly providing additional funds to core cash-poor programs themselves. Although the literature suggests the primary *raison d'être* of nonprofit commercial enterprise is to generate revenue to cross-subsidize other programs, this pattern was not in evidence in any of the commercial activities observed in our research. All of the commercial and quasi-commercial programs were also *bona fide* mission-fulfilling activities.

Third, the case studies broaden our understanding of the multiple origins of nonprofit commercialization. Zimmerman and Dart (1998) suggest that nonprofit commercialization can have its origins in either financial scarcity (i.e., responding to funding cuts) or ideology (i.e., wanting to be more like a business). These were, in fact, part of the origin of nonprofit commercialization in our cases. However, we also found that nonprofit commercialization can have its origin in two other quite distinct concerns. Changes in CO's clinical services and financial counselling which could be characterized as commercial had their origins in the desire for improved program effectiveness. In addition, the particular nature of the changes in clinical services were also attributed to changes in professional norms. This suggests that the origins of nonprofit commercialization are likely to be as complex and diverse as the nonprofit enterprises which we observe.

Fourth, the case studies highlight the distinction between nonprofit enterprise and nonprofit commercialization. A variety of past studies blur the distinction between nonprofit enterprise (i.e., the activity undertaken for-profit) and nonprofit commercialization (i.e., the mode of thinking derived from for-profit businesses). Evidence from both of our cases suggests that the distinction between the two needs to be sharpened. Much of the commercialization uncovered in our study had its origin in something other than explicitly commercial enterprise. In fact, in several instances, the nonprofit mission-based programs seemed more commercialized than the nonprofit enterprise activities themselves. Since commercialization in nonprofits has multiple and distinct origins, we should not expect that commercial activities themselves will be the sole or primary source of broader commercialization in nonprofit organizations.

Fifth, the case studies highlight a continuum between nonprofit/for-profit and charitable/commercial modes of organizing. The nonprofit enterprise literature typically presents a dichotomy between nonprofit and for-profit, and between charitable and commercial.[14] In our case studies, we found no evidence for the existence of distinct and mutually exclusive modes of organizing. We found no core mission-based programs that seemed uninfluenced by elements of commercialization. Even such a normatively charged area as abuse counselling was organized in a quasi-commercial manner. Paralleling this, we found no nonprofit commercial enterprise activity that was without some kind of mission-related, pro-social underpinning. Even selling used textiles for money had to be good for the environment as well. The fact that all program areas studied exhibited both commercial and pro-social elements suggests that future research examine the structural, cognitive and functional continuum that is found between the pure nonprofit and for-profit types.

Notes

We would like to thank the Kahanoff Foundation for their financial support of this project. We also wish to thank Keith Banting and the School of Policy Studies at Queen's University for organizing a workshop which provided useful feedback for the paper. Kevin Davis' reviewer's comments were also very helpful.

[1] For a survey of more than 100 sources on the nonprofit enterprise phenomenon, see Zimmerman and Dart (1998).

[2] While this time period was sufficient to capture some of the dynamics of this changing phenomenon, we note that it is inadequate to assess the origins of any of the nonprofit commercial activities studied (since they were initiated before this study began) or the long-term impact of these activities in the environmental organization site.

[3] Unrelated diversification refers to activities (such as business ownership, property leasing, licensing, etc.) (Crimmins and Keil 1983) which are relatively peripheral to a nonprofit organization's mission and therefore of less central interest to this research.

[4] See "Top Line versus Bottom Line Thinking," Zimmerman and Dart (1998, p. 30).

[5] The question to be asked is whether the overhead would be incurred regardless of accepting these contracts. If so, and if no additional overhead costs are incurred as a result of the contracts, then the opportunity cost of accepting the contracts is minimal.

[6] Elements of this deregulation and restructuring include the incursion of large American HMOs into the Canadian EAP marketplace as well as competitive bidding for local EAP contracts by many of the out-of-work social workers and psychiatric nurses who have been "downsized" in recent public sector funding cuts.

[7] This fund is distinct from an endowment because there was never an intention to simply use the interest/income that the fund generated.

[8] The chair of EO's board noted that the subsidy is to be used on an ad hoc basis whenever programs and administration are unable to fully fund themselves. As of late 1998, all areas of EO had become financially self-sustaining, although the chair has doubts that this will be the case through all of 1999.

[9] Creditors "donate" money to the financial counselling program based on a percentage of the money that the program collects for them through debt management plans.

[10] Revenue was suggested as the primary objective in other instances.

[11] CO staff suggest that market conditions on the supply-side (i.e., the abundance of unemployed and underemployed social workers) are the reason for this.

[12] The executive director of CO did believe that the origin of cognitive therapy was in the more cost-conscious American for-profit health marketplace.

[13] The financial counselling program has developed a proposal for a home economist position to provide budget counselling in order to service this client group which could not get comparable service elsewhere.

[14] Some commentators (e.g., Brinckerhoff 1990; Budd 1996; Emerson and Twersky 1996) discuss the ways that mission-based activities can be profitable, or the way that commercial activities can serve pro-social goals.

References

Adams, M. 1997. *Sex in the Snow: Canadian Social Values at the End of the Millennium.* Toronto: Penguin Books.

Anheier, H. and W. Seibel, eds. 1992. *The Third Sector: Comparative Studies of Nonprofit Organizations.* Berlin: Walter de Gruyter.

Baum, J. and C. Oliver. 1996. "Toward an Institutional Ecology of Organizational Founding," *Academy of Management Journal*, 39(5):1378-427.

Brinckerhoff, P. 1990. "Mixing Business and Mission: How Should a Board Decide?" *Nonprofit World*, 8(3):9-10.

_____ 1994a. "How to Turn Your Entrepreneurial Skills Toward Your Mission," *Nonprofit World*, 12(4):17-19.

_____ 1994b. "Is 'Profit' a Dirty Word? (and Other Questions to Answer Before You Start a Business)," *Nonprofit World*, 12(1):18-20.

_____ 1994c. "How to Keep Your Funders Happy as You Develop a New Business," *Nonprofit World*, 12(6):18-20.

Budd, J. 1996. "How are Nonprofits Using Business Ventures? Advice from the Front," *Nonprofit World*, 14(3):40-42.

Canadian Centre for Philanthropy (CCP). 1990. *Law, Tax and Charities: The Legislative and Regulatory Environment for Charitable Non-profit Organizations.* Toronto: CCP.

Crimmins, J. and M. Keil. 1983. *Enterprise in the Nonprofit Sector.* Washington, DC: Partners for Livable Places.

Day, K. and R. Devlin. 1996. *The Canadian Nonprofit Sector.* Ottawa: Canadian Policy Research Network.

Dees, J. D. 1998. "Enterprising Nonprofits," *Harvard Business Review*, (January-February):55-67.

DiMaggio, P. and H. Anheier. 1990. "The Sociology of Nonprofit Organizations and Sectors," *Annual Review of Sociology*, 16:137-59.

Emerson, J. and F. Twersky, eds. 1996. *New Social Entrepreneurs: The Success, Challenge and Lessons of Non-profit Enterprise Creation*. San Francisco: The Roberts Foundation.

Goodman, W. 1994. *When a Charitable Organization Carries on a Business: United Way of Toronto* – PEP Program.

Horton Smith, D. 1997. "The Rest of the Nonprofit Sector: Grassroots Associations as the Dark Matter Ignored in Prevailing 'Flat Earth' Maps of the Sector," *NVSQ*, 26(2).

Jacobs, J. 1992. *Systems of Survival: A Dialogue on the Moral Foundations of Commerce and Politics*. New York: Random House.

Jorgenson, D. L. 1989. *Participant Observation: A Methodology for Human Studies*, Vol. 15. Newbury Park: Sage Publications.

Kuttner, R. 1997. *Everything for Sale: The Virtues and Limits of Markets*. New York: Random House.

Mintzberg, H. 1996. "Managing Government, Governing Management," *Harvard Business Review,* (May-June):75-83.

Neuman, L. 1994. *Social Research Methods: Qualitative and Quantitative Approaches*. Needham, MA: Allyn & Bacon.

Salamon, L. 1995. *Partners in Public Service: Government-Nonprofit Relations in the Modern Welfare State*. Baltimore, MD: Johns Hopkins University Press.

Salamon, L. and H. Anheier. 1996. *The Emerging Nonprofit Sector: An Overview*. Manchester, UK: Manchester University Press.

Saul, J.R. 1995. *The Unconscious Civilization*. Toronto: House of Anansi Press and the Canadian Broadcasting Corporation.

Skloot, E. 1987. "Enterprise and Commerce in Nonprofit Organizations," in *The Nonprofit Sector: A Research Handbook*, ed. W. Powell. New Haven: Yale University Press.

Soros, G. 1997. "The Capitalist Threat," *Atlantic Monthly*, 279:45-58.

Yin, R. K. 1994. *Case Study Research: Design and Methods*. 2d ed. Thousand Oaks: Sage Publications.

Zimmerman, B. and R. Dart. 1998. *Charities Doing Commercial Ventures: Societal and Organizational Implications*. Ottawa: Canadian Policy Research Network and the Trillium Foundation.

5

Hand-in-Hand: When Accountability Meets Collaboration in the Voluntary Sector

Susan D. Phillips and Katherine A. Graham

The voluntary sector in Canada is undergoing a profound restructuring in virtually all aspects of its operations — in how it raises money, how it serves its communities and clients, and how it relates to the public and private sectors. These changes have come in response to an environment in enormous flux that has produced rising demands for services, more diverse constituencies, clients with more complex needs, shrinking funding, and attacks upon the sector's credibility. In many fundamental ways, the traditional roles of the public, private, and voluntary sectors have been altered and the boundaries between them blurred. Governments have shed many of their long-standing service roles and replaced direct provision of services with contracting. Private sector firms have begun to enter "markets" once occupied almost exclusively by voluntary organizations and are increasingly marketing their products through identification with causes and organizations in the voluntary sector. Voluntary organizations have had to become more business-like, not only in undertaking more commercial activities, but in their governance and management practices. This transition has spawned two critical, and related, challenges for voluntary organizations.

First is a growing pressure to work collaboratively — in partnerships, joint ventures and, in the extreme, mergers — with other voluntary organizations, governments, and corporations. Collaboration cannot be expected to happen spontaneously or necessarily be implemented smoothly, however. Voluntary organizations are by nature particularistic and dependent upon the passion and commitment of volunteers on boards and in program delivery to work for the specific cause or community that is the motivation for their involvement. Thus collaboration is a delicate balance between being able to serve the particular, while being more expansive and collective in order to inject new resources or reduce costs in meeting increasing service demands. While appealing conceptually, collaboration may be difficult to achieve because the environment in which voluntary organizations operate has become increasingly competitive and organizations feel the need to protect their own competitive advantage. Implementation of collaborative arrangements must thus overcome a certain degree of "turf" protection. Nevertheless, the pressures to be more effective and efficient are driving a wide range of experimentation with collaborative arrangements.

The second key challenge for voluntary organizations is to demonstrate and enhance accountability for their operations and activities. Increasingly, pointed questions are being asked by the public, the media, funders, and from within the sector itself. Does an organization spend its fundraising dollars wisely? Are the programs it provides effective? Is the organization fulfilling its mission and representing its constituency appropriately? The growing interest in accountability of the voluntary sector advanced by such questions is not simply the result of an absence of existing accountability or even questionable behaviour by a few wayward organizations that captured media headlines. Like the push for partnerships, it is reflective of a fundamental change in the relationships between the public, private, and voluntary sectors. Although accountability has been a central operating principle of the voluntary sector and innovations in practice are ongoing, recent shifts in roles and responsibilities have made accountability within the sector both more visible and more complex.

This paper takes a critical look at accountability in the context of collaboration in the voluntary sector. The first part of the paper provides conceptual frameworks for analysis of accountability and of collaboration in the sector. We develop the notion of accountability regimes to help understand the numerous and varied ways in which voluntary organizations are accountable to their multiple audiences. Next, the possibilities and types of collaboration under experimentation in the sector are outlined along a continuum that ranges from insular to merger. The second section turns to the intersection of accountability and collaboration. Why have both become central issues at the end of the millennium and how are they interconnected? How does accountability play out in the context of collaboration? In this discussion, we explore some of the emerging challenges and issues of the accountability-collaboration nexus by studying eight diverse cases of collaborations in the social services and health fields. Based on this exploration, the paper offers suggestions for ways in which accountability practices in the new forms of collaborative arrangements might be improved, speculates on potential contradictions between the imperatives of accountability and of collaboration, and outlines directions for future research.

CONCEPTUAL FRAMEWORKS: ACCOUNTABILITY AND COLLABORATION

Accountability Regimes

Accountability is the requirement to explain and accept responsibility for carrying out an assigned mandate in light of agreed upon expectations (Panel on Accountability and Governance in the Voluntary Sector 1999, p. 11; see also Canada 1997, p. 5; Kearns 1994, p. 185; Taylor 1996, pp. 58-59). Its application involves three basic elements:

- taking into consideration the public trust in the exercise of responsibilities;

- informing and explaining by providing detailed information about how responsibilities have been carried out; and

- accepting the consequences for problems created, not avoided or not corrected.

Voluntary organizations must exercise accountability for at least four basic aspects of their operations: political, financial, process, and program matters (see Milofsky and Blades 1991). Political accountability refers to responsibility for the mission, priorities, and overall viability of the organization. Accountability for financial matters includes both how revenues are raised and how they are spent, and has been the focus of most of the recent debate over accountability. The third category, accountability for process, refers to how the organization is run and how it discharges its mandate including, for example, fair and equitable treatment of staff, volunteers, and clients. The final category relates to the impacts or results of programs and services on beneficiaries: How well are they served by the programs, at what cost, and with what change in their condition or quality of life?

Accountability, particularly in the voluntary sector, is not a single or straightforward principal-agent relationship with one body imposing specific rules and standards of accountability on a voluntary organization for all of its activities. By necessity, accountability in the voluntary sector depends upon a combination of self-regulation and external regulation. As self-governing bodies, accountability in voluntary organizations starts with leadership by, and accountability of, their boards of directors. Beyond this, voluntary organizations have a broad span of accountabilities to multiple audiences — upward to the public, funders, umbrella organizations, and governments; outward to partners and affiliated organizations; and downward to clients, constituencies, and volunteers (Edwards and Hulme 1996, p. 8).

This complexity of accountability in the voluntary sector can appropriately be conceived of as a "regime" — the formal and informal arrangements by which voluntary and intermediary organizations, funders, governments, and the public function together to be able to make and enforce policies and practices concerning accountability (Stone 1989, p. 6). A regime consists not only of sets of the rules and relationships among actors, but also of the norms, cultures, and expectations created as a result of these relationships. Complexity is central to the concept of a regime (Stoker 1995, p. 8). Authority is fragmented and although a degree of coordination among the regime actors may exist, in most cases there is a lack of direction and control by any particular member over the entire regime. As a result, some aspects of accountability may fall through the cracks or, alternatively, inefficient double reporting to different actors for the same thing may occur.

A range of accountability mechanisms or tools are available, including: legislation and regulation, legal liability of boards of directors, contracts, rules imposed by funders, professional standards, accreditation, voluntary codes, communication and transparency, complaints processes, the norms of partnership, and ongoing stewardship by boards of directors. Seldom does a regime rely only on a single tool. Nor are the requirements of accountability in a regime uniform for every voluntary organization; rather they vary to some extent depending on an organization's specific place in the network of relationships. Regimes also have a temporal dimension. As a regime, its relationships and norms are relatively stable, slow to change, but nevertheless capable of change. Over time, regimes evolve as they are established, institutionalized, weakened, and displaced.

The implication of the complexity of accountability regimes, coupled with the enormous diversity of Canada's voluntary sector, is that there is no single regime of accountability governing all voluntary organizations. Rather, there are — in both concept and practice — a variety of types of regimes. Although not an exhaustive topology, three general forms of accountability regimes may be identified: (i) funder-dominated; (ii) accreditation-based; and (iii) self-regulating. These are general types rather than discrete categories: some exercise of accountability by funders, by accrediting organizations, by governments, and by an organization's own board of directors is normally found in every regime.

Funder-dominated regimes are common for voluntary organizations that depend heavily on a particular funder — be it government, the United Way, or a foundation — for the bulk of their program and project support. This is not to say that funders are the only significant players in these regimes, but their requirements have the greatest and most immediate influence on the behaviour of the organizations to whom they apply. These types of regimes tend to be particularly good at controlling financial and program accountability since, through the use of contracts and project funding, they generally have very formalized rules governing budget allocations and reporting requirements.

Accreditation regimes are defined by the existence of a "parent," intermediary or other organization which has the legitimate authority to set standards for its members and affiliates, evaluate their practices and programs and, on this basis, permit or deny the member to advertise itself as accredited (often by calling itself a member organization). Accreditation regimes are often found in services that are directed to potentially vulnerable populations in which control over both process and program outcomes are important. Examples include mandatory accreditation by the Big Sisters/ Big Brothers of Canada and the voluntary program of Family Services Canada.[1]

The self-regulating regime is characterized by adherence to voluntary codes of conduct for fundraising and ethical behaviour, to the expectations of partner organizations, and to professional standards for staff. As a mix of objective and subjective, explicit and implicit standards, these regimes are in many respects the most complex. Given the need for internal guidance, the boards of directors of individual organizations assume an even more critical role in these regimes than in the others. Self-regulating regimes are likely to develop where there is a heavy reliance on fundraising from the public and from corporations, where the organizations are relatively well established and mature, and where collaborative arrangements are key to achieving an organization's core mandate. The strength of self-regulating regimes is in maintaining political accountability for the mission and for program outcomes since the ability to attract funding from multiple sources is closely tied to demonstrating the value of both the cause and program outcomes. And, in order to maintain public or corporate confidence and donations, certain activities and political positions will be tempered or avoided.

In all three types of regimes, governments also play an important role, although seldom the defining one. For Canada's 78,000 registered charities, a common element of all three regime types are the rules imposed under the *Income Tax Act* and supervised by Revenue Canada (Panel on Accountability and Governance 1999, p. 8). In exchange for the opportunity to issue tax receipts for donations, registered charities must complete annually a lengthy information return (the T3010 form) and comply with certain regulations. These include: meeting a disbursement quota that 80 percent of a charity's receipted revenues be spent on charitable purposes, thus limiting the amount that can be spent on overhead, administration, or fundraising; restricting ancillary political activities to no more than 10 percent of all the organization's resources; and refraining from engaging in unrelated business activities. Violation of these regulations may result in the revocation of an organization's charitable status, the only sanction currently available to Revenue Canada for non-compliance.[2] In spite of the potential severity of penalties, Revenue Canada is not the only, or even the most important force shaping the day-to-day activities and accountability practices of most charities, but it does set basic parameters.

The creation of any particular type of accountability regime for a specific set of voluntary organizations is not automatic. Its development depends to a large extent on the missions, constituencies, and capacities of the member organizations, as well as the existence of competitors and intermediary organizations. No one regime is *prima facie* more effective than others. The value of the concept of a regime is that it directs attention to the conditions under which effective mechanisms of accountability emerge and are sustained. We argue that, in all regimes, the sound exercise of accountability is facilitated by several conditions. First, relatively clear definitions of roles and responsibilities make it widely understood when the obligations of accountability apply, for what, to whom and by what means they should be exercised. As Day and Klein note, "[t]here has to be agreement about the context, the reason why one actor owes explanation to another since it is precisely this sense of obligation which translates the giving of accounts into accountability"(1987, p. 5). Second, effective accountability implies shared expectations of what is acceptable performance and standards by which it is to be justified. For this reason, accountability is facilitated by an informed public who can ask appropriate questions and demand answers by those who carry out public services. Third, meeting the obligations of accountability requires the capacity to do so. If specific rules, standards, and other reporting requirements are beyond the resources of most organizations, full accountability cannot be met simply by imposing standards.

Accountability requires both strong voluntary sector organizations which can instil an internal sense of obligation *and* bodies with legitimate authority, within or external to the sector, capable of imposing sanctions on organizations that fail to comply with accepted obligations of accountable behaviour. But accountability is not merely a response to externally imposed rules and regulations. Rather, it requires subjective accountability, an internal and self-driven sense of obligation. As the Panel on Accountability and Governance (1999, p. 11) notes, accountability can be a constructive tool for organizational development, enhancing management practices, self-evaluation and strategic planning. At its best, suggests Taylor, accountability becomes "a multi-track learning process, which searches for good practice rather than constraining it within preconceived formulae" (1996, p. 68).

No one size fits all, no single set of accountability practices can be applied equally to all parts of the sector or can be enforced by a single body either inside or outside the sector. Rather, accountability must be negotiated as legitimate and thus accepted as an obligation by self-governing boards with adequate capacity available to fulfil its standards and obligations. Moreover, a set of accountability practices or a regime that works for a particular organization may not work so well when that organization enters into collaborative arrangements with others, depending on the nature of the collaboration, the expectations of new partners, and the incongruities between the accountability regimes in which the collaborators are already embedded. Rather, new expectations, mechanisms, and regimes may need to be developed and given time to evolve.

Before turning to an examination of some of the issues of accountability in the context of collaboration, we need a conceptual framework for understanding and differentiating collaboration.

In Collaboration: A Continuum

Like accountability, collaboration in the voluntary sector takes a variety of different forms and serves a multiplicity of objectives. During the 1990s, the extent and variety of collaborative arrangements expanded rapidly as voluntary organizations were both pushed and pulled into partnering and other collaborative arrangements.

By the late 1990s, the idea of collaboration had become so popular that the word "partnership" and related terms were mentioned no less than 25 times in the 1997 Speech from the Throne (Zussman 1997, p. 1). Indeed, the language of partnership has become so pervasive in recent years that it is, in effect, a plastic word, becoming synonymous with any form of collaboration and, at times, meaning almost anything the user wants. As Zussman and others (see Armstrong and Lehnihan1999) have noted, one of the challenges associated with making the concept of partnership a workable one, has been to press for elaboration of the details of how partnerships will actually work, including identification of the most suitable accountability regime in each case.

In order to establish greater precision in the definition and use of concepts, we conceive of a continuum of collaboration among voluntary organizations and with governments and corporations, of which partnership is one specific type. This continuum ranges from insular, indicating a lack of collaboration, as an anchor on the left, to mergers as the ultimate form of organizational consolidation on the right.

Figure 1: Organizational Collaboration: A Continuum

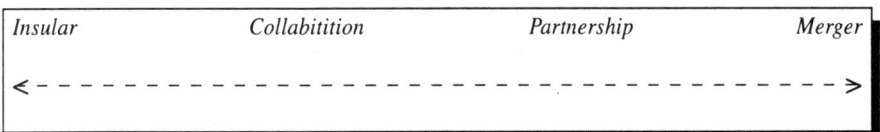

Clearly, organizations in the voluntary sector are shifting toward the right side of this continuum. Relatively few organizations today exist in insulated autonomy, without support from others or without some degree of contact with others over programs, political activities, and accountability. Those that are engaging in "collabitition" may be collaborating for some purposes but are still in head-to-head competition for many of their fundamental organizational needs, such as program resources.[3] Most of this type of collaboration takes place as joint ventures around specific programs, projects or events and generally is quite informal. Because the underlying competitive stance of the collaborators is not conducive to laying down a firm foundation of trust, collabitition arrangements are inherently unstable and transient, usually disbanded after the project has been completed, and sometimes falling apart before that. In accountability terms, this relationship imposes limits on the sharing of information among the organizations involved, as each tries to use the arrangement, in part, to enhance its comparative advantage.

Although also aimed at combining forces to achieve a particular purpose, partnerships can be characterized as inherently less conflictual and as requiring a higher level of sharing than collabitition arrangements. For our purposes, a partnership can be described as a relationship involving the sharing of power, work, support and/or information with others for the achievement of joint goals and/or mutual benefits (Ekos Research 1998, pp. 5-6; Kernaghan 1993, p. 61; Phillips 1991, p. 190; Waddock 1988, pp. 19-20). Its essential elements are: common objectives; expectations of mutual benefits, joint action, shared contribution, and some degree of shared power and shared risk — and therefore some measure of shared accountability. We need to be careful in specifying the particularities of partnerships because they, in fact, encompass a broad range of forms and functions. The purposes of partnerships may vary widely and include, among others: joint efforts to raise money and lever new sources of funding, improved delivery of programs and services by pooling the differential expertise of partners, reduction of program costs by joint delivery of existing programs, undertaking entirely new programs and services that might be too big or risky for one partner alone, increased influence with a target audience, and collective efforts to increase a community's political voice and enhance participation in social change and policy making (Mintz *et al.* 1998, pp. 11-16; Tjorman 1998, pp. 5-10).

The precise model of partnership may also take several forms. A partnership may be a joint venture; there may be a new "delegate" organization with specific responsibilities and operational arrangements mandated by participating organizations; alternatively, it may take the organizational form of a new "trustee" organization, with more autonomy from the original partners. Different kinds of partners — voluntary organizations, philanthropic foundations, businesses, government departments, and educational institutions — may be involved, combined in small intimate dyads, or in complex arrangements involving many, diverse players. Partners bring very different needs and resources to this type of relationship. For instance, their contributions might include money, staff, volunteers, program experience, credibility, and connections to specific social or business communities.

Mergers are the ultimate form of collaboration as they involve the fusion of two or more organizations and are thus at the end of our continuum. A merger is the most permanent form of collaboration since it involves giving up existing organizational identities and structures to the creation of a new entity with its own legal status and personality. Since a merger involves the unknown and the inability to revert back once consolidated, it is also the arrangement that involves the greatest degree of uncertainty and risk. Theoretically at least, a merger should result in an open and widened accountability regime, as clients and other stakeholders grow and become familiar with the new organizational enterprise. At least as important are the cultural dimensions. For example, partnering or merging organizations that provide a similar service, such as counselling, to different clientele may involve quite different organizational cultures even though from the outside they may appear to have similar structures and interests. Such cultural differences may require innovative thinking regarding accountability relationships and related organizational practices.

Neither accountability nor collaboration are new processes for the voluntary sector. In recent years, however, the saliency of each has increased and the two have become increasingly interdependent. In the next section, we examine the reasons for this attention and the pressures upon voluntary organizations when accountability meets collaboration.

Shared Roots: Accountability and Collaboration in Context

It is not a coincidence that pressures for greater collaboration and enhanced accountability began to be acutely felt by voluntary organizations starting in the early 1990s. Both emanate from a fundamental shift in the relations between the voluntary sector, the state, and the private sector. In order to understand how these pressures intersect and produce particular responses by voluntary organizations, it is useful to examine briefly the underlying causes giving rise to both.[4]

State Restructuring

The prepotent factor that has led to both increased collaboration and accountability is the restructuring of the state. Driven by fiscal exigencies and neo-liberal ideologies, governments around the world have restructured the delivery of many public services with an eye to reducing costs, making them more efficient and effective, and shrinking the size and reach of the state in general. The direct consequences were to cut, often dramatically and without much warning, government support for voluntary sector organizations, particularly for intermediary and advocacy organizations not directly engaged in service delivery, or to shift the form of support from core to project funding (Jenson and Phillips 1996, pp. 118-20). Since governments, both federal and provincial, had provided almost 60 percent of the revenues of the sector, the impact of these cuts has been far reaching (Sharpe 1994, p. 21). The loss of government funding has had to be made up by increased fundraising, corporate sponsorships, and business activities; and by reducing costs in every way possible, including joint programming and other forms of collaboration. This, in turn, has raised questions about accountability.

For many citizens, the solicitation of donations is their only point of contact with voluntary organizations and, given a limited knowledge of the sector, they naturally ask questions about how as well as how effectively the money will be spent (Hall and Parmegiani 1998, pp. 1-2). Along with concerns about accountability for money donated come questions about potential rationalization of the sector. Are there too many organizations chasing the same fundraising dollars? Would the public be better served by some form of rationalization, such as joint or umbrella campaigns or organizational mergers?

State restructuring has also resulted in governments shedding many services completely and in the provision of others under contract with voluntary or private sector organizations. Government off-loading has left many voluntary organizations with more clients and clients with more difficult and complex needs (Picard 1997, pp. 35-39; Rekart 1993; Municipality of Metropolitan Toronto *et al.* 1997). In order to meet the needs of new clients and address gaps in existing services, voluntary organizations have been experimenting with new forms of delivery and in many cases have begun joint programming to fill the gaps. Competitive contracting has forced voluntary organizations both to specialize in order to compete better, and to diversify in order to enhance their chances of winning at least some of the contracts on which they bid (see Jenson and Phillips, this volume). For many organizations, a negative consequence is what Smith and Lipsky (1993 pp. 127-46) call the "dance of contract management" — the chase for contract money which drives the activities of the organization toward greater diversification in order to win more contracts to subsidize core operations of the organization, spinning it further and further from its original mission and expertise. To prevent such mission drift, boards of directors have had to do more strategic planning and focus on policy directions, not simply administration. The discussion, adoption, and commercialization of the Carver (1997) strategy advocating policy governance models reflects the struggle faced by many boards to rethink their roles and structures.

At the same time, governments have been enticing and, on occasion, mandating voluntary organizations into partnership arrangements as a form of alternative service delivery that is presumed to be at once more client-centred and less costly. Not only have governments directly initiated their own partnerships with voluntary organizations, but they are increasingly making program support to voluntary organizations conditional on those organizations attracting partners. In addition, governments have been actively inducing rationalization of the voluntary sector as a counterpart to their own downsizing. If hospital services are consolidated, for instance, as they have been in most provinces, voluntary organizations providing such services as hospice care or outpatient transportation have cause to examine their operations and structures.

A final implication of the restructuring of the welfare state has been a perceived need for more advocacy. As many social programs have been eliminated, off-loaded or significantly cut back and as economic and social disparities have increased, many voluntary organizations have chosen to act as advocates for their constituencies in order to make the consequences of cutbacks apparent and subject to public debate. Not surprisingly, such criticism has not been warmly welcomed by governments which have in many cases attempted to "divide and conquer" the voluntary sector critics by attacking their credibility or limiting their access to policy forums (Pierson 1994, p. 158). Advocacy by registered charities has come under particular scrutiny because current federal government rules place limitations on such activity and these rules are being interpreted by the courts in ways that are more, not less restrictive.[5] These regulations have generated tensions between the centuries old model of charity — to help others less fortunate — and modern conceptions of civil society in which representation and participation, by nature political activities, are valued contributions alongside service to others. What is the legitimate role that citizen organizations should play in public policy debates relative to parties and parliamentariàns? This has become a central question in the sector's transition from a charity-based to a civil-society model.

THE CHANGING NATURE OF PHILANTHROPY

Another underlying factor in shining a spotlight on both accountability and collaboration has been the changing nature of philanthropy. Corporations have been relatively minor players in supporting the voluntary sector, providing a mere 1.5 percent of the revenues of the sector (Hall and Macpherson 1996, p. 2). Although its level of support has not increased significantly in recent years, its form of assistance has changed. The current trend in corporate giving is toward cause marketing. This involves tying support or sponsorships to causes and organizations that help a corporation sell its products or build a positive image among a target group of potential consumers. As one major corporate sponsor told us, both business and voluntary organizations have "to go in with both eyes open and recognize that corporate giving is not simply about cheque writing. The charity has to understand that there has to be a business link."[6] Cause marketing has not only created new opportunities for voluntary organizations to work collaboratively with corporations, but has also forced boards to ask themselves about the appropriate limits of such support. Corporations have also begun to support volunteerism as part of their contribution, covering some of the costs of the time of their staff to volunteer or encouraging participation by staff as a group. This makes accountability linkages even more extended and tenuous.

The New Volunteerism

The rising participation by and changing expectations of volunteers has been a third factor focusing attention on both collaboration and accountability. The 1997 National Survey of Giving, Volunteering and Participating found that the percentage of Canadians volunteering their time with an organization has risen almost 5 percent over the past ten years, from 26.8 percent to 31.4 percent.[7] Not only numbers, but expectations of volunteers have changed. In addition to being able to work for a cause to which they are personally committed, volunteers have sophisticated expectations that their volunteer experience will be meaningful, permitting them to use their skills and explore their own strengths. About one-fifth of volunteers, and particularly youth, are seeking to learn new skills that could be transferred to paid employment (Canadian Centre for Philanthropy *et al.* 1998, p. 37). At the same time, many organizations are also grappling with how to integrate the "non-voluntary volunteer" — the person on workfare or other compulsory community placements who often has limited skills or work experience.[8]

Although increasing numbers may be regarded as a positive trend, volunteers are not free resources. Rather, they must be trained, organized, supervised, and rewarded, requiring the input of both financial and human resources and more attention paid to the accountability of the organization to its volunteers. This task has been exacerbated, however, by the changing nature of funding. Indeed, the positions that have been hardest hit by reduced funding are the managers of volunteers and training programs since project funding often does not include allocations for the management of the volunteer component (see Rekart 1997, pp. 75-94). Accountability in the relationship between organizations and their volunteers has been accentuated by legal issues, particularly around revelations of sexual abuse of children by hockey coaches, educators, and youth workers, which have directed attention toward the need for improved volunteer screening programs.[9]

The Rise of Populism

Finally, changing models of democracy have had significant implications for the voluntary sector. The rise of populism (which posits that individual citizens should have direct access to and control over elected officials through mechanisms such as townhalls, referenda, and recall) has challenged the role of intermediary associations in interpreting and articulating the interests and identities of communities. Some elected officials have become self-appointed watchdogs over the voluntary sector because they feel that they have to compete with voluntary organizations to be heard in public policy debates.[10] Their conclusion has been that the activities of voluntary organizations must be closely monitored and highly regulated with strict limits imposed on advocacy. Concerns have also been perpetuated by an aggressive media whose love of a scandal and search for conflict have produced a number of sensational stories, absorbed by a public with very limited knowledge of the sector. This has resulted in all voluntary organizations being painted with the derogatory brush of "special interests," questioning who they really represent and the nature of their motives. This trend has presented serious challenges, particularly in partnering arrangements, for balancing service responsibilities and political activities when the latter are denigrated.

Collectively, these fundamental changes have presented voluntary organizations with a series of contradictions. They have had at once to be more specialized and more diverse. Finding new resources, meeting greater client needs and having a political voice in a more hostile environment has required greater innovation and risk-taking. But at the same time, increased scrutiny, extended reporting requirements, and concerns about legal liability have encouraged organizations to be more conservative and cautious. Voluntary organizations are simultaneously more collaborative and more competitive, more autonomous and more regulated. At a time when governments need the voluntary sector more than ever — as service providers, as agents for building social capital and cohesion, and as policy experts — its credibility is under attack. Even though the role of the sector and its influence on the everyday lives of citizens is growing, the public knows very little about the sector or what it does (Brem 1998, p. 2).

ACCOUNTABILITY IN THE CONTEXT OF COLLABORATION

What happens when accountability meets collaboration? Has collaboration forced changes in accountability regimes? In order to look at the intersection of accountability and collaboration, we examined accountability practices in eight cases of collaboration involving voluntary organizations.[11] The cases were chosen to be representative of a variety of types of collaboration and to include collaboration among different sets of actors — voluntary organizations with others in the sector, with governments, and with corporations. Although we cast our net widely, we did not wish to have such a broad diversity of organizations, jurisdictions, and policy fields that few relevant comparisons could be made. Thus our selection of cases was limited to three provinces, Ontario, Alberta, and British Columbia (and more specifically Toronto, Ottawa, Calgary, and Vancouver).[12] We have also confined our selection to two policy areas, social services and health, for two reasons. Voluntary organizations are important deliverers of services in both areas, and they have been hard hit by recent state restructuring. The voluntary organizations involved in the collaborations are mainly medium-sized organizations with both staff and volunteers, and thus typical of the bulk of the sector. The specific cases were identified by key informants in the sector whom we asked to tell us about "interesting experiments," whether successful or not, of partnerships and other forms of collaboration. How the collaboration is made to work and how accountability is addressed within it were explored through structured interviews with the executive directors of the lead organizations, as well as those of their partners.

Our research has two main objectives. First, we aim to determine current practices regarding accountability in these relationships. In particular, our goal is to ascertain if partnerships and mergers tend to induce innovation in working through accountability issues, either when the collaboration is under initial consideration or subsequently. Our second purpose is to identify gaps between need and practice. In short, is there a need for new thinking regarding accountability regimes, as partnerships and mergers become more commonplace in the voluntary sector? It is evident that this relatively small sample of cases cannot yield definitive answers to these questions. The results of our research do, however, start the process of illuminating accountability issues which result from these new forms of engagement and point to an agenda for future research.

A brief introduction to each of the cases provides a sense of the diverse contexts in which partnerships and mergers in the health and social service sectors are occurring. We will discuss the cases along the continuum of increasing collaboration, starting with examples of collabitition and ending with mergers.

The Regional Case Management Service (RCMS) in Ottawa-Carleton is a collaboration to which several local organizations providing housing, health care, and other supports to persons requiring mental-health services have delegated responsibility for case management. Yet, the underlying competitive relationship among the delegating organizations leads to this collaboration being characterized as one of "collabitition."

This collaboration was initially induced by the Ontario Ministry of Health in 1990. Local organizations had submitted numerous funding proposals for client services and staff development for community mental-health workers. The ministry indicated that it wanted to entertain only one such proposal from the region. Two years later, the RCMS came into being. Participating organizations, such as the Canadian Mental Health Association, Salus (a nonprofit group-home agency), the Royal Ottawa Hospital, and area health and community service centres utilize the service for managing the cases of clients requiring mental-health outreach. As this collaboration developed, however, several participating agencies continued to compete with each other for funding and volunteers.

In the original partnering arrangement, issues concerning what different partners would bring to the collaboration, overall expectations, and how participating organizations would report back to their respective boards were never really addressed. In short, there is no protocol for agency boards to deal with each other or with policy issues concerning services that the RCMS provides to their clientele. For example, there is no policy for agencies to use in dealing with complaints regarding RCMS staff or with issues which "crossed jurisdictions" into such areas as sheltered housing or immigration services. An inter-agency committee of agency executive directors was created. Both its policy and accountability roles are limited, however, being restricted to the mandate that each senior staff person has with her/his board, rather than carving out new responsibilities for itself.

By the late 1990s, a number of factors had coalesced to prompt re-examination of the original arrangement. Increasing rivalry among some agency partners for funding, the addition of a group of new agencies which were not seeing any appreciable benefit from the collaboration in terms of increased funding for themselves or for staff development, and the sense that the provincial government would not look favourably on termination of the troubled partnership all contributed.

Participating agencies are currently re-examining the mission and values of the partnership and exploring the merits of preparing written protocols for some of the issues identified above. There is some interest in re-conceptualizing the RCMS as a consortium, with more explicit and more direct linkages among the agencies. As in any relationship that has become difficult due to problems with trust and communication, these and related accountability issues are difficult to address.

Collingwood Neighbourhood House Project in Vancouver is a collaborative joint venture, involving the community-based Collingwood Neighbourhood House Society, a private developer, and the City of Vancouver. The basic aim of the venture is to provide a range of human services to area residents. The project, which opened in September 1995, emerged over a five-year period as the result of an urban redevelopment controversy. When the developer, Greystone Properties, submitted a rezoning application to create Collingwood Village, a high density, mixed-use area, an opportunity was created to construct, as part of the development, a new home for the existing Collingwood Neighbourhood House which required room to expand in order to meet growing community needs. This project became part of the negotiation of a development agreement between the City of Vancouver and Greystone with both parties working with the Collingwood Neighbourhood Society and the community to plan the facility.

The relationships among the developer, the city, and the community organization were initially quite challenging. Different agendas and different cultures among the three partners meant that trust and recognition of others' accountability relationships and practices took time to develop. The impetus to finally launching the project was a zoning bylaw change and formal lease agreement for the facility, both of which gave credence to the needs and interests of the three parties. As the project moved into the construction phase, a multi-party management committee was established to oversee creation of the facility. This committee responded to the recommendations of a series of residents' committees which brought forward views concerning such diverse matters as capital assets, recreation, child care, and fundraising. As the community became mobilized, over 1,000 residents volunteered to participate in the project in some way.

This case provides an example of collaboration borne out of potentially competing interests. Initially, Collingwood Neighbourhood House Society and the community perceived themselves as disadvantaged in the negotiations between the developer and the city. They lacked information and resources but had a vision of what they wanted to achieve. As community advocates became more experienced in the negotiating process and became more accustomed to dealing with the developer's representative, the parties began to build a relationship. This proved to be the cornerstone for being more open and creative in negotiations and moving to a collaborative joint venture. The collaboration worked because all of the parties endeavoured to reach consensus and were willing to make compromises when necessary.

Formal accountability was to a large extent maintained through the legal instruments of the lease agreement and the zoning bylaw which required no less than 14 appearances before city council, and by central management of the funds for the project by the city. More important than these formal mechanisms, however, were the personal efforts to create trust and openness. In addition to simple patience in working through the initial rough spots of differences in organizational cultures and interests, the openness of the management committee as a forum for discussion and the relationships of respect among the three central personalities representing each of the parties were key.

As a result of its success, new issues of accountability have emerged. The legacy of the collaboration has been a facility that has made a positive contribution to the delivery of local community services and, for the developer, enhanced public relations. During the process, Collingwood Neighbourhood House Society evolved into a successful service-driven organization. But there is now an emphasis on getting back to its original community-development focus — empowering, not simply delivering services to residents. To achieve this, however, its board recognizes that it would have to give up some control which has sparked concerns over liability related to financial and human resource issues.

The AIDS Committee of Toronto (ACT) has grown to become Canada's largest community-based AIDS service organization, while remaining close to its roots as an activist organization rooted in a broader social movement. ACT is unusual among voluntary organizations because almost two-thirds of its $2 million annual budget comes from private sources with only one-third from governments. It has established partnerships with a number of corporations for different purposes, most notably for fundraising (for example, with Molson Breweries and MAC Cosmetics, among others) and for client education (with Glaxo-Wellcome pharmaceuticals). These partnerships can be characterized as collaborative joint ventures around specific purposes. The accountability regimes associated with these collaborations are segregated; ACT and each of its partners have their own accountability regimes, with little shared terrain or joint liability. In the case of the relationships with Molson and Glaxo-Wellcome, there is mutual recognition between ACT and the corporate partner that the collaboration is part of a broader corporate public relations or marketing strategy. The benefits for the pharmaceutical company relate primarily to the education about proper use of drugs and are increasingly targeted on special events and projects. ACT approached the relationship by being clear about the sponsor's role and encouraging them to sponsor events, rather than specific programs. In this way, the corporations remain once removed from the organization's core activities, a particular concern with the pharmaceutical companies whose interests in collaboration may be looked upon with some suspicion by members of the AIDS community.

The relationship with Molson is quite different, in part because there is not as much perceived conflict of interest. Molson was one of the first major corporations to support AIDS service organizations in Canada. Its major contributions are what it does best — selling products through advertising. Molson commissions its ad firms — firms that ACT could never afford — to publicize and sponsor ACT events. In other words, they "take a social issue and make it a consumer issue." It is interesting to note that this partnership does not dissuade ACT from taking money from Molson's competitors, however, because "AIDS is too big to give anyone exclusivity."[13] ACT's relationship with MAC Cosmetics is exceptional in corporate partnerships because it is closer to true philanthropy than cause marketing; the cosmetics company is quite hands-off, giving significant amounts of money to ACT for major events and being supportive of the roughly half of its employees who volunteer their time in organizing these events.

Success of these partnerships depends on two main factors: recognition and mutual respect for different interests of the partners, and clarity about what each partner is expected to contribute. In particular, while the links with the corporate sponsors have an atmosphere of informality, formal letters of agreement are signed nevertheless to clarify expectations. This appears to contribute to the generally constructive relations between ACT and their sponsors. The main source of tension is the extent to which ACT and other AIDS organizations engage in advocacy of a type which some of their corporate partners might perceive to be inappropriate or threatening. ACT has successfully maintained a balance by self-regulation of its own behaviour to some extent — knowing where the lines are — and leaving the more radical action to others.

The Regional Umbrella Group for Childcare (RUG) in Vancouver is a partnership involving 15 community childcare organizations and the local and provincial governments. It is one component of a four-year initiative, the Vancouver Childcare Regional Delivery Model Pilot Project, which was jointly funded through March 1999 by the Canada/British Columbia Strategic Initiatives Program of Human Resources Development Canada (HRDC) and BC's Ministry for Children and Families. RUG is intended to develop best practices for the administration and management of voluntary/nonprofit organizations working in childcare, and in this context has looked mainly at management and administrative structures for coordinating services, management leadership training, and financial/cost analysis.

The RUG project has a number of important elements that can be characterized simultaneously as strengths and challenges. Community groups, for example, were concerned at the outset whether the project would result in something useful to them, given the time they would have to commit to the project and the program activities associated with it. The transaction costs involved in negotiating the various legal contracts were high for all parties but particularly for community organizations. These costs were offset somewhat by the allocation of a "participation" contribution of $2,000 a year to each community member from the project's annual budget. Although this was merely a token for all the time, expertise, and commitment each made, it was also an important recognition by government of the cost of collaborative work. The outcome-based evaluation regime, required by the federal and provincial government partners, has also proven difficult to mesh with some of the more process-oriented objectives of the participating community organizations.

Accountability is more formalized in this collaboration than most of the other cases with, among other things, protocols about how to make decisions and resolve problems. The accountability regime hinges on the role of the City of Vancouver, to a considerable degree, as federal/provincial funds for RUG flow through the city. Vancouver's Child Care Coordinator has been involved since the very beginning and has served as chair of the

RUG steering committee. This committee seems to have dealt successfully with the challenges of building trust, respect, and openness among its members. A sense of equality among the David (community) and Goliath (government) partners has been created — too often a rarity in collaboration between community organizations and governments. The relationship did not reach this mature state until the last two years of the project, however, illustrating that successful collaboration often must allocate considerable time for relationships to develop and solidify. Moving forward and building trust was aided by giving more autonomy to subcommittees to determine priorities and work through specific projects, rather than trying to achieve consensus by the full RUG group on every issue. It was also aided by ensuring that the key staff-person, the RUG coordinator, was an independent contractor, clearly working for and accountable to the partnership, rather than an employee of a member organization whose first loyalty might have been seen as questionable. One salutary outcome of the interaction between the funding governments and the community organizations involved in RUG is an enhanced ability for the community sector to undertake advocacy. The community sector now speaks with a common voice on more issues and has identifiable interlocutors in government. The community sector is currently exploring ways to sustain the RUG initiative after the initial funding ends.

The Immigrant Services Society (ISS) of Vancouver was established in 1972 to assist with the settlement and training of recent immigrants, and it has grown to a staff of between 125 and 140 with a volunteer component of 450. ISS went through two unsuccessful partnerships with neighbourhood houses and community centres in early attempts to secure federal funding for immigrant settlement under the Host Program. The host program, which is 100 percent funded by the federal government, started in 1985 with a mandate to serve government-sponsored refugees. In 1991, the program's funding was expanded to include not only refugees but landed immigrants and organizations such as ISS were required to "work with the community" by establishing partnerships with neighbourhood houses and community centres. The government went so far as to dictate four organizations with which the ISS should partner. Two of these forced collaborations failed. In one case, the community centre "partner" felt that it received nothing from the initiative and had no spare resources to contribute. In the other case, the community felt there was no need for the program. These failures resulted in withdrawal of funding by the federal government for the landed immigrant component, although the host program still required ISS to provide these services.

The ISS has since established two viable partnerships, both of which receive federal funding under the host program. The accountability regime for these initiatives is determined by the funding agreement between the Government of Canada and the ISS. The mission and overall direction of the program is set by the federal government while ISS is responsible for strategic planning. The Immigrant Services Society uses the funds it receives to place its immigration counsellors and other resources in the two participating community centres. However, the centres receive no direct support, such as a contribution to overhead, from the program and are not involved in the formal accountability regime.

In short, this case is characterized by a very asymmetrical accountability relationship. It illustrates the danger of lopsided partnerships in which one party, in this case the Government of Canada as the funder, has excessive control over less than willing partners and in which the funder and other partners lack a shared vision. As a result of its dependence on government funding, the ISS board has shied away from advocacy, resulting in conflict between the board and the staff. For ISS, an emerging imperative therefore is to diversify funding and to find a way to have an advocacy voice to press the federal government on public policy issues. Moreover, the government's provision requiring specific partnerships within the voluntary sector, as a condition of funding, does not always bode well for success. When collaboration does occur at the community level, accountability relationships between the ISS and community centres are informal, dependent largely on personal relationships, and are rarely put to the test. But this also makes them somewhat fragile because if personnel leave, new relationships of trust with replacement staff have to be built in order to keep the collaboration going.

SUCCESS is a 25-year old Vancouver organization dedicated to assisting new Canadians to overcome language and cultural barriers to participating in the community. Over that time SUCCESS has grown to a staff of 204, an annual budget of $7 million and some 6,000 volunteers. It has no long-term institutionalized partnerships but is currently involved in over 50 collaborative projects on an "as needed" basis. These include: supplying Chinese volunteers to some 150 organizations, including hospitals and the meals-on-wheels program; providing staff for counselling and public awareness programs aimed at the Chinese community; and undertaking cross-cultural training activities with public agencies and private sector firms.

SUCCESS has no model or policy for collaborations and partnerships. If a partnership involves funding, the accountability arrangements are very formal and there is a clear allocation of responsibilities and roles. Without funding, the relationship is usually very informal. In some cases, the partners are accountable to their own boards, communities, and funders. In other cases, SUCCESS does joint evaluations on initiatives and actively collaborates with partners to plan and/or monitor a program. In all cases, a clear understanding of what is expected from every partner is essential and sought out.

On a project-by-project basis, the issue SUCCESS and its partners have had to face most frequently concerns how to define and operationalize an appropriate accountability relationship for shared project staff. Problems are more likely to arise when the staff, ostensibly working for the partnership, are actually employed by one of the member organizations. The relationship can become particularly troubled if the partners become dissatisfied with staff performance, but the employer refuses to address the problem. More generally, SUCCESS is concerned about the imposition of collaboration by funders and the burden of some accountability regimes for voluntary organizations with scarce resources.

The rise of imposed collaborations as a criterion for access to government funding is an increasing problem for SUCCESS. This organization shares the view of the ISS that these will not work. In many cases, the government wants an organization seeking funding to get ethnic communities or organizations involved in their programs. As one such organization, SUCCESS has been swamped with requests that it lend its name to an initiative or write a letter of support. Agreement to provide support has resulted in one of two contradictory, but equally troubling consequences. Often requesting organizations have little genuine interest in working with SUCCESS or having it take a role in the project. On the other hand, SUCCESS does not have the time or staff to sit on another organization's advisory committee or on a joint committee to ensure accountability. The transaction costs associated with concluding and monitoring partnerships are a matter of concern.

The Big Sisters, Aunts and Uncles at Large organizations in Calgary represent the extreme of collaboration with a three-way merger in 1994. This case illustrates some of the key factors in making mergers work and, in particular, the critical role to be played by funders when they are prepared to assist and facilitate, rather than mandate collaboration. Successful merger negotiations occurred after an earlier effort had broken down as a result of vested interests and personality differences. The City of Calgary, the Calgary Foundation, local Progress Clubs, and the Muttart Foundation all played a key role in the merger and, in some cases, in its aftermath. They encouraged collaboration among the three original organizations and the Muttart Foundation required it, as a condition of funding. Both the Muttart and Calgary Foundation provided critical funds for organizational support, during the merger negotiations and in the early months of the merger. They also encouraged the organizations to engage the services of a facilitator/mediator who had been through a similar merger. The one-time costs of transition were also covered. Another key ingredient was senior staff in the original organizations who along with their board chairs, became committed to the merger, and guided their respective boards through the process by keeping the focus on the shared mission of the three organizations. They were willing to take a risk on consolidation, but were always mindful to ensure that the quality of programs was not in jeopardy. Since these organizations are closely overseen by an accreditation process by a national organization, a decline in the ability to meet standards for process or program accountability most likely would have been caught, with serious implications for the new organization.

The success of the merger talks was due, in part, to acknowledgement of points of difference among the parties and concerted efforts to resolve them. In addition, all parties showed goodwill by each being prepared to give up something, but non-negotiables were also put on the table from the start. There were strong and frequent accountability links back to the boards of the three participating organizations during the merger process. The relatively smooth implementation of the merger also can be partly attributed to a determination to merge all aspects of the organization — including case management, personnel, and financial resources and management. The facilitator played a key role in working with the new board, from the outset, on how to best blend three distinct organizational cultures. Fortuitously, staff issues were resolved by having two of the former executive directors who wanted to stay with the merged organization work as co-directors. The parties agreed that if any of the three organizations were dissatisfied within a year, it could withdraw (although there naturally would be some sunk costs forfeited). None did so and the long-term benefits of the merger are becoming evident. Within the first year, there was a 20 percent reduction in overall operating costs, a budget surplus, and a doubling of corporate donations as well as a sense by the new organization that it is delivering better, more integrated service.

The Family Service Association (FSA) of Metropolitan Toronto and the *Toronto Counselling Centre for Lesbians and Gays (TCCLG)* merged in 1996. In contrast to the last case, this merger involved organizations of vastly different size and culture: FSA was an established multi-service agency with a full-time equivalent staff of 130, and the TCCLG was a newer organization with a staff of 2.5 serving an oppressed minority constituency. In fact, it is better described as a transfer of programs from the TCCLG to FSA, rather than a true merger. Nevertheless, most of the issues that arose are similar to those experienced in mergers. The impetus for the "merger" stemmed from the TCCLG's perennial difficulties in securing adequate funding. At the point of dissolving the organization after a 15-year struggle to survive, its board sought to ensure the survival of its programs in another organization, leading it to seek out the FSA. The Family Service Association was a willing participant in the merger because it had been seeking ways to broaden its responsiveness to particular communities. The United Way of Greater Toronto, the Municipality of Metropolitan Toronto, and the AIDS Bureau of the Ontario Ministry of Health were also important catalysts providing encouragement and transitional grants to facilitate the merger. Issues of funding, the continuing integrity of the lesbian and gay program, and the blending of differing organizational cultures were prominent during the negotiations. The formal agreement to merge captures many of the issues involved, including the requirement for FSA to "hire Counselling Centre volunteers and the requirement for training for FSA Board members, staff and volunteers concerning the former Centre's clientele and mandate." Homophobia and fear of HIV/AIDS were a particular concern. This training and a formal policy review to ensure that the transformed agency meets the needs of lesbians, gay men, and people affected by HIV/AIDS was to be completed by March 1999.

An important challenge in this merger was establishing the *modus operandi* of the board. One FSA board member who was uncomfortable with merging with a lesbian and gay organization resigned at the time of the merger. The others and incoming members including several from ethnoracial communities have embraced the program. The FSA made a specific undertaking to include lesbian and gay members on its board, although numbers were not identified. Given the very different realities of the two organizations, the extent to which the new board will operate on the policy-based Carver model already in place at FSA or be more operationally oriented was an issue. TCCLG had been characterized by advocacy and activism at the board, staff, and volunteer levels. In the new blended organization which serves a variety of constituencies, the Carver model may be a barrier to potential board members who are inclined to activism on the part of particular communities. On the other hand, FSA has a strong tradition of public policy advocacy and maintains a social action manager. There is little risk that board elections will become subject to efforts by particular communities to seize control because attention is given to ensuring all voices are heard. Some of this is addressed through the creation of community advisory committees not only for the lesbian, gay, and HIV/AIDS communities, but for several ethno-racial communities as well.

A major issue for the smaller unit was how it could carve out its unique identity as part of a much larger organization. The new organization continues to work on these issues of accountability and organizational culture and, indeed, sees this work as open-ended. In spite of transition difficulties involved in overcoming cultural differences, the general sense by participants is that the merger is working well. The benefit to the FSA has been greater access to the lesbian, gay, and HIV/AIDS communities and the programs once provided by the TCCLG have obtained a greater degree of legitimacy and visibility, not to mention greater security of funding, as part of a larger, more mainstream organization.

WHAT HAVE WE LEARNED?

These cases have illuminated some important issues concerning accountability in collaborations involving voluntary sector organizations. Our first objective was to determine current practices regarding accountability in these relationships and examine the implications for accountability regimes. Our most fundamental finding in this regard is that, despite the variable accountability arrangements among the cases, accountability issues were of universal concern. The specifics of this concern have informed our second objective of identifying gaps between need and practice.

Three general observations are pertinent before we turn to specific lessons about accountability practices. First, what all of these cases demonstrate is the importance of self-regulation and self-adherence to mutual expectations and standards of accountability. In many cases, formal agreements have assisted in setting out the expectations and formalized accountability arrangements have helped to ensure compliance. But, given the importance of mutual obligation and trust in collaborations, legalisms and other formal arrangements are not a prerequisite to functional accountability regimes and, indeed, mean little if they are not built on a solid foundation of good will and self-regulation.

The second general observation is that forced, imposed or token collaborations seldom work. The Immigrant Services Society, SUCCESS and, to a lesser extent, the Regional Case Management Service cases reveal the inherent problematic nature of such partnerships. In all three cases, participants have grown increasingly wary of token or "showcase" partnerships, which maintain the pretense of collaboration but do not involve real joint action, because they seldom help achieve their mandates or directly benefit the organizations in other ways. Interestingly, problems with imposed partnerships may have the unintended consequence of making some participating organizations more insular.

Third, no specific type of collaboration, nor any particular set of partners seems *a priori* more likely to succeed or develop more effective accountability mechanisms than others. The exception is the type of collaboration labelled collabitition, in which an underlying competition among the collaborators serves to undermine the establishment of long-term relationships and trust. In general, accountability regimes seem most well-developed in partnerships taking the form of joint ventures. Joint ventures with the private sector, as illustrated by the AIDS Committee of Toronto, are particularly interesting. They show evidence of recognition of both shared ground and points of departure between the partners. This includes, in the ACT case, a *modus vivendi* on issues related to advocacy. As partners, governments have been both flexible, as demonstrated by the Regional Umbrella Group for Childcare collaboration and rigid, as illustrated by the federal government's relationship with ISS.

In reflecting upon specific accountability practices, we see that the factors that produce effective accountability are the same elements that contribute to making the collaboration succeed in the first place. This is not surprising because both hinge on shared responsibility, joint action, and mutual benefit. The first practical lesson is the importance of getting off on the right foot by choosing appropriate partners, being clear about the purpose of the collaboration, and establishing agreed upon expectations about roles and responsibilities from the start (see Ferronato 1999, pp. 89; National Center for Nonprofit Boards 1994). In some cases, such as the RCMS, it is evident that, although accountability may be a concern, the boards of the collaborating organizations have not actively thought through the specifics or mechanisms. What appears to be vital to success, however, is not attention to detail, but the establishment of clear expectations, confidence that such specifics can be worked out based on the underlying trust among the partners, and respect for different interests and types of contributions.

The case studies dealing with mergers (Big Sisters, Aunts and Uncles at Large, and the Family Service Association, and the TCCLG) involve groups with somewhat different mandates and histories. Both show the importance of setting the accountability roadmap on the table for each organization negotiating a potential merger. Equally important to examining accountability issues before the merger occurs is the resolution to continue to work on accountability issues post-merger. At this stage, accountability issues become linked with those of developing a positive internal organizational culture and providing appropriate service to the clients and constituencies of the merged organizations who may have differing needs and interests.

Leadership is a key ingredient here, not only in the beginning but also during the follow-through. Collaborations entail both vision and risk and, as we move from collabitition to merger, the degree of risk increases. In the merger of three organizations to become Big Sisters and Brothers, a few board members and senior staff were willing to take the risk because they had a vision of how consolidation would improve services and, through this commitment, were able to bring along the rest of their boards. But the risks had been realistically assessed. They were also minimized by a system of accreditation: the quality of programming was subject to standards and evaluation by a parent accrediting body so that any decline in service was likely to be noticed and remedies required. Even in less than full consolidation, however, boards have to risk giving up some control to the collaboration. RCMS illustrates a case in which the participating boards did not cede enough authority to an inter-agency committee of executive directors to allow it to push the collaboration forward, largely because they saw little need to do so. Although the partners need to maintain accountability to their own boards, in this case the collaboration was unduly restricted by the collaborators' control over the delegation of policy roles.

A collaboration, even a merger, is not an event, but a process in which trust is a foundational element of accountability. Of course, building trust takes time, and depends in large measure on communication and personal relationships (see Ekos Research 1998, p. 24). We saw, for example in the Collingwood Neighbourhood House Project, how potential conflict could be transformed into a successful collaboration among a community organization, a municipal government and a developer. Increasing familiarity and mutual respect among the three key actors was vital in moving the relationship to a new, more collaborative footing and these were fostered largely by the openness of communication in the management committee. When a collaboration or a specific partner runs into difficulty, communication and reaching out to the partner may be what saves the whole thing from divorce. Recognition that the RCMS may be a marriage in trouble as a result of inter-agency competition among participants, for instance, may lead to reformulation of the partnership to reflect the inherent differences and tensions among the organizations that participate.

An important aspect of building trust is respecting and valuing differences — of contributions, cultures, and relationships with constituencies. Accountability frameworks need to be built on a recognition that different partners may make different sorts of contributions. A common complaint is that voluntary organizations whose primary contributions are connections to community and volunteer resources often feel undervalued by those partners making financial contributions. In particular, governments are often guilty of assuming that the weight of their dollars gives them the authority to dictate accountability mechanisms and policy directions, rather than to negotiate them. Respecting and working through differences in organizational cultures is a recurring theme in the cases. Perhaps the most extreme example is the culture clash of the more mainstream Family Service Association with the more political, activist culture of the Counselling Centre for Lesbians and Gays, but it was a factor in other collaborations as well. In several cases, the corporate or government partner often complained that the community organizations were too "process" focused, meaning that they were overly concerned with encouraging the participation of and getting the reaction of their members or communities before proceeding. Although the resulting slow pace can be frustrating for the partners, community involvement needs to be understood as a resource and one of the inherent strengths of the voluntary sector, rather than an impediment.

Although specific structures do not necessarily generate trust, they can help. The importance of a forum for sharing ideas and concerns and for solving problems is a common aspect of effective partnerships and accountability. Generally, this takes the form of a management committee comprised of the senior staff of the collaborating organizations. The cases illustrate, however, that this committee needs to be greater than the sum of its parts; while maintaining accountability links to the member boards is important, the committee should also have the capacity to act in the interests of the collaboration, rather than for a collection of individual interests. The role played by the staff to the collaboration also matters considerably. First, simply having staff helps. Second, staff is more effective if they are attached to, and understood to be working for, the collaboration not for specific members. Where problems and misunderstandings arose with staff in our cases, it was because the staff were employed by, and thus under the control of a member organization, rather than having unequivocal first loyalties to the collaboration.

This brings us to the issue of capacity more generally. Capacity, defined as "the assets, strengths, qualities or characteristics" that enable a voluntary organization to survive and thrive (Ramsey and Reynolds 1997, p. 14), is essential to achieving real accountability. Collaboration is not costless; in fact, the transition costs can be substantial. Without sufficient infrastructure, knowledge and skills, organizations will have difficulty meeting their accountability obligations and perhaps participating in collaborations at all. A compounding factor is that organizations have had few places to turn to get the information and support they need to help work through the issues created by collaboration. When assistance in the form of expertise as well as financial support was forthcoming, as in the case of the merger of Big Sisters, Aunts and Uncles, the chances of a successful collaboration with appropriate accountability mechanisms in place were increased enormously. While capacity is important for all organizations, it is a much bigger issue for small, community-based associations. The positive relationships and continued commitment of the community organizations in the RUG group, for instance, were greatly enhanced by government's provision of a small "participation" contribution which, even if it did not begin to cover the actual draw on organizations' time and resources, was a valued recognition of the cost of collaborative work.

The need for capacity building to promote accountability is nowhere more evident than in the growing interest in evaluation. Although evaluation is recognized as important, voluntary organizations partnering with government funders sometimes find that the evaluation criteria and requirements do not address their interests and are burdensome in terms of time and resources. Specifically, we see in the RUG case and in its umbrella project, the Vancouver Childcare Regional Delivery Model Pilot Project, real concerns that the achievements in developing collaborative relationships and opening up enhanced possibilities for collaboration in the future will be undervalued in the formal evaluation process. "Results-based evaluation," undertaken over a four-year project may also give insufficient recognition to the amount of time required to build collaborative relationships which may eventually lead to better results.

Our final observation is the difficulty of balancing advocacy and service responsibilities within a collaboration. The problem stems from differences in basic roles: while most governments and corporations involved in partnerships are primarily interested in cutting costs, enhancing service delivery or in improving public relations, the voluntary sector partners have a more complex set of responsibilities to balance. Not only do they provide services to communities, but they have responsibilities to represent the interests and identities of these constituencies and enable them to participate in the organization's governance and decision making (Phillips 1995). Although voluntary organizations take on an accountability to the partnership, they do not forego their accountability to their communities. Yet many voluntary sector partners found that their ability to be advocates on behalf of their communities was explicitly or implicitly constrained once they were part of a collaboration, or that their government and corporate partners were often frustrated by how much time they spent on issues of community engagement. Setting out boundaries that maintain a space for advocacy, as ACT successfully did with its corporate partners, helps to ensure that the responsibilities to communities are not compromised. Although the boundaries for advocacy often do not become clear until they are tested with a specific issue, they are an important aspect of accountability frameworks that, to the extent possible, should be a part of the shared expectations at the outset.

Does collaboration induce innovation in working through accountability issues, either at the time of the partnership/merger or subsequently? Our tentative answer is yes, although the innovation seldom comes in the form of elaborate rules and procedures. Often invention comes from experience, and sometimes adversity, during implementation of a partnership or merger. Nevertheless, cases as diverse as the Big Sisters, Aunts and Uncles merger, the FSA-TCCLG merger, and the RCMS partnership suggest it is still important to think through accountability issues during the negotiation phase. Three basic questions need to be put on the table: accountability for what? accountability to whom? and accountability by what means? The specifics may initially be less important than the articulation of basic guiding principles and creation of effective means of communication to establish common expectations and solve problems as the collaboration evolves.

The Changing Nature of Accountability Regimes

So far, we have discussed lessons about accountability practices within regimes. Our cases also provide insight, albeit speculative given our limited number of cases, into the changing nature of accountability regimes. First, it appears that funder-dominated accountability regimes are becoming more complex and their requirements more onerous: governments have moved from service providers to contract managers and grantors of project funding which require accounting; the growing preference for sponsorships over philanthropy by corporations brings with it more strings attached to funding; and most funders are not only requiring accountability for sound financial management but for outcome-based performance assessment. Where there is simply a proliferation of rules and regulations without co-ordination among funders, the result is more onerous and time-consuming reporting, but not necessarily better practices. Our case studies demonstrate that where funders step beyond the activities of simply grant-making/grant-monitoring to more facilitating roles — helping to build capacity by contributing to overhead, lending expertise to voluntary organizations to engage in strategic planning and problem solving, and providing assistance with research for performance measurement — greater innovation in both collaboration and accountability results. As collaboration increases, moving from collabitition to genuine partnerships or mergers, the effectiveness of funder-based accountability regimes will depend, in our view, on their ability to adapt to these new roles of capacity-building and facilitating.

The other major regime shift is that collaboration gives greater primacy to self-regulating accountability regimes. Although it is relatively easy to impose and enforce accountability rules in relationships based on formal instruments such as contracts, in partnerships which are dependent primarily on trust and mutual benefit, regulation by one partner or by an external actor is not the most useful vehicle for accountability. Strong self-regulatory regimes rely on four important elements: skilled and attentive boards of directors capable of guiding and monitoring their organizations, willingness to cede adequate space and authority to the partnership for some aspects of operations and accountability, strong intermediary associations which can develop standards and lead innovation on best practices, and transparency and easy access to information about specific organizations so that practices can be observed and monitored by the public. In our view, all of these elements need some work and are part of the capacity-building we discussed above. In this respect, the evolution of self-regulating regimes is closely tied to the enhancement of capacity by funder-dominated regimes.

Practice and Theory: Bridging Gaps

Our final objective is to identify gaps between need and practice. In this context, the cases yield at least four areas where further research and deliberation would assist the voluntary sector and its public and private sector partners.

First, there is a need to identify and document best practices in successfully negotiating and implementing partnerships and mergers.[14] For the most part, organizations have learned by doing and, through experimentation, have developed effective partnerships accountability processes. Yet, most of their external communication is limited to the requirements of financial reporting to Revenue Canada and to funders, rather than sharing information across the sector and with the public. We need more information, not only on the new and often relatively invisible partnerships that have been created, but on what has actually occurred to develop and implement accountability regimes in them.

A second need is for models of evaluation which balance the concerns and interests of the sector and its public and private sector partners. Specifically, we need models of evaluation that address concerns about both outcome and process, and that are not overly burdensome on voluntary organizations with limited human resources and time to devote to the process. In this undertaking, foundations and other funders as well as universities could make significant contributions.

Third, our research suggests the need to track the effect of particular models of board governance on organizations which merge but serve distinct communities. This emerged from our study of the Family Service Association, where adoption of the Carver model may have important effects on the politics of board membership and accountability to communities. In our view, this issue is of broader concern, as voluntary organizations continue their preoccupation with board governance issues.

Finally, we think that more exploration is required on the role and treatment of advocacy activities by voluntary organizations who participate in partnerships and mergers. A recurring theme, particularly with governments as partners, is how to balance service delivery with the legitimate role and, indeed, responsibility of voluntary organizations to be public policy advocates for their constituencies. Do advocacy activities impose limits on collaboration with other organizations, legally, culturally or for other reasons? Under what circumstances do partnerships and mergers help in advocacy? How do organizations involved in partnerships and mergers deal with controversies surrounding advocacy? These are just some of the important questions which need further examination.

CONCLUSION

Neither the trends toward greater collaboration nor the interest in increasing accountability in the voluntary sector are passing fads. Rather, they are the consequences of deeper structural changes in the relationship of the sector to government, business, and society. As the implications of these fundamental shifts continue to unfold, accountability practices and collaboration arrangements will also evolve. Collaboration is not a uniform type of relationship, but is multi-faceted, taking the form, we suggest, of a continuum that ranges from competitive cooperation to organizational mergers. In order to better understand the pluralistic and complex nature of accountability in the voluntary sector, we have applied the concept of a regime, a set of relationships among multiple actors that is relatively stable but flexible over time, and that creates its own norms and expectations. How the regime is experienced by any specific organization depends, in part, on how that organization is situated among the other actors in the regime. Collaborations can change an organization's situation in the accountability regime, as their boards sort out new relationships with partners, funders, and constituencies, thereby making accountability even more complex and subject to a wide range of experimentation.

The joint rise of accountability and collaboration has created many contradictions for voluntary organizations: in particular, to become at once more risk-taking and more rule-following. One limitation of our study is that we looked only at those organizations that have sorted out some of these contradictions, at least to the extent that they all have been sufficiently risk-taking to enter into collaborative arrangements. Nevertheless, even in our case studies certain contradictions remain unresolved. One is to find greater clarity amid greater complexity. The need for clear expectations and understanding by the board of its role and those of its partners is more important than ever in collaborations. Some boards have been able to rise to this challenge, while others struggle. Another persistent contradiction is undertaking policy advocacy without alienating cautious government and corporate partners.

Within the emerging models of collaboration, it is evident that subjective or self-directed accountability is more important than externally imposed rules and regulations. As we observed in our cases, there is no one uniform approach or set of rules for effectively addressing accountability issues in joint ventures, partnerships, and mergers: some approaches are formal, others informal; some were pre-specified, others evolved; some were extensive, others minimal. But in all cases, the boards and senior staff were critical to the success of the partnership. It is the boards of directors and the staff of the partnerships who must champion, set priorities, keep to the mission, promote constructive outcomes, and help to shape organizational cultures in collaborations. This stewardship cannot be regulated. But it can be nurtured. The challenge of board development in coming years should not be underestimated. This does not imply, however, that there is no role for other actors in improving the effectiveness of accountability regimes. Issues of transparency and the capacity of voluntary organizations to meet accountability commitments and requirements remain significant shortcomings of most regimes. Both governments and the private sector can play an important part in expanding capacity in the sector through supporting sectoral infrastructure, assisting with technology, facilitating information exchange, and helping to develop and refine performance-based outcome measures.

The evolution of collaboration, we suggest, will continue to move to the right of our continuum. As rationalization of the public and private sectors continues, governments and other funders are likely to promote — indeed, explicitly to require — consolidation of organizations, rather than merely collaboration around projects and programs. Yet, as we have seen, many of the government-mandated collaborations have produced uncomfortable and unhappy relationships, often ending in divorce. The challenge for governments and other funders will be to provide incentives and support for collaboration and consolidation, where appropriate, but at the same time respect the autonomy of the organizations and leadership of their boards. More importantly, they also need to recognize that partnerships are not substitutes for more substantial capacity-building in the sector.

Notes

This paper benefited from the assistance and support of a number of people. First, we gratefully acknowledge the financial support of the Kahanoff Foundation Nonprofit Sector Research Initiative which was critical in enabling us to develop the case studies. Research assistance was expertly provided by Elizabeth Dandy and Michael Orisini. The comments of the participants at the authors' workshop and, in particular Alasdair Roberts and Keith Banting, helped us address the many flaws of the first draft. Finally, we thank the participants in our case studies who gave generously of their time in interviews and later kindly read and corrected our accounts of their experiences. Accountability for the errors or misinterpretations which remain, however, rests with us.

[1] Agencies external to the sector, notably the Better Business Bureau, have attempted (albeit with limited success) to develop and impose their own accreditation systems by requiring voluntary organizations in a particular locale to report on how well they meet a set of standards and to publish the comparative ratings of the organizations on these standards.

[2] These regulations are discussed in the Panel on Accountability and Governance in the Voluntary Sector (1999, pp. 66-72).

[3] We are grateful to Michael Hall for suggesting this term which has been used by the Canadian Centre for Philanthropy.

[4] The following discussion is to a large extent based on the presentations made to the Panel on Governance and Accountability during its consultations with hundreds of voluntary organizations across the country in the fall of 1998 and in the briefs presented to the panel. The authors had access to this information as Susan Phillips served as Research Director to the panel and attended the consultations. The briefs presented to the panel are available at www.pagvs.com.

[5] A 1998 decision by the Federal Court of Appeal in the Human Life International case further restricted the definition of permissible advocacy activity by stating that "activities designed essentially to sway public opinion on a controversial social issue are not charitable but are political." On appeal, the case was dismissed by the Supreme Court.

[6] Personal communication with study participant.

[7] The most significant rise in the volunteering rate is for youth (aged 15 to 24 years) which almost doubled from 18 percent in 1987 to 33 percent in 1997. The survey reports that although the percentage of citizens who volunteer and the total hours volunteered has increased, the average number of hours contributed per volunteer has decreased from 191 hours per year in 1987 and 149 hours in 1997 (Canadian Centre for Philanthropy *et al.* 1998, pp. 27-28).

[8] We could find no Canadian literature that discusses the impact of workfare and other programs of mandatory volunteerism on voluntary organizations. In the American case, see Dundjerski and Gray (1998, pp. 1, 29).

[9] Recent court decisions in British Columbia, now under appeal, have created the real possibility that boards of directors could be held vicariously liable for the misconduct of employees and, by extension, volunteers, even for acts that predate their terms as directors. See *WRB v. Plint* 1998 BCJ no. 1320, BC Supreme Court, June 1998.

[10] The backbench Liberal MP, John Bryden, was a very vocal critic of the sector. By his own statement, his concern was that he was in competition to be heard. See Susan Delacourt, "Losing Interest," *The Globe and Mail*, 1 April 1995, p. D5.

[11] We initially included 15 partnerships, but the data for some were incomplete or the cases are very similar, so for purposes of brevity, we are reporting only eight cases here.

[12] The fact that there are more in Vancouver than the other cities reflects the networks we used and the completeness of interview data, not the level of collaboration taking place in the four cities.

[13] Personal communication with study participant.

[14] We note that the merger establishing the Big Brothers and Sisters of Calgary is currently being documented and analyzed by the co-directors, Jim Campbell and Sherry Ferronato, who have received a Muttart scholarship to develop the case study. This will be a valuable addition to knowledge about mergers in the sector.

References

Armstrong, J. and D.G. Lenihan. 1999. *From Controlling to Collaborating: When Governments Want to be Partners*. Toronto: IPAC.

Brem, M. 1998. "In the Dark: Role and Value of Charitable Sector Little Known Among Public," *Inter Sector: A Newsletter for Imagine Community Partners*, 4(3):2.

Canada. Task Force on Public Service Values and Ethics. 1997. *A Strong Foundation: Report of the Task Force on Public Service Values and Ethics*. Ottawa: Supply and Services Canada.

Canadian Centre for Philanthropy. Non-Profit Research Initiative, Volunteer Canada Canadian Heritage, Health Canada, Human Resources Development Canada and Statistics Canada. 1998. *Caring Canadians, Involved Canadians: Highlights from the 1997 National Survey of Giving, Volunteering and Participating*. Ottawa: Minister of Industry.

Carver, J. 1997. *Boards that Make a Difference*. 2d ed. San Francisco: Jossey-Bass.

Day, P. and R. Klein. 1987. *Accountabilities: Five Public Services.* London: Tavistock.

Dundjerski, M. and S. Gray. 1998. "A Lesson in Mandatory Service," *Chronicle of Philanthropy,* 10(22):1-29.

Ekos Research Associates Inc. 1998. "Lessons Learned on Partnerships: Final Report." Ottawa: Report Prepared for the Voluntary Sector Roundtable.

Edwards, M. and D. Hulme. 1996. "Introduction: NGO Performance and Accountability," in *Beyond the Magic Bullet: NGO Performance and Accountability in the Post-Cold War World.* London: Kumarian Press.

Ferronato, S. 1999. "Nonprofit Mergers: Perils and Possibiliites," *Front and Centre,* 6(1):1, 8-9.

Hall, M.H. and L.G. Macpherson. 1996. "What Types of Charities Are Getting Corporate Donations?" *Research Bulletin,* 3(4):2. Toronto: Canadian Centre for Philanthropy.

Hall, M.H. and M. Parmegiani. 1998. "Public Opinion and Accountability in the Charitable Sector," *Research Bulletin,* 5(2):1-2. Toronto: Canadian Centre for Philanthropy.

Jenson, J. and S.D. Phillips. 1996. "Regime Shift: Citizenship in Canada," *International Journal of Canadian Studies,* 14(Fall):111-36.

Kearns, K.P. 1994. "The Strategic Management of Accountability in Nonprofit Organizations: An Analytical Framework," *Public Administration Review,* 54(2):185-92.

Kernaghan, K. 1993. "Partnership and Public Administration: Conceptual and Practical Considerations," *Canadian Public Administration,* 36(1):57-76.

Milofsky, C. and S.D. Blades. 1991. "Issues of Accountability in Health Charities: A Case Study of Accountability Problems among Nonprofit Organizations," *Nonprofit and Voluntary Sector Quarterly,* 20(4):371-93.

Mintz, J., M. Hudson and B. Lebrun. 1998. "Partnerships: Governments' New Math," *Perspectives on Partnership.* Ottawa: Caledon Institute of Social Policy, Social Partnerships Project.

Municipality of Metropolitan Toronto. City of Toronto and Social Planning Council of Metropolitan Toronto. 1997. *Profile of a Changing World: 1996 Community Agency Survey.* Toronto: Municipality of Metropolitan Toronto.

National Center for Nonprofit Boards. 1994. *Nonprofit Mergers: The Board's Responsibility to Consider the Unthinkable.* Washington, DC: National Center for Nonprofit Boards.

Panel on Accountability and Governance in the Voluntary Sector. 1999. *Building on Strength: Improving Governance and Accountability in the Voluntary Sector*. Ottawa: Voluntary Sector Roundtable. Also available at www.pagvs.com.

Phillips, S.D. 1991. "How Ottawa Blends: Shifting Government Relationships with Interest Groups," in *How Ottawa Spends 1991-92: The Politics of Fragmentation*, ed. F. Abele. Ottawa: Carleton University Press.

_____ 1995. "Redefining Government Relationships with the Voluntary Sector: On Great Expectations *and* Sense and Sensibility." Paper prepared for National Voluntary Organizations.

Picard, A.1997. *A Call to Alms*. Toronto: Atkinson Charitable Foundation.

Pierson, P. 1994. *Dismantling the Welfare State? Reagan, Thatcher, and the Politics of Retrenchment*. Cambridge: Cambridge University Press.

Ramsey, G.R. and R. Reynolds. 1997. *The Social Reconnaissance Project: Discovering Philanthropic Leadership Opportunities*. Vancouver: Vancouver Foundation.

Rekart, J. 1993. *Public Funds, Private Provision*. Vancouver: UBC Press.

_____ 1997. *The Transformation of the Voluntary Sector*. Vancouver: Social Planning and Research Council of BC.

Sharpe, D. 1994. *A Portrait of Canada's Charities: The Size, Scope and Financing of Registered Charities*. Toronto: Canadian Centre for Philanthropy.

Smith, S.R. and M. Lipsky. 1993. *Nonprofits for Hire: The Welfare State in the Age of Contracting*. Cambridge: Harvard University Press.

Stewart, J. 1995. "Accountability and Empowerment in Welfare Services," in *British Social Welfare: Past, Present and Future*, ed. D. Gladstone. London: University College London Press.

Stoker, G. 1995. "Regime Theory and Urban Politics," in *Theories of Urban Politics*, ed. D. Judge, G. Stoker and H. Wolman. London: Sage.

Stone, C. 1989. *Regime Politics*. Lawrence, KA: University of Kansas Press.

Taylor, M. 1996. "Between Public and Private: Accountability in Voluntary Organisations," *Policy and Politics*, 21(1):57-72.

Tjorman, S. 1998. *Partnerships: The Good, the Bad and the Uncertain*. Ottawa: Caledon Institute of Social Policy.

Waddock, S.A. 1988. "Building Successful Social Partnerships," *Sloan Management Review*, 17 (Summer):17-23.

Zussman, D. 1997. "Ensuring Successful Partnerships Through Performance-Based Management," *The Alternative Network*, 2(3):1-5.

6

The Nonprofit Sector in Manitoba: A Baseline Survey

Laura K. Brown, Elizabeth S. Troutt and Attah K. Boame

Over time, nonprofit organizations (NPOs) have come to form a thriving sector of the economy. The nonprofit sector (NPS) affects the lives of all citizens in Canada as they seek health care, participate in sports, or belong to a professional organization. NPOs also interact with other actors in the Canadian economy, including business and government. As researchers have only recently begun to recognize the influence of the NPS, information about the sector, particularly in Canada, is quite limited. Sharpe (1994) focuses on a sectoral breakdown of charitable organizations in Canada without any regional analysis. Ross (1990) provides only limited information that is confined to volunteer work in Manitoba. More recently, the Canadian Centre for Philanthropy (CCP) has reported findings on Canadian charities (CCP 1997*b*) and on Canadian voluntarism (CCP 1998). Virtually no research has been conducted on the nonprofit sector (NPS) in Manitoba, or indeed in any specific geographic region of Canada. This paper examines the nonprofit sector in Manitoba, exploring its basic dimensions and characteristics, and examines two issues in greater depth: the level of government funding in the sector and the perceived influence of various parties on decision making within NPOs.

DEFINING THE NONPROFIT SECTOR

Definitions of the NPS or of the nonprofit organizations (NPOs) which make up the NPS are not yet clear. In the literature, there is neither consensus as to what constitutes an NPO nor as to what characteristics an NPO must possess. The one point of agreement is that NPOs, like government, face what Weisbrod (1988) and Hansmann (1987) call "the non-distribution constraint." That is, while NPOs are not prohibited from *earning* profits, they do not *distribute* profits to any set of owners.

As various authors build on this one point of agreement, however, they offer or imply vastly differing definitions of NPOs. Ben-Ner and Van Hoomissen "regard [NPOs], *at their inception*, as coalitions of individuals who associate to provide themselves and others with goods or services that are not adequately supplied by either for-profit or government organisations" (1991, p. 521). According to Anheier, Germany's System of Economic Activities (GSEA) defines NPOs as "associations and institutions which either provide public goods and serve the common weal, or meet the specified interests of their members or other groups" (1987, p. 676). Knapp and Kendall recognize the difficulty in defining what they refer to as the voluntary sector, and suggest that the organizations which comprise the sector "should be formally constituted, self-governing, private (independent of government), not distributing profits to those who control them, benefiting from voluntarism, and producing some public or external benefits" (1991, p. 712). Rutherford (1992) defines a "non-profit enterprise" as an organization whose members, because they lack private property rights in the organization, are not entitled to any of its profits, thereby limiting his definition to organizations that face Weisbrod's and Hansmann's non-distribution constraint. However, he describes motives for the establishment of such organizations which would seem to add to his working definition of a nonprofit enterprise. These motives include the desire or need to provide "merit goods" and subsidize goods and services such as religion and the arts. James and Rose-Ackerman (1986) use the legal definition of the United States Internal Revenue Code (USIRC), which includes organizations that have the three characteristics of adhering to the non-distribution constraint, providing "socially useful" goods or services, and receiving at least some of their revenue from (tax deductible) donations.

In part, this lack of consensus as to definition may reflect the diversity of the NPS. Every sector of the economy possesses the traits of breadth and variety, but the NPS is almost entirely a subsector of the service sector, which is itself marked by extreme breadth and variety. It is not surprising therefore to find that the NPS is extremely diverse and that definitions of the sector should permit this variety. Many authors point out that their definitions rightly allow room for, as Rudney says, "religious, educational, health, scientific, cultural, and social service organisations" (1987, p. 55); or, as Salamon puts it, "hospitals, universities, museums, arts groups, foster-care providers, health clinics, youth training centres, private nursing homes, advocacy groups, neighbourhood revitalization organisations, and many more" (1987, p. 100). The definition we use in our conceptualization of the NPS is:

The non-profit sector is an economic grouping of organizations whose purpose is to provide a good or service either for its members or for non-members, where each of these organizations

a) is recognizable as an organization in that the organization exists independently of any individual member,

b) faces a non-distribution constraint in that profits may not be distributed among either members or owners, and

c) is self-governing, or is an independently defined part of a larger self-governing organization which satisfies criteria (a) and (b).

This definition follows Ben-Ner and Hoomissen and the GSEA. It rejects the constraints implied by Knapp and Kendal that the NPS includes only organizations that use volunteers, and by the USIRC that the NPS includes only organizations which are legally permitted to issue tax receipts for donations. The definition therefore recognizes the existence of NPOs which, over a period of time, receive 100 percent of their income from the government, but which are not a part of government. It also avoids the difficulty that could be raised by Rutherford's definition by recognizing that members of NPOs face a non-distribution constraint, irrespective of whether that constraint is self-imposed because owners choose to be a part of the NPS or whether it has been imposed by some other authority. Finally, by stating that the organization is self-governing, the definition makes a clear distinction between government agencies and government-financed NPOs.

The NPS might be viewed as consisting of many subsets of more homogeneous groups of NPOs. Clearly, the NPS can be divided into the subgroups of NPOs along a number of dimensions. For example, the sector could be subdivided into NPOs that are registered charities and those that are not; or those that benefit from volunteer labour and those that do not. Alternatively, it could be divided along primary service lines or according to the amount of government funding the organization receives with, for example, organizations that receive more than 75 percent of their funding from government sources being considered "quasi-governmental" and being assumed to be of a different nature than those that are less dependent on government funding. An additional way in which the sector might be subdivided is according to range of function; under this subdivision, there might be three groups of NPOs. The first category would contain any NPO which provides goods or services to some group other than itself or its membership. This category would contain NPOs such as women's centres and poverty relief organizations. The second category would include NPOs that provide benefits to themselves or their members; examples are religious organizations, sports clubs, and professional associations. The third category would contain organizations which deliver services, goods, or benefits on behalf of government; these NPOs might be viewed as "middlemen" between government and the public. This category would contain educational and health organizations, for example. There are probably numerous other ways in which the NPS could be subdivided.

Regardless of the classification system used, a critical question is whether NPOs in one category in fact differ from those in other categories. That is, does one type of NPO differ from other types, or are the differences among NPOs within a given category at least as significant as those among NPOs across the sector? Throughout the analyses we present here, we categorize NPOs in various ways in an attempt to examine whether there are operative differences across the various types of NPOs it is possible to identify.

CONTEXT AND RESEARCH QUESTIONS

In this paper, we report the findings of a sample survey of Manitoba NPOs that was designed to examine resource flows into and out of the NPS, the role of government funding, and the extent of NPO autonomy in administration and decision making. We also establish a baseline of information on the NPS in Manitoba which should allow for follow-up research through case studies to probe more deeply into the organizational behaviour of selected types of NPOs, through further survey research to track trends in the sector over time, or through comparisons of Manitoba's experience with the NPS in other places.

Manitoba is characterized by a number of features that make it very conducive to studying the NPS. Although the population of the province is only about one million, there are at least 7,506 active nonprofit organizations in the province[1] and the Canadian Centre for Philanthropy (1997b) reports that there are 4,114 registered charities. In addition, Manitoba's population includes a number of distinct populations. Indigenous groups are important: Winnipeg has the largest urban aboriginal population in Canada (Statistics Canada 1996), and the rural aboriginal population is large, well-organized, and growing fast. The province is home to large Eastern European and Finnish communities, as well as the largest francophone population outside Quebec; and according to the 1996 Census, 90 percent of Manitobans identify themselves with at least one ethnicity other than Canadian. Additionally, Manitoba is a hub for several national organizations which serve or represent disabled people, and the worldwide Mennonite Central Committee is headquartered here. All of these groups have traditions of community cohesion and providing "for the common good" of the society of which they are a part. The presence of these cultural influences in Manitoba provides a setting in which a variety of NPOs might be expected to flourish. Manitoba has a history of grass-roots initiatives and strong social activism. This may have become more apparent to the rest of Canada during the flood of 1997 and the 1999 Pan American Games, but it has always been a part of the province's social fabric. This is not to say that our research findings are necessarily unique to Manitoba. We conducted our research in Manitoba because it is a place with which we are familiar and because Manitoba offers an NPS that is well-suited to study. Our findings may well reflect patterns that are true of the NPS in other places, and the numerous unanswered questions that arise from this research can be posed about the sector elsewhere.

Researchers agree on the importance of NPOs throughout the world (Powell 1987; Ben-Ner and Gui 1991; Pryor 1994; Sharpe 1994; Salamon and Anheier 1996). Across countries, the size of the NPS in 1982 varied from 15 percent of GNP in the Netherlands to 1.6 percent of GNP in Sweden (James 1987). In Canada, the charitable sector comprises 75,000 organizations (CCP 1997*b*) and represents 13 percent of GDP (Sharpe 1994). Because not all NPOs are registered charities, Canada's NPS must account for an even larger share of Canadian gross domestic product (GDP) than does the charitable sector.

Clearly, the funding sources of such a large sector of the economy need to be better understood. The literature on the NPS documents that in most Western economies, the largest proportion of NPO funding comes from government. In Canada, 60 percent of funding for registered charities was obtained from government sources, while Manitoba charitable organizations receive roughly 55 percent of their revenue from government sources (CCP 1997*b*). These numbers are of critical importance to both governments and NPOs. The NPS is often viewed as a substitute for government services. If government is truly the largest source of NPO funds, then NPO services may be viewed as an inexpensive *substitute* for government-provided (often unionized) service provision. However, this is not the only possibility. It may be the case that the NPS is in fact a *complement* to the public sector. In this case, government can be viewed as providing some administrative and regulatory services directly, and as complementing these services with NPO funding for front-line service provision. Which of these views is more accurate cannot be assessed because of a general lack of systematic research on the NPS.

While theories abound about the relationship between government and the NPS, very little evidence has been amassed. In this paper, we seek to contribute to this process by presenting findings about two basic elements of the NPS in Manitoba: government funding and perceived influences on decision making.

Manitoba NPOs' Reliance on Funds from Government Sources

This first area examines the degree of reliance on government funding by the Manitoba NPS. Across countries, governments are the largest source of funding to the NPS. A number of theories have been advanced to explain the predominance of government funding. One theory (Weisbrod

1988) is that the NPS serves a gap-filling role in the provision of public services. If demand is heterogeneous, government provides funding to satisfy the needs of the median voter, and private funding supplies the remaining demand for each subgroup of the population. Douglas (1987) lists a number of theories stressing the political reasons for government funding of the NPS. Government is seen to help finance (rather than deliver) activities when direct public provision would be politically untenable. Political theories also emphasize the flexibility of the nonprofit sector. NPOs provide a channel through which government can experiment with programs that may not justify a long-term funding commitment. Also, the reduced accountability required by NPOs decreases their degree of bureaucratization and allows them more flexibility in responding to the needs of their clients. Finally, governments channel services through NPOs because the latter are better able to serve groups and individuals who either distrust government or for whom a social stigma is attached to receiving government services (Hansmann 1987; Ben-Ner and Van Hoomissen 1991).

The degree of funding provided to NPOs by government raises the question of whether this sector is truly separate from (i.e., is a substitute for) the public sector, or whether its services are complementary to government services in that both government services and NPO services are significantly influenced by government funding and government priorities. From the NPS' perspective, the degree of NPO dependence on government funding can be viewed as an indicator of the NPS' vulnerability to government budget cuts.

A related question is whether all NPOs are equally dependent on government funding. Two NPO characteristics may be related to dependence on government funding. First, it is possible that NPOs in different sectors exhibit different funding patterns. For example, while health and education NPOs are generally thought of as being dependent on government for the largest proportion of their funding, NPOs in other service areas such as the environment may rely more heavily on non-government sources. If the degree of NPO reliance on government funding does vary with the type of service the NPO delivers, then it may be reasonable to begin to distinguish between a semi-public type of NPO and a semi-private type of NPO.

Second, it is possible that NPOs whose services benefit different types of populations vary in their reliance on government funding. NPOs that deliver benefits to more narrowly defined segments of the population may rely less on government funding than do NPOs that benefit a broader cross-section of society. One might expect that government funds would be directed more toward NPOs with a broad target population than toward NPOs that serve a narrower group. However, it is also possible that government funds are spread across many organizations serving small subgroups in the population.

Influence Exerted by Various Parties over Manitoba NPO Decision Making

This second area of our research examines the level of autonomy that NPOs in Manitoba have. It is possible that an NPO's largest contributor (be it government, a foundation, individuals, or a corporation) may exert considerable influence over the NPO's orientation and administration. In this research area, we explore whether there are significant limits to an NPO's autonomy resulting from and/or varying with the type of agency that makes the largest contribution to the NPO's funds.

As with funding, contributions of labour may affect the orientation and governance of an NPO. In this case, however, the link is not clear. It is possible that organizations requiring a large number of volunteers respond quickly to the needs and desires of their volunteer workforce, but it is also possible that these organizations develop a top-down administration for efficiency purposes. The same uncertainty exists with respect to decision-making control being shared between an NPO and its paid workforce.

METHODOLOGY

In this study, we employ a sample survey methodology to gather data on resources flowing into and out of Manitoba NPOs. We focus on NPOs' funding, services, labour resources (both paid and volunteer), and autonomy in decision making. Our objective is to establish baseline information on the Manitoba NPS as a whole. Therefore, we were interested in sampling the widest possible variety of NPOs, rather than focusing on a subset of the NPS such as the charitable sector. The challenge we faced was to find a sampling frame that would reflect the diversity of the NPS that we wanted to capture.

In Manitoba, as throughout Canada, organizations may register under law as NPOs if they are non-share capital corporations (that is, if they adhere to the non-distribution constraint by not distributing profits to any set of owners) and if they declare that they provide a service to the community. A subset of NPOs are also registered charities. Registered charities gain their status under the federal *Income Tax Act*, and have the right to issue tax-deductible receipts for donations. While some analysts regard the charitable sector as equivalent to the NPS, charities constitute only one part of the overall sector. As noted earlier, much of the literature on the NPS supports the idea of the NPS being defined to include a much broader array of NPOs than merely those that are charitable; our conceptualization of the NPS certainly does. Using a list of Manitoba charities as a sampling frame for the NPS would therefore have been incomplete.

Accordingly, the sampling frame for our survey was derived from a list of all types of NPOs registered with the Companies Office of Consumer and Corporate Affairs of the Government of Manitoba.[2] As of April 1998, this list contained 10,690 organizations that share two characteristics. First, they are non-share capital corporations (i.e., they adhere to the non-distribution constraint). Second, they have declared that they provide a good or service that is of value to the community or some subset of it. The information we were able to obtain from the Companies Office for each of the 10,690 NPOs on this list included the organization's name, its registration date, and its status. The status code indicated whether the organization is active from the perspective of the Companies Office. The Companies Office deems organizations that fail to file reports with the Office in three consecutive years to be inactive.

To transform this list into the sampling frame, we eliminated all NPOs that had lost their active status in the eyes of the Companies Office, which left 7,506 NPOs. We randomly selected 2,000 NPOs from this group, and used phone directories, a local publication that lists charitable organizations,[3] and Internet resources to search for contact information for these NPOs.[4] Our search yielded contact information for 415 of the 2,000 initially selected NPOs. These organizations were mailed a questionnaire (in the Appendix) and received ongoing follow-up phone calls to increase our response rate. In the end, 118 NPOs responded to our survey, for a 28 percent response rate.

Several biases are inherent in this sampling procedure. First, bias is introduced by sampling from among only those NPOs that have registered with the provincial government. Clearly, this list was incomplete; we ourselves know personally of several NPOs that have opted not to register. How much non-registration bias is present in the sampling frame is unknown. It is also unclear whether this non-registration bias is more significant for certain types of NPOs than for others. It may be, for example, that health and education NPOs, which typically face certification requirements, might be more predisposed than other types of NPOs to register. Alternatively, because registration may be required for certain grant programs, cultural or environmental NPOs may be more likely than other types to have registered. Additional biases arise from the sampling method we employed. It is very likely that certain NPOs are more likely than others to have contact information kept up-to-date and available through the sources we were able to access. Here again, however, the pattern and extent of bias are unclear. Another potential bias could be introduced by the individuals who completed our questionnaire. Most of our respondents answered most, if not all, of the questions. However, some respondents left occasional questions unanswered, and a few left entire sections of the questionnaire blank, sometimes citing time constraints or lack of adequate records to answer the questions. In follow-up phone calls with respondent NPOs, we verified the position held by the person who filled out the questionnaire. Of the 102 telephone respondents, 78 were paid employees of the NPO, and 52 sat on the NPO's board of directors (15 in a non-voting *ex officio* capacity). The respondent at 96 NPOs (81 percent) was a senior manager who could be assumed to know a great deal about the NPO and could therefore be expected to have supplied informed responses to our questions. Nevertheless, the findings presented in the balance of this paper should be interpreted with these biases in mind.

The questionnaire completed by the NPOs in our sample contained questions designed to gather information about the amount of funds the NPO receives from different sources, the number of employees and volunteers the NPO has, the services the NPO offers, the beneficiaries of the NPO's services, and perceptions of the influence that different parties exert on various management aspects of the NPO. The information we gathered on these topics is presented in the remaining sections of this paper. The small number of respondents means that all results reported here should be interpreted as preliminary. Because some subgroups in the sample are extremely small, we have not performed any econometric analysis of the data. This study's major contribution is to provide an initial description of the NPS in Manitoba and to identify characteristics of the sector and issues pertaining to it that can enlighten future research.

OVERVIEW OF THE DATA SET

The data obtained from our respondents confirm our expectation that Manitoba's NPS is extremely varied. Of the 118 respondent NPOs, 82 (69 percent) are from Winnipeg, while the remaining 36 (31 percent) are located outside the City of Winnipeg. The 36 NPOs from outside Winnipeg are from a wide variety (28) of towns and rural municipalities throughout the province; four are in Portage la Prairie and three are in Selkirk. While only eight NPOs reported that they target their services at specific ethnic groups varying from First Nations people to Mennonites to recent immigrants, 19 NPOs could be identified as ethnically-oriented by their organization name or target population. Sixty-four of the 102 telephone respondents are registered charities.

The respondent NPOs offer a wide range of services. Figure 1 shows the number of NPOs listing various services as their primary or main service. The primary service category containing the most NPOs in our sample is education. The educational services most commonly provided by NPOs in this category are daycare (12 NPOs) and adult education (four NPOs). The second most common NPO activity in our sample is the provision of leisure services. Of the 28 NPOs in this service category, 12 are sports clubs and eight are cultural organizations. There are 17 NPOs whose primary service is health-related. Of these, four provide elder care, four provide support to the disabled, and others provide services as wide-ranging as women's health care, maintenance of a health registry, and health-related

Figure 1: Number of Sampled NPOs in Primary Service Categories

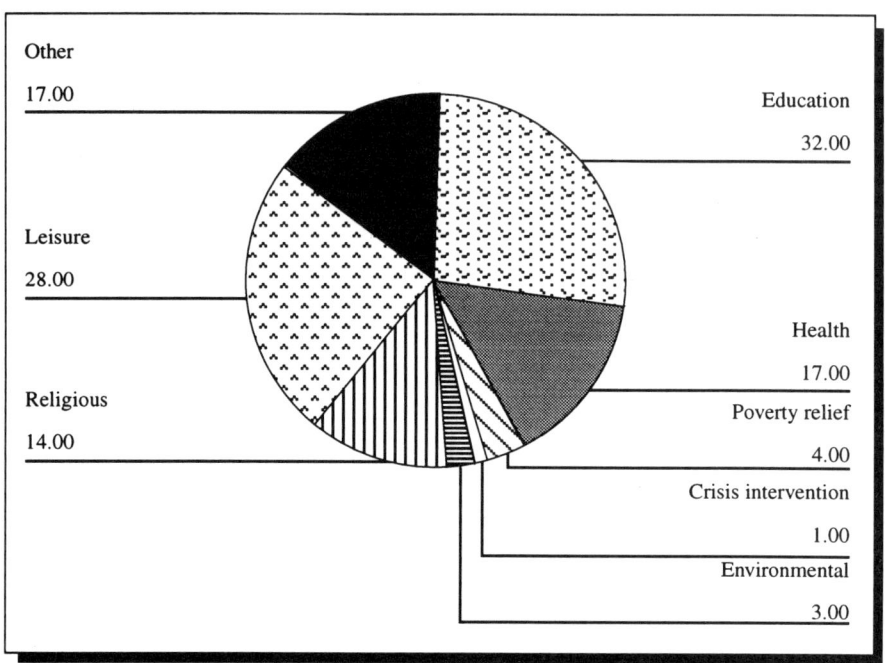

research. Finally, the 17 NPOs who provide "other" primary services further illustrate the variety of the NPS. Their primary services range from advocacy to cat care to artistic and cultural activities and services.

Forty-one (35 percent) of our respondent NPOs report that individuals require membership in their organization in order to benefit from the services they provide or to participate in their programs. Of these, 35 charge fees for membership (one of these charges fees to adult members but not to juniors).

The NPOs also vary in the composition of their labour force. Seventy-two NPOs (84 percent of respondents who answered this question, and 61 percent of all respondent NPOs) reported that they benefited from the labour of volunteers during 1997, and 103 NPOs (87 percent) relied on part-time and/or full-time paid labour during 1997. Of the 72 organizations reporting the use of volunteer labour, six (8 percent) are run exclusively by volunteers. Of these six, two are poverty relief providers and three are leisure-related NPOs. The average number of volunteers "employed" by the NPOs in our sample in 1997 was 177. Both the number of volunteers working in the NPO and their number of hours change from peak to non-peak periods throughout the year. During weeks of peak activity, the number of active volunteers ranges from 2 to 5,000; during weeks of non-peak activity, the maximum number of active volunteers is only 200. The pattern is similar for the number of hours volunteers work. During peak periods, up to 50,000 hours of volunteer labour may be employed by NPOs, with an average of 1,138 hours; during non-peak weeks, the maximum number of volunteer hours is 1,500, with an average of 55 hours.

NPOs in different primary service categories also make differential use of volunteer labour. Table 1 shows the average number of volunteers and the average number of volunteer hours in peak and non-peak weeks in various primary service categories. NPOs whose primary service category is health care had far more volunteers active in 1997, on average, than NPOs in any other service category. However, these data are strongly skewed by one organization, which held a very large volunteer event during the year.[5] NPOs who provide leisure activities and poverty relief also had large numbers of volunteers active in 1997. The three environmental NPOs in our sample had the fewest volunteers. Interestingly, five religious organizations declined to express how many volunteers they have; they wrote in the margin of their questionnaire that they consider their entire congregation to be volunteers working in a ministering capacity.The pattern of volunteer use also varies significantly by primary service category. While health-related NPOs had the most volunteers active overall in 1997, they show the greatest variations in use of volunteers between peak and non-peak periods, followed by NPOs in the leisure category. The difference between the number of volunteers and volunteers' hours in peak and non-peak weeks is much smaller for NPOs in the other primary service categories. Poverty relief NPOs exhibit an interesting pattern of behaviour. During weeks of peak activity, they have fewer volunteers working longer hours than during weeks of non-peak activity.

As a way of estimating the size of their annual budgets, we asked NPOs to report their 1997 expenditures. The 101 NPOs who completed this question had expenditures ranging from $1,000 to $3.5 million, with average expenditures of approximately $365,000 and a median expenditure

Table 1: Average Number of Volunteers and Volunteer Hours by Primary Service Category

NPOs' Primary Service Category	n	Average number of volunteers active in 1997	Average number of volunteers active in a peak week	Average number of volunteers active in a non-peak week	Average volunteer hours in a peak week	Average volunteer hours in a non-peak week
Education	12	58	38	12	32	24
Health[a]	14	456 (98)	398 (13)	12 (7)	4,232 (60)	31 (24)
Poverty Relief	3	206	120	175	250	150
Environmental	2	10	8	2	12	2
Religious	8	136	88	54	368	261
Leisure	21	292	151	11	86	25
Other	11	22	15	8	35	22

Note: [a]The numbers in parentheses are calculated with the outlier excluded.

Figure 2: Number of NPOs with 1997 Expenditures in Specified Ranges

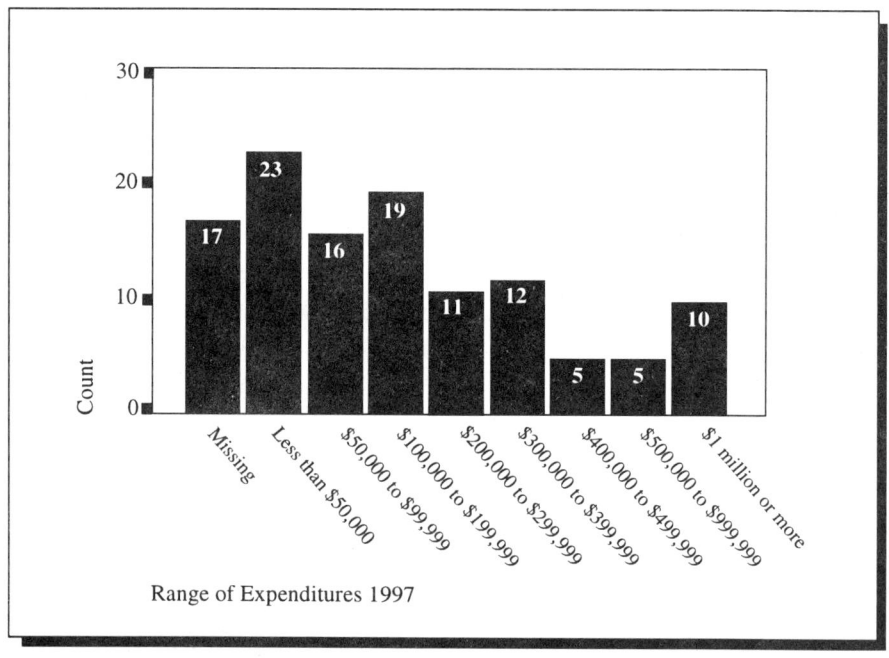

level of $150,000. Figure 2 shows the number of NPOs with expenditures falling within specific ranges.

Table 2 shows the average expenditures by NPOs in various primary service categories. NPOs in different service categories tend to have different sized budgets, with those providing education and poverty relief having the highest budgets, on average. Environmental NPOs have the lowest budgets by far, although the three respondents here may not be representative of environmental NPOs in general. In general, however, the variation in budget size within each service category is greater than the variation in budget size between categories, as Table 3 shows.

Table 2: Average 1997 Expenditures by NPOs in Primary Service Categories

NPO's Primary Service Category	Count	Mean	Std Deviation	Minimum	Maximum
Education	32	$479,664	$779,675	$20,000	$3,500,000
Health	17	$223,452	$381,039	$ 6,000	$1,600,000
Poverty relief	4	$596,356	$789,913	$65,000	$1,504,069
Crisis intervention	1	.	.	.	.
Environmental	3	$ 17,500	$ 10,607	$10,000	$ 25,000
Religious	14	$176,747	$183,163	$39,748	$ 700,000
Leisure	28	$360,098	$651,973	$ 1,000	$2,053,900
Other	17	$492,935	$904,239	$18,000	$3,324,000

Table 3: Number of NPOs Receiving Funds from Federal, Provincial and Local Governments

	Missing	Number of NPOs Who Receive No Funds From:	Number of NPOs Who Receive Some Funds From:	Total
Federal government	9	80	29	118
Provincial government	9	47	62	118
Local government	9	88	21	118

Manitoba's NPOs' Reliance on Funds from Government Sources

In our survey, we asked NPOs to state the proportion of their budget obtained from various sources during 1997. These sources included federal, provincial, and local levels of government, corporate or business sources, private individual donors, earnings from commercial activities, fundraising events such as lotteries, bingos, or raffles, and other sources. Many NPOs reported that they received some funds from "other sources," including service fees, membership fees, the United Way or a foundation, and income from investments. Where service fees, membership fees, or investment income were specifically mentioned (with percentages provided), we broke them out as additional distinct sources of funds. Since we did not explicitly ask about these sources of funds, not all NPOs who received such funding may have explicitly reported it. As such, the service fee, membership fee, and investment income sources of funding reported here can be taken as conservative estimates for the NPS in Manitoba.

The respondent NPOs in our sample rely, on average, on government sources for 34 percent of their funding. Of the 102 respondent NPOs we followed up by phone, those registered as charities rely on government sources for 38 percent of their funding, while those not registered as charities rely on government sources for 35 percent of their budgets. Since most religious NPOs do not receive any funding from government, it makes sense to look at average NPO reliance on government funding with religious NPOs excluded from the analysis. Our non-religious respondent NPOs received an average of 39 percent of their budgets from government sources, while non-religious non-charities and non-religious charities relied on government sources for 35 percent and 46 percent of their funding, respectively. These findings compare to the Canadian Centre for Philanthropy's (1997*b*) finding that government grants and payments contributed 60 percent and 55 percent of Canadian and Manitoba charities' budgets, respectively.

Figure 3 shows the proportions of respondent NPOs who rely to varying degrees on federal, provincial, and/or local governments for funding. Approximately one-third of respondents (39 NPOs) do not receive funding from any level of government. The remaining two-thirds of respondent NPOs (69) rely to some extent on funding from some level of government, with slightly over half of these (37 NPOs) being more than 50 percent

Figure 3: Number of Sample NPOs with Varying Dependence on Government Funding

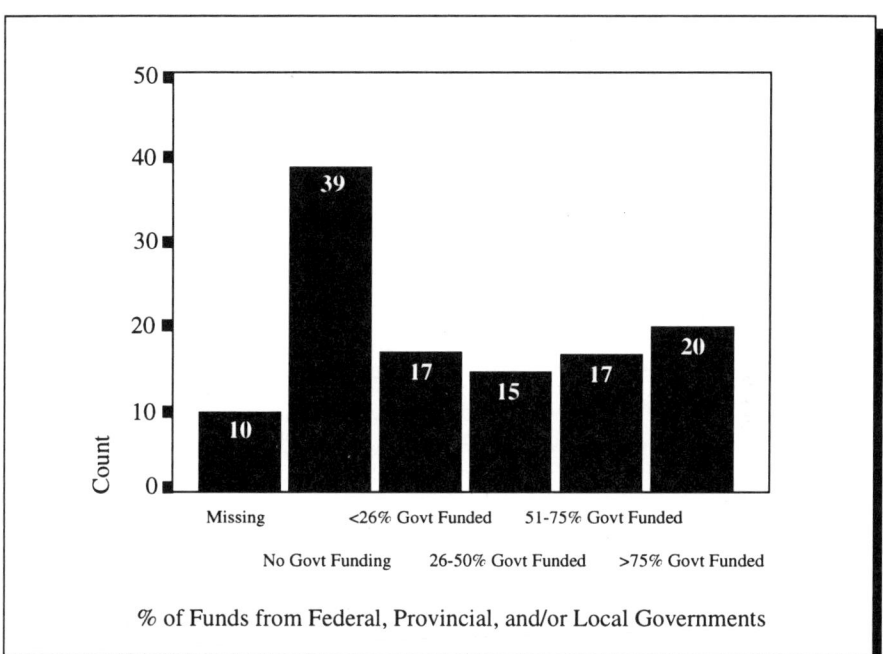

government-funded. Thus, while a sizeable portion of the NPS in Manitoba operates without financial assistance from any level of government, it is clear that the sector as a whole relies significantly on government sources of funding to operate.

To examine the distribution of government funding by size of NPO, we looked at the correlation between government funding and NPO expenditures. There was no evidence of any relationship between these variables. We also examined the relationship between overall government funding and size of the NPO (in terms of budget), and again found no correlation. The independence of government funding (and indeed, any other variable) from the size of the NPOs in our sample as measured by their expenditures is one of the more surprising results of this study. It helps to dispel the myths that governments only fund large organizations, that larger organizations are more likely to be registered charities, and that the size of an NPO is related to its primary service category.

Reliance on funding from different levels of government varies dramatically among Manitoba NPOs, as is evident in Tables 3 and 4. Table 3 shows the number of NPOs reporting that they receive funding from local, provincial, and federal governments. Almost all (62) of the 69 respondent NPOs who receive government funds are funded at least in part by Manitoba's provincial government. Of these, half (31) report that the provincial government is their main source of funds. The number of NPOs receiving funds from federal and local governments is much smaller, suggesting that the federal and local governments may serve as substitute funding sources to the provincial government. Analysis shows that the correlation between funding from the federal and provincial levels of government is -0.32 (significant at the 1 percent level), and between funding from the provincial and local levels of government is -0.298 (significant at the 5 percent level). There is no correlation between federal and local government funding of organizations. Because these various levels of government are substitute funding sources, the overall effect of governmental influence on the sector is likely to be stronger than the effect of funding from any specific level of government.

Table 4 shows average proportional reliance on funds from specific governmental and non-governmental sources by NPOs with varying overall levels of reliance on government funding. Naturally, as the proportion of an NPO's budget funded from government sources rises (moving across the columns in Table 4), reliance on other sources decreases. For NPOs who are 50 percent or less reliant on government funding, money from commercial activities and service fees is very important. In fact there is a significant negative correlation (-0.260; 1 percent level of significance) between funding from commercial activities and government funding, and between membership fees and funding from government sources (-0.241; 5 percent level of significance).

Further information on funding patterns in Manitoba's NPS can be observed from looking at the contribution of different funding sources in different service categories. Table 5 shows the average reliance on funds from different sources by NPOs in eight primary service categories. On

Table 4: Average Percentage of Funds from Different Levels of Government, by NPOs with Varying Levels of Reliance on Government Funding

	Proportion of Funds from Federal, Provincial, &/or Local Governments				
Percent of Funds from:	No Govt Funding (n = 39)	< 26% Govt Funded (n = 17)	26-50% Govt Funded (n = 15)	51-75% Govt Funded (n = 17)	> 75% Govt Funded (n = 20)
	Mean	Mean	Mean	Mean	Mean
Federal government	—	1	3	11	18
Provincial government	—	10	30	46	68
Local government	—	2	6	6	5
Commercial activities	14	31	22	9	—
Service fees	11	14	9	6	2
Fundraising activities (raffles, etc.)	5	15	11	6	1
Membership fees	17	4	5	—	2
Investment income	1	—	—	—	—
Contributions from private individuals	38	11	4	7	2
Businesses and corporations	8	8	4	4	2
Other sources	7	4	6	4	1

Table 5: Average Reliance by NPOs in Different Primary Service Categories on Funds from Different Sources

Percent of Funds from:	NPOs Primary Service Category						
	Education (n = 32)	Health (n = 17)	Poverty Relief (n = 4)	Environmental (n = 3)	Religious (n = 14)	Leisure (n = 28)	Other (n = 17)
	Mean	Mean	Mean	Mean	Mean	Mean	Mean
Federal government	14	1	8	—	—	4	1
Provincial government	33	35	28	60	—	20	24
Local government	—	1	3	—	—	8	6
Commercial activities	10	12	22	3	6	25	13
Service fees	15	6	—	—	—	5	16
Fundraising activities (raffles, etc.)	3	10	24	3	1	12	3
Membership fees	6	6	—	33	—	9	16
Investment income	—	2	—	—	—	—	—
Contributions from private individuals	12	10	4	—	85	6	4
Businesses and corporations	4	10	2	—	—	5	11
Other sources	3	6	9	—	8	3	5

average, religious NPOs were far more likely to receive no government funding. The sampled environmental NPOs received the most government funding, on average, followed by NPOs in the education, poverty relief, and health service categories. The provincial government was the largest single source of funding for sampled organizations in all categories, except, of course, religious services. The federal government concentrated most of its funding on education, while the local government directed funding mainly toward leisure services.

Table 6 addresses the issue of whether government funding is directed toward NPOs who deliver benefits to narrowly defined segments of the population. The survey asked respondents to indicate if their services or activities are targeted to particular groups defined according to age, gender, socio-economic grouping, ethnicity or culture, profession, or shared experience. Respondents who target specific groups exhibit greater reliance on government funding than respondents who do not target specific groups. This provides some support to the theory that government may provide funding to a variety of organizations each of whom is capable of targeting a specific group.

Table 6: Reliance on Government Funding by NPOs Who Target Specific Groups in their Activities

Proportion of Funds from Federal, Provincial and/or Local Governments	Does the NPO Target a Specific Group?[a]			
	Yes		No	
	Count	% of NPOs	Count	% of NPOs
No government funding	15	25	11	34
< 26% Government funded	10	16	7	22
26-50% Government funded	8	13	7	22
51-57% Government funded	13	21	2	6
>75% Government funded	15	25	5	16

Note: [a]Target a particular group in terms of age, gender, ethnicity, or shared experience.

Perceived Influence over NPO Decision Making

Given government's role as a significant contributor of funds to Manitoba's NPS, it is important to ask how autonomous the NPOs that receive such funding are from government influence in their decision making. The same question can be asked about the influence exerted by other funding sources, as well as by volunteers and paid employees.

To explore these questions, we asked sampled NPOs about the degrees of influence that certain groups have over five decisions the NPO makes: (i) the accounting methods/practices used by the NPO; (ii) the composition/membership of the NPO's decision-making body; (iii) the types of fundraising activities the NPO undertakes; (iv) what activities, services, or programs the NPO delivers/performs; and (v) how the NPO's activities are carried out. We inquired into the relative control over decision making by five groups: volunteers, paid employees, government sources of funding, corporate or business donors, and private individual donors. The sampled NPOs were asked to express the amount of influence each group has on each of the decisions, using a scale of one to ten, with one reflecting that the group's input is not requested or considered, and ten reflecting that the decision is completely determined by the group. Table 7 summarizes the responses to these questions.

Two trends in Table 7 are particularly interesting, and somewhat different from what we expected. First, of the five groups, volunteers are seen as wielding the greatest overall influence over NPO decision making. This may reflect that volunteers really are a backbone of the NPS, and because they are so relied upon, they are empowered. Organizations that rely on volunteer labour may indeed respond to the needs and desires of their volunteer workforce by establishing decision-making systems and processes that permit their volunteers to have a large impact on critical elements of NPO operations. This may be because volunteers are involved with the NPO out of a strong belief in the mission and services of the NPO, and the NPO perceives that, in order to retain volunteer labour as well as harness volunteer enthusiasm, the volunteers must be sufficiently empowered to participate in the operation of the organization.

Volunteers may also possess specialized skills and knowledge that enable them to contribute to NPO decision making in concrete and meaningful ways. This is especially the case where NPOs' boards of directors are largely

Table 7: Average Perceived Influence[a] Over Decision Making Wielded by Five Different Groups

		Average Degree of Influence by Volunteers over NPO Decisions About:				
Group	n	NPO's Accounting Methods	Composition of NPO's Decision-Making Body	Types of Fundraising Activities the NPO will Undertake	NPO's Activities, Services, and Programs	How NPO's Activities Are Carried Out
Volunteers	99	6.2	8.2	7.8	7.1	6.9
Paid Employees	98	4.3	2.9	4.6	5.9	6.3
Government	66	4.4	2.0	1.6	4.1	3.9
Corporate or Business	30	2.3	2.3	2.8	2.9	2.8
Individuals	79	2.5	3.4	3.0	3.1	3.1

Note: [a]Respondents were asked to express decision-making influence on a scale from one to ten, with one meaning that the party's input is not requested or considered in the decision, and ten meaning the party has power to completely determine the decision.

comprised of volunteers. In follow-up phone calls, 45 percent of the 89 responding NPOs with volunteers reported that they answered the question about volunteers' influence based on volunteer board members' influence, 5 percent stated that their response reflected task-oriented volunteers' influence only, and 50 percent some combination of the two. Of this 50 percent of NPOs whose response reflected a combination of board members and task-oriented volunteers, those with fewer than 100 volunteers reported that their volunteers have greater overall influence than did NPOs with 100 or more volunteers. This suggests that NPOs requiring large numbers of volunteers become more centralized in their decision making while those with fewer volunteers use decision-making processes that are empowering to volunteers. Alternatively, it may indicate simply that the group of NPOs with fewer than 100 volunteers is more likely to have volunteer boards of directors who are particularly empowered.

These responses capture the *perceptions* of influence held by central participants in NPOs. Obviously, these perceptions may be shaped not only by the actual experience of decision making but also by the norms, values, and beliefs that animate the NPS. Our respondents may *want* to believe that volunteers are significantly empowered, and this faith may influence their interpretation of decision making in their organizations. In addition, the particular role of our respondents may influence their perceptions; for example, senior employees may see the organization differently than senior volunteers. To shed some light on these factors, we broke down the responses to questions concerning influence by the organizational position of the respondent, and found that the perceived influence of volunteers was higher, on average, when volunteers answered the question than when the respondent was an employee. However, follow-up telephone interviews also revealed that much depended on which group of volunteers the respondent was thinking about when answering the question. When the respondent was considering the role of volunteers who sit on the board of directors, both employee and volunteer respondents reported the same degree of influence for volunteers in each decision-making category (there is no correlation between status of the respondent and the influence responses). However, if the respondents were considering the influence of a combination of the board of directors and other volunteers, we find that volunteer respondents tend to attribute greater influence to the volunteers in the organization than do paid employees. This finding hints at an interesting tension about the role of volunteers within the internal culture of NPOs.

The other interesting trend in Table 7 is that NPOs reported considerably less influence by government funding sources than we expected. In particular, since government mandates the accounting practices of businesses including for-profit and nonprofit organizations, we expected respondent NPOs to report that their government funding sources have much more influence over their accounting methods than they did. It may be the case that NPOs are generally aware of government-mandated accounting practices, but that these principles are then specifically interpreted or implemented by a volunteer or employee.

Table 8 presents government's perceived level of influence over NPO decision making for all NPOs who receive government funding. This group is divided into "quasi-government organizations," which receive more than

Table 8: Average Perceived Influence[a] Over Decision Making Wielded by Government Funding Sources Overall, in Non-Quasi-Governmental NPOs and in Quasi-Governmental NPOs

Degree of Government Influence in:	n	Average Degree of Government Influence over NPO Decisions about:				
		NPO's Accounting Methods	Composition of NPO's Decision-Making Body	Types of Fundraising Activities the NPO will Undertake	NPO's Activities, Services, and Programs	How NPO's Activities Are Carried Out
NPOs who receive funds from government	63	4.4	2.0	1.6	4.1	3.9
NPOs who are not quasi-governmental	44	3.8[b]	1.6[b]	1.4	3.7	3.3[b]
NPOs who are quasi-governmental	19	5.8[b]	3.0[b]	2.2	5.2	5.3[b]

Notes: [a]Respondents were asked to express decision-making influence on a scale from one to ten, with one meaning that the party's input is not requested or considered in the decision, and ten meaning the party has power to completely determine the decision.
[b]Average degrees of influence by quasi-governmental NPOs and non-quasi-governmental NPOs differ significantly at the 0.05 level.

75 percent of their funding from government sources, and non-quasi-governmental NPOs. Quasi-governmental NPOs perceive their government funding sources to have a greater degree of influence over their decision making than do other NPOs. As expected, the difference is most marked for NPO accounting methods, but it is also significant for the composition of the NPO's decision-making body and for the process by which the NPO's activities are carried out. Nevertheless, it is still striking that perceived governmental influence is relatively low, even when government funding

represents the bulk of the budgets of NPOs. This finding probably reflects the nature of governmental influence in the NPS. The primary form of governmental influence is unlikely to be regular intervention into the detailed decision making of each organization. Rather, it is likely that the government influence over an NPO's service or program is indirectly determined through the selection process; like any funder, government is unlikely to provide funding to an NPO unless it approves of the services it delivers. If this is the case, the primary form of government influence over the NPO sector as a whole involves influence over which NPOs expand their activities rather than direct intervention in individual organizations. In this context, it would not be surprising to see government-funded NPOs reporting low direct government influence over their service or activity decision.

The observation that perceived government influence is greater in NPOs that rely on government for at least 76 percent of their funds raises the general question of whether this phenomenon transcends the case of government funding. Are the largest contributors of any kind seen as exercising greater influence over the NPO's decision making than other funding sources? Table 9 presents information on this question. Since we asked about influence on decision making only for government, corporate, and individual sources of funding, Table 9 contains the average perceived influence of these three sources, both when they are the main funding source for the NPO and when they are not.[6] Table 9 shows that the major funding source is, in fact, perceived to have greater influence over decision making than other sources. The change is most striking for organizations whose main funding source is corporate or business. We also examined the degree of volunteer and employee influence on decision making for different major funding sources. Volunteers are seen as having the most influence in NPOs that rely mainly on individuals for funding, and the least influence in NPOs who rely on corporations for funding (though the sample of organizations who have both volunteer labour and a major corporate funding source is very small). Employee decision making is highest when corporations are the major source of funds (for decisions over accounting methods, composition of decision-making body, and fundraising activities) or when the government is the main source of funds (for decisions over choice of activities and process).

Table 9: Average Decision-Making Influence by Major Funding Source

Influence by:	NPO's Accounting Methods	Composition of NPO's Decision-Making Body	Types of Fundraising Activities the NPO will Undertake	NPO's Activities, Services, and Programs	How NPO's Activities Are Carried Out
Main Funding Source: Government					
Government	4.7	2.3	1.8	4.1	4.2
Corporate	2.7	1.0	1.9	1.9	2.4
Individual	2.0	2.4	1.7	2.4	2.5
Main Funding Source: Corporate or Business					
Government	1.0	1.0	1.0	4.5	3.0
Corporate	1.3	6.0	5.3	5.5	5.5
Individual	1.3	1.7	1.0	2.3	2.3
Main Funding Source: Individuals (Donations, Membership Fees, and Service Fees)					
Government	4.0	1.3	1.1	3.9	3.9
Corporate	1.0	1.0	2.0	1.0	1.0
Individual	2.6	4.9	3.6	3.4	3.2

Note: Respondents were asked to express decision-making influence on a scale from one to ten, with one meaning that the party's input is not requested or considered in the decision, and ten meaning the party has power to completely determine the decision.

CONCLUSIONS

This paper presents the results of a small survey of the NPS in Manitoba. Due to the paucity of research on the NPS and the limited scale of the survey, our research raises many more questions than it answers. Because the NPS is both broad and diverse, we used existing work to provide a working definition of the sector. We recognize that the NPS is not synonymous with either the charitable sector or the volunteer sector, though there is considerable overlap between the three, just as there is overlap between the NPS and the equally heterogeneous service sector. We surveyed 118 NPOs in Manitoba chosen from a list of those NPOs actively registered or incorporated in the province. Our sample size is small, so our findings must be interpreted with caution. However, the results reported here provide some guidance for future research on similar questions, and open avenues for wider, comparative, and/or time series studies of the NPS.

The survey results reported here help illuminate the issue of the independence of the NPS. We examined government funding of the NPS and the perceived influence of various stakeholders in the NPOs on the decisions made within the organizations. Consistent with the results of other studies of the NPS, we found the respondent NPOs in our survey to be heavily reliant on government funding. Surprisingly, the average percentage of the budget of NPOs provided by government did not differ significantly by the size of the organization, by the number of volunteers working for the NPO, or by major service category, with the exception of religious services whose funding is mainly provided by individual contributors. Also surprisingly, the three environmental organizations in our survey received the highest proportion of their budgets from government funding.

Government funding did differ, however, according to whether or not the NPO targets services toward a defined group of people, with those organizations that target their services receiving more government funding than those whose services benefit a broader cross-section of society. This provides some support for the idea that government can directly provide services or programs to the broad populace, but that NPOs may complement government services because each can target its services to a different subgroup of the population. It would be interesting to know whether government funding is related to the particular group targeted; however, our small sample precluded such an analysis.

Government funding also seems to be negatively related to NPOs' reliance on membership fees and commercial activities. When a group is willing and able to pay for services to its members, it is possible that government financing is neither needed nor sought. Finally, in our sample, government funding of registered charities is higher than government funding of other NPOs. This could indicate that registered charities are viewed as more trustworthy by governments, or that organizations undertake the somewhat arduous process required to obtain charitable status, in part, to obtain government funding. This issue, too, requires further research.

The provincial level of government is the highest funder of NPOs in our sample, which coincides with its role as the major funder of social services. The federal and municipal governments seem to be substitutes rather than complements for the provincial level in funding the NPS. The federal government provides a larger proportion of the funding for NPOs in the education category than in any other category, which may be a reflection of its role in adult education. The municipal government plays its role as a funder of leisure activities, again an area that is mainly a municipal responsibility.

While government is, in general, the largest single funder of NPOs, it was not perceived as wielding the most influence over decisions made by the organizations. Overall, in organizations that use volunteer labour, volunteers are seen as having more influence over NPO decision making than paid employees, government funding sources, corporate donors, or individual contributors. Nevertheless, when NPOs in the survey were categorized by *major* funding source, it seemed that "he who paid the piper" did have greater influence over naming the tune. When compared with other funding sources, the influence of an NPO's major funding source (be it government, corporations, or individuals) was seen as markedly stronger compared with other sources of funding. Further research could also examine whether and how funding sources influence NPOs' work, and whether changes in an NPO's mix of funding sources changes its orientation or activities.

The influence questions asked in the survey also provide some evidence as to perceptions of volunteer influence in NPOs. Both volunteer and employee respondents report the same degree of influence for volunteers who are members of the NPO's board of directors. But volunteer and paid employee respondents differ in their assessment of the influence of non-board volunteers; volunteer respondents perceive volunteers to have greater influence than do paid employee respondents. Our findings about influence point to areas that require further research. It is not surprising that volunteer members of the board of directors are seen as being more influential than non-board volunteers. However, more work is needed on whether the different interpretations of the role of non-board volunteers affects the number of volunteers attracted to an organization, the efficiency of the organization, and the extent to which volunteers feel empowered by their experience.

One area for research is hinted at by our data and by observations made by other researchers in this volume. In our survey, the small number of respondents from environmental organizations received a high proportion of government funding. This is a relatively new area for NPO activity. When this is combined with the anecdotal evidence that for at least ten years NPOs have repeatedly described themselves as suffering due to cutbacks in government funding, a different theory of government funding of NPOs arises. It is possible that government funding of the NPS is in fact a form of "seed money." Perhaps government encourages initiatives by funding organizations for a limited (and perhaps unspecified) period, after which the public is expected to pick up the cost through private donations. If this is the case, we would expect younger NPOs to have a higher proportion of their budgets funded by government than older NPOs.

Finally, more research is needed simply to enable researchers to work from a more complete list of NPOs when studying the NPS. The Canadian Centre for Philanthropy has done a good deal of work to compile a data set of charitable organizations in Canada. This list could be used as a base for the compilation of a database listing names and contact information for NPOs across Canada. Since this survey sample, which is drawn from only those NPOs registered or incorporated in Manitoba, contains almost as many non-charitable NPOs as registered charities, we would expect the CCP data to provide about half of the required data for a complete listing of the broad array of organizations in the NPS.

According to the Canadian Centre for Philanthropy (1998), Canadians donated almost $5 billion and more than 1.1 billion hours in 1997. Considering its size, therefore, the contribution of the NPS to the Canadian economy and to society is in dire need of greater examination. This paper is one of the first steps on a long road toward better understanding of the nonprofit sector.

Notes

We express sincere gratitude to the Kahanoff Foundation for financial support of this research; to the Companies Office of Consumer and Corporate Affairs of the Government of Manitoba for assistance with the sampling frame and other information; to Roger Gibbons of the University of Calgary and the Canada West Foundation for reviewer comments; to participants of the Nonprofit Research Initiative Workshop and the University of Manitoba Economics Department's Seminar Series for insightful criticism and suggestions; and to Manitoba nonprofit organizations, who were the most vital contributors to this research.

[1] Nonprofit organizations who desire to can register with the Government of Manitoba through the Companies Office of Consumer and Corporate Affairs of the Government of Manitoba. The Companies Office has had 10,690 nonprofit registrations. Of these, 7,506 remain active in the sense that they file reports with the Companies Office annually, or have not failed to file in three consecutive years. What is not known is what proportion of NPOs opt not to register with the Companies Office. If registered NPOs are a high proportion of all NPOs, then the number of active NPOs in Manitoba is quite close to 7,506. If a minority of NPOs opt to register with the Companies Office, then the number of NPOs in Manitoba could be significantly greater than 7,506.

[2] "Registered" can mean either of two things. First, an NPO may opt to incorporate in the province. Second, NPO may opt simply to register its name, which is referred to as name notation or registration. These options have different benefits and costs associated with them. Less than 5 percent of NPO registrations with the province have been name notations. See also note 1.

[3] *Contact: A Community Resource Guide for Manitobans.* April 1998. Contact Community Information. Volunteer Centre of Winnipeg. Winnipeg, Manitoba, Canada.

[4] The Companies Office informed us that a number of the NPOs that register with the province provide a lawyer's address or some other address (e.g., a former member of the board of directors) at the time they register. The Companies Office believes that the contact information they have in their records for many NPOs is out of date.

[5] This organization is included in our analyses because, although it is an outlier, we believe it accurately represents some health-care sector NPOs whose major fundraising activities make short-term use of a large number of volunteers.

[6] Organizations who reported individual donations, membership fees or service fees also answered the questions on influence, so these three groups are included among individual funders. If service fees are removed from individual main funding source, (i.e., if service fees are considered to be a commercial activity), the relationship between average degree of influence by funders is unchanged.

References

Anheier, H.K. 1987. "Indigenous Voluntary Associations, Nonprofits, and Development in Africa," in *The Non-Profit Sector*, ed. Powell.

Ben-Ner, A. and B. Gui, eds. 1991. *The Nonprofit Sector in the Mixed Economy*, 62(4) in *Annals of Public and Cooperative Economics* Series. DeBoeck University.

Ben-Ner, A. and T. Van Hoomissen. 1991. "Nonprofit Organisations in the Mixed Economy: A Demand and Supply Analysis," in *The Nonprofit Sector in the Mixed Economy*, ed. Ben-Ner and Gui.

Canadian Centre for Philanthropy (CCP). 1997*a*. *Annual Report*. Ottawa. http://www.ccp.ca/join/ann1997.htm.

⎯⎯⎯⎯ 1997*b*. *Research Bulletin*, 4(2 & 3).

⎯⎯⎯⎯ 1998. *Caring Canadians, Involved Canadians: Highlights from the 1997 National Survey of Giving, Volunteering, and Participating*. Catalogue no. 71-542-XIE. Ottawa: Statistics Canada.

Douglas, J. 1987. "Political Theories of Nonprofit Organization," in *The Non-Profit Sector*, ed. Powell.

Hansmann, H. 1987. "Economic Theories of Nonprofit Organization," in *The Non-Profit Sector*, ed. Powell.

James, E. 1987. "The Nonprofit Sector in Comparative Perspective," in *The Non-Profit Sector*, ed. Powell.

James, E. and S. Rose-Ackerman. 1986. *The Nonprofit Enterprise in Market Economics*. New York: Harwood Academic Publishers.

Knapp, M. and J. Kendal. 1991 "Policy Issues for the UK Voluntary Sector in the 1990s," in *The Nonprofit Sector in the Mixed Economy*, ed. Ben-Ner and Gui, pp. 711-732.

Kramer, R. and P. Terrell. 1984. *Social Service Contracting in the Bay Area*. Berkeley, CA: Institute of Governmental Studies.

Powell, W.W., ed. 1987. *The Non-Profit Sector: A Research Handbook*. New Haven: Yale University Press.

Pryor, F. 1994. "Reflections on the Non-Profit Sector," *Comparative Economic Studies*, 36(1):69-81.

Ross, D.P. 1990. *Economic Dimensions of Volunteer Work in Canada*. Ottawa: Department of the Secretary of State of Canada.

Rudney, G. 1987. "The Scope and Dimensions of Nonprofit Activity," in *The Non-Profit Sector*, ed. Powell.

Rutherford, D. 1992. *Dictionary of Economics*. New York: Routledge.

Salamon, L.M. 1987. "Partners in Public Service: The Scope and Theory of Government-Nonprofit Relations," in *The Non-Profit Sector*, ed. Powell.

Salamon, L.M. and H.K. Anheier. 1996. *The Emerging Nonprofit Sector: An Overview*. Manchester, UK: Manchester University Press.

Sharpe, D. 1994. *A Portrait of Canada's Charities*. Toronto: Canadian Centre for Philanthropy.

Smith, L. 1992. *Canada's Charitable Economy: Its Role and Contribution*. Toronto: Canadian Foundation for Economic Education.

Statistics Canada. 1994. *International Conference on the Measurement and Valuation of Unpaid Work: Proceedings*. Cat. No. 89-532E. Ottawa: Supply and Services Canada.

_____ 1996. http://www.statcan.ca.

Weisbrod, B. 1988. *The Nonprofit Economy*. Cambridge, MA: Harvard University Press.

Appendix

NPO QUESTIONNAIRE

Non-Profit Organisation Questionnaire   Identification # _____
++

Part A. Administrative Information

Name of organisation: _____

Mailing address: _____

Contact person (optional): _____ Phone number: _____

Email address: _____ Fax number: _____

Part B. Services, Participants, and Activity Pattern

Services. Using the following number system, please indicate which of the following types of services you provide. (Numbering system: Put a "1" in the blank next to the primary type of service you provide; a "2" next to your next-most-important service; and so on. Please number as many service types as apply to your organisation.)

Poverty relief: ____ Health Care: Education: ____
  Foodbank: ____   Elder care: ____   Ages 0-4 yrs.: ____
  Clothing: ____   Disabled support: ____   Primary age: ____
  Other: ____   Psychological   Secondary age: ____
    support: ____   Adult education: ____
  Health fund raising: ____   Other (please
  Health research: ____   specify_____): ____
  Other (please
    specify _____): ____

Leisure: ____   Crisis intervention: ____
  Sports: ____ Environmental: ____   Women's shelter: ____
  Artistic: ____   Suicide prev: ____
  Cultural: ____   Addiction: ____
  Religious: ____   Natural disaster: ____
  Other (please   Other (please
    specify _____): _____   specify_____): ____

Other (please specify _____): ____

Membership.
Do individuals require membership in your organisation in order to benefit from your services and/or to participate in your programs?   Yes ____   No ____

If yes, is a fee charged for membership?   Yes ____   No ____

Recipients of services OR participants in programs. Are your services and/or programs
  a. targeted to particular age group?   Yes ____, Age(s) _____   No ____
  b. targeted to a specific gender?   Yes ____, M/F _____   No ____
  c. targeted to particular ethnic/cultural group?   Yes ____, specify _____   No ____
  d. targeted to a particular profession?   Yes ____, specify _____   No ____
  e. targeted to people who share a particular experience or disease (for example, parent group, cancer
     survivors, etc.)?   Yes ____, specify _____   No ____
  f. targeted to a particular social grouping?   Yes ____, specify _____   No ____
  g. targeted to serve as many persons as possible?   Yes ____, specify _____   No ____

Non-Profit Organisation Questionnaire   Identification # _____
++

Pattern of Activity. If your organisation had (a) peak period(s) of activity in 1997, please list these peak periods (mm/dd) below:
Peak 1: From: _____ To: _____
Peak 2: From: _____ To: _____
Peak 3: From: _____ To: _____

Part C. Staffing

Volunteers.
Number of volunteers your organisation has in Manitoba:
  Registered with your organisation: _____
  Active during the last week: _____
  Active in an average week during peak period: _____
  Active in an average week during non-peak period: _____
  Active in 1997: _____

Total number of hours which your organisation's volunteers worked:
  In the last week: _____
  In an average week during peak period: _____
  In an average week during non-peak period: _____

Of the total hours volunteers worked, please enter the percentage of those hours spent in each of the following activities (please ensure that the percentages in each column total 100%):

	In last week	In peak period week	In non-peak period week	In last year
A. Management:	_____	_____	_____	_____
B. Clerical:	_____	_____	_____	_____
C. Professional:	_____	_____	_____	_____
D. Technical:	_____	_____	_____	_____
E. Sales:	_____	_____	_____	_____
F. Service:	_____	_____	_____	_____
G. Transportation:	_____	_____	_____	_____
H. Manual labour:	_____	_____	_____	_____
I. Crafts:	_____	_____	_____	_____
J. Teaching/coaching:	_____	_____	_____	_____
K. Counselling:	_____	_____	_____	_____
L. Other	_____	_____	_____	_____
	100%	100%	100%	100%

Number of volunteer hours spent in recruiting, training and coordinating volunteers in your organisation:
  In the last week: _____
  In an average week during peak period: _____
  In an average week during non-peak period: _____
  In 1997: _____

Non-Profit Organisation Questionnaire   Identification # _____
++

For each of the following types of decisions that get made in your organisation, please indicate the amount of input that volunteers have in the decision by circling a number on the scale from 1 to 10, where 1 means that volunteers' input is not at all requested or considered, and 10 means that the decision is made completely by volunteers.

	1-Volunteers' input not requested or considered							10 - Completely determined by volunteers		
A. accounting methods used by your organisation	1	2	3	4	5	6	7	8	9	10
B. deciding who will be on the organisation's decision-making body	1	2	3	4	5	6	7	8	9	10
C. the types of fundraising activities the organisation will undertake	1	2	3	4	5	6	7	8	9	10
D. what activities the organisation will perform	1	2	3	4	5	6	7	8	9	10
E. how the organisation's activities are carried out	1	2	3	4	5	6	7	8	9	10

Paid employees.

Number of paid employees your organisation has in Manitoba:
    Active during the last week: Part-time _____ Full-time _____   Total _____
    Active in an average week during peak period: Part-time _____   Full-time _____ Total _____
    Active in an average week during non-peak period: Part-time _____   Full-time _____ Total _____
    Active in 1997: Part-time _____ Full-time _____   Total _____

Total number of <u>hours</u> your organisation's paid employees worked:
    In the last week: Part-time hours _____ Full-time hours _____ Total hours _____
    In an average week during peak period:
        Part-time hours _____   Full-time hours _____ Total hours _____
    In an average week during non-peak period:
        Part-time hours _____   Full-time hours _____ Total hours _____

Of the total <u>hours</u> which paid employees worked, please enter the <u>percentage</u> of those hours spent in each of the following activities (please ensure that the percentages in each column total 100%):

	In last week	In peak period week	In non-peak period week	In last year
A. Management:	_____	_____	_____	_____
B. Clerical:	_____	_____	_____	_____
C. Professional:	_____	_____	_____	_____
D. Technical:	_____	_____	_____	_____
E. Sales:	_____	_____	_____	_____
F. Service:	_____	_____	_____	_____
G. Transportation:	_____	_____	_____	_____
H. Manual labour:	_____	_____	_____	_____
I. Crafts:	_____	_____	_____	_____
J. Teaching/coaching:	_____	_____	_____	_____
K. Counselling:	_____	_____	_____	_____
L. Other	_____	_____	_____	_____
	100%	100%	100%	100%

Non-Profit Organisation Questionnaire   Identification # _____
++

Number of paid employee <u>hours</u> spent in recruiting, training and coordinating volunteers in your organisation:
   In the last week: _____
   In an average week during a peak period: _____
   In an average week during a non-peak period: _____
   In 1997: _____

For each of the following types of decisions that get made in your organisation, indicate the amount of input that paid employees have in the decision by circling a number on the scale from 1 to 10, where 1 means that paid employees' input is not at all requested or considered, and 10 means that the decision is made completely by paid employees.

	1 - Paid employees' input not requested or considered						10 - Completely determined by paid employees			
A. accounting methods used by your organisation	1	2	3	4	5	6	7	8	9	10
B. deciding who will be on the organisation's decision-making body	1	2	3	4	5	6	7	8	9	10
C. the types of fundraising activities the organisation will undertake	1	2	3	4	5	6	7	8	9	10
D. what activities the organisation will perform	1	2	3	4	5	6	7	8	9	10
E. how the organisation's activities are carried out	1	2	3	4	5	6	7	8	9	10

Part D. Funding

Annual Budget. What was the total of your organisation's expenditures (in Manitoba) in your 1997 accounting year? (If you don't not know the exact figure, please approximate.) $_____

Source of funds. For the sources listed below, please record the approximate percentage of your annual budget that comes from each (please ensure that the percentages total 100%):

    A.   Earnings from commercial activities: _____%
    B.   lotteries, raffles, bingos, tag-days, etc. carried out by your organisation: _____%
    C.   Individual contributors: _____%
    D.   Corporate or business donations: _____%
    E.   Federal government: _____%
    F.   Provincial government: _____%
    G.   Municipal/Local government: _____%
    H.   Other (please specify_____):   _____%

                                                                                    100%

Funding sources' influence on organisation's decision-making. Three funding sources are listed below. For each of the decisions listed in each of the three tables, indicate how much influence that funding source has in that decision by circling the appropriate number on the scale from 1 to 10. (1 means that the funding source's input is not at all requested or considered, and 10 means that the decision is made completely by the funding source.)

Individual contributors:

	1-individual contributors' input not requested or considered					10 - Completely determined by individual contributors				
A. accounting methods used by your organisation	1	2	3	4	5	6	7	8	9	10
B. deciding who will be on the organisation's decision-making body	1	2	3	4	5	6	7	8	9	10
C. the types of fundraising activities the organisation will undertake	1	2	3	4	5	6	7	8	9	10
D. what activities the organisation will perform	1	2	3	4	5	6	7	8	9	10
E. how the organisation's activities are carried out	1	2	3	4	5	6	7	8	9	10

Business/Corporate Donors:

	1-Business'/Corps' input not requested or considered					10 - Completely determined by businesses/corps				
A. accounting methods used by your organisation	1	2	3	4	5	6	7	8	9	10
B. deciding who will be on the organisation's decision-making body	1	2	3	4	5	6	7	8	9	10
C. the types of fundraising activities the organisation will undertake	1	2	3	4	5	6	7	8	9	10
D. what activities the organisation will perform	1	2	3	4	5	6	7	8	9	10
E. how the organisation's activities are carried out	1	2	3	4	5	6	7	8	9	10

Government Funding:

	1-Government's input not requested or considered					10 - Completely determined by government				
A. accounting methods used by your organisation	1	2	3	4	5	6	7	8	9	10
B. deciding who will be on the organisation's decision-making body	1	2	3	4	5	6	7	8	9	10
C. the types of fundraising activities the organisation will undertake	1	2	3	4	5	6	7	8	9	10
D. what activities the organisation will perform	1	2	3	4	5	6	7	8	9	10
E. how the organisation's activities are carried out	1	2	3	4	5	6	7	8	9	10

Further research. We are planning future research on volunteers' contribution to non-profit organisations in Manitoba. Would you be willing to permit us to contact some of your volunteers for this project? (Their participation would be entirely voluntary, as would be any cooperation you would be willing to give. Any information would be kept strictly confidential.)   Yes_____   No_____

Thank you for completing our questionnaire!!
We appreciate your time and effort!

7

Advocacy from the Margins: The Role of Minority Ethnocultural Associations in Affecting Public Policy in Canada

Audrey Kobayashi

National ethnocultural associations represent a relatively unnoticed and unstudied segment of the nonprofit sector in Canada. Although such organizations have been in place as long as the communities they represent, that is, since the communities were first established through immigration, present-day associations are direct products of the rise of federal multiculturalism policy as official recognition of the role played by non-Charter groups in Canadian society. This paper is a preliminary attempt to examine aspects of ethnocultural group participation in Canadian public policy issues, with an emphasis on the role of the Canadian Ethnocultural Council (CEC) over the past five years.[1]

My contention is that because multiculturalism policy has by and large failed, this failure has implications for a wide range of policy issues of significance to ethnocultural organizations. These groups address public policy issues from a position that has them constantly playing catch-up to the dominant political agenda. Their marginality thus places them at a disadvantage and subject to the negative effects of government cutbacks, restructuring, and ideological backlash against human rights. In this paper,

I explore the recent activities of the Canadian Ethnocultural Council, arguably the volunteer group that has been more active than any other in lobbying to strengthen the multiculturalism policy, with a view to understanding some of the factors that have conditioned their public policy lobbying efforts. Many, if not most, of these factors are external to the organization itself and include the broad orientation of the government as well as the wider political context shaping that policy. When policy trends are reasonably sympathetic, the CEC has been able to advance its goals; when wider political currents shift the policy environment, the CEC has had much greater difficulty, not only in advancing its policy goals but also in maintaining itself as a vibrant organization.

The Canadian population has always comprised a wide range of ethnocultural groups, but over the past two decades diversity has increased as a result of the direct and indirect effects of shifts among immigrant source countries. At the same time, the public policy agenda has received greater emphasis on questions of diversity, including human rights issues (especially racism), immigrant settlement services, language and job training, employment equity, and multiculturalism generally. Nearly every aspect of public policy, from health care, education and social services to cultural development, international affairs and trade, demands that the diversification of the population be taken into account.

Currently, about 47 percent of Canada's population is of non-English and non-French background, and nearly one-third of those are also non-white. Most of these Canadians are represented in some way by national ethnocultural organizations. Little is known, however, about how effective such organizations are in influencing the direction of public policy on behalf of their constituencies or in providing, through voluntarism, services that meet needs that would not be filled, or would be filled inadequately, by other agencies. Furthermore, while there seems to be general recognition that fiscal restraint has made it more difficult for all nonprofit groups to function, little is known about the kinds of adjustments that such groups are making in the current economic and political context.

Ethnocultural associations also need to be understood in light of the changing Canadian imagery with regard to national identity, citizenship, human rights, the role of the state in defining that imagery, and evolving public attitudes and mores concerning the public policy agenda (Stasiulis

1997). Recent trends indicate that minority ethnocultural communities are engaged in discourse that transcends the established debate between liberal and communitarian philosophies, to work toward new forms of participatory democracy. This trend is in direct conflict with the movement to oppose the needs of "special interest" groups. Before presenting the case to illustrate this point, however, I wish to relate two anecdotes, which for me say a great deal about the "multicultural" context in which ethnocultural groups operate.

TWO TALES OF EXCLUSION

Several years ago, following the failure of the Meech Lake Accord and the Charlottetown Accord, Prime Minister Mulroney asked Constitutional Affairs Minister Joe Clark to chair a task force to travel the country assessing the mood of Canadian citizens with respect to constitutional reform. I was part of a delegation from the Canadian Ethnocultural Council which met with Mr. Clark in Ottawa in 1992, to reiterate a request that the government make multiculturalism a "fundamental characteristic" of Canadian society. A group of about 30 individuals, most of them representing their respective ethnocultural associations, gathered at a horseshoe-shaped table in a room in the West Block, and waited patiently for about 15 minutes until Mr. Clark, accompanied by several aides, entered the room and took his place at the head of the table, the flag of Canada providing a dramatic backdrop to his serious demeanor. The president of the CEC made a presentation informing him that members of Canada's ethnocultural minority groups felt that their concerns had been left out of the constitutional discussions. The theme of the presentation was similar to many others that had been placed before an assortment of politicians since the late 1970s, when ethnocultural minority groups fought and failed to have multiculturalism guaranteed in the *Charter of Rights and Freedoms*.[2]

Mr. Clark leaned across the table, extending the forefinger of his right hand. "What you people need to understand," he intoned, "is that your issues are not on the agenda this time around." He then proceeded to explain to us that our concerns could not be given serious consideration until the issues of Quebec's constitutional status and aboriginal land claims had been addressed.

I shift scenarios now to the Queen's University Club during the summer of 1998. The occasion is a conference on Canadian unity sponsored by the Queen's University Institute of Intergovernmental Affairs. The Honourable Stephane Dion had been invited as an after-dinner speaker. Prior to dinner, I found myself bemused by the curious behaviour of those gathered for cocktails, the vast majority of them political scientists and middle-aged white men mingling with a sprinkling of bureaucrats, some of whom were women, and a handful of supportive spouses. The "boys" jostled around Minister Dion, subtly elbowing themselves into more advantageous positions. I noticed at the edge of the crowd a professor from India, recently arrived at Queen's on a Canadian Studies grant, who looked quite uncomfortable. We struck up a conversation and eventually moved together into the dining room.

Over dinner, we listened to Minister Dion give a very impressive speech outlining his federalist position. He credited the work of a number of individuals in the room and expressed how honoured he felt to be in the presence of such a group of major players in the field of intergovernmental relations in Canada. Afterwards, the Indian visitor turned to me with a puzzled expression to ask whether the concerns of minority racial and ethnocultural groups were part of the discussions over constitutional issues, and whether our official policy of multiculturalism had any effect upon the outcomes.

I was taken aback. Certainly I had been feeling somewhat uncomfortable at that gathering and, as is often the case, had been remarking to myself upon the obvious patterns of male bonding and power brokering that I saw around me. But I was more profoundly disturbed as I replied to him that, no, I did not think those concerns were of particular relevance. My Indian colleague had come to Canada hoping that he would find in our well-established practices of diversity and multiculturalism some basis for advancing parliamentary reform based on pluralism in India. He left, somewhat disappointed.

This conversation struck me with the harsh realization that Joe Clark's pronouncement was being acted out in that room and most of the players were not even aware of the script; just as it is acted out throughout the country on a daily basis, with the issues that concern minority groups receiving diminishing attention as the national stakes get higher and they move closer to the centres of power. The concerns of those communities exist at best on the very fringes of the Canadian public policy agenda. Multiculturalism is not yet a mainstream policy. It is tolerated with a kind of forbearance that lasts only as long as we can avoid major contradictions between multiculturalism and issues higher on the list of national priorities.

ETHNOCULTURAL ASSOCIATIONS AND CITIZENSHIP

Scholarly research on nonprofit ethnocultural organizations in Canada is very limited. Writings on nonprofit associations tend to concentrate on their ability to expand or augment the role of the state in social service provision (e.g., Lenk and Andrew 1995), although the role of local ethnocultural organizations in this area has been much neglected. Questions of legal status and financial organization have received extensive coverage, but they ignore ethnicity or address it only in passing (e.g., Anheier and Knapp 1990; Bernd and Kenis 1994; Randon 1994; Salamon and Anheier 1992*a,b*; Taylor 1992). Similarly, studies of public policies that concern ethnocultural groups tend either to be restricted to the official realm of policymakers (e.g., House 1992; Marger 1993), or to address how policies affect ethnocultural populations generally, by-passing representative associations in the process. Research at the community level has placed very little emphasis on representative associations, at least in a contemporary context. A small number of studies has addressed issues of community voluntarism (Calliste 1996; Ujimoto 1978). The role of associations in ethnic conflict has received passing glances (Sharma 1995; see also Mentzer 1993), but the role of ethnocultural associations in public policy has barely received notice (however, see Blanshay, PhD dissertation in progress; Stasiulis 1982; Kobayashi 1992, 1993*b*). There is a limited literature on the broader issue of consultation between governments and interest groups (Coleman and Skogstad 1990; Stanbury and Fulton 1987; Finkle *et al.* 1994).

In contrast, the literature on public policy and diversity is vast. It includes, for example, discussions of the impact and cultural politics of immigration (Black 1987; Castles and Miller 1995; Castles and Fontaine 1995; Chui, Curtis and Lambert 1991; Helly 1997), the efficacy of multiculturalism policy (Dorais, Foster and Stockley 1994; Kobayashi 1993*a*; McLelland and Richmond 1994), the problem of racism for visible minority groups (Guillaumin 1995; Henry *et al.* 1995), the politicization of multicultural issues (Bannerji 1996; Legare 1995; Rahim 1990), the role of ethnocultural minorities in political processes (Abu-Laban 1997; Stasiulis 1994; Stasiulis and Abu-Laban 1991), and the direct relationship between the efficacy of ethnocultural organizations and their ability to mobilize political action (Clarke, Kornberg and Stewart 1985). Debates over diversity, human rights, and citizenship have become a major preoccupation of social theorists. It is far beyond the scope of this paper to examine these theoretical issues in depth, but there is a general recognition that multiculturalism is part of the process of globalization (Waters 1993), and that it has a major impact on social relations, especially in large cities (Sassen 1994; Zukin 1995). Most significant for the present project are emerging challenges to the traditional liberal/communitarian debate over democracy and human rights. While most Canadian theorists have rejected communitarianism for a re-vamped liberalism (Kymlicka 1995*a,b*; Taylor 1993), both positions marginalize the central role of communities as actors defining rights and, as a result, also contribute to the social and policy marginalization of those groups. On the other hand, human rights groups such as the Canadian Ethnocultural Council tend to be more strongly influenced by those who advance new definitions of democracy (e.g., Minow 1990; Mouffe 1994; Young 1990). These approaches suggest that a "politics of difference" can result in minority groups' inclusion in the public policy agenda on their own terms, with full recognition of contemporary forms of difference ("race," gender, sexuality, ability) which both constitute historic oppression and signal new forms of social identity. If those new forms are to move away from the margins where public policy and other powerful social mechanisms have kept them, however, they need both to be recognized by society as a whole as full social partners and to find a means of expressing, or negotiating their legitimate social place.

These discussions address many aspects of how diversity can be conceptualized and addressed in contemporary society, from changes in the law to restructuring government (Lijphart 1995), and they recognize the *very* important point that any discussion of diversity needs to address the layers of diversity created through "difference" (Canadian Council on Social Development 1997; Phillips 1995). There is very little discussion, however, of who is actually engaged in the project of changing social conditions. There is a need for empirical evidence of the role of ethnocultural associations, not only in working to achieve rights for their constituents, but in changing (or attempting to change) the way Canadians define democracy (Stasiulis 1997), for democracy means not only specifying the rights and responsibilities of social actors, but also developing means for such actors to act effectively. The issue is not so much thereby in specifying the differences between what Kymlicka and Norman (1994) call "citizenship-as-legal-status" and "citizenship-as-desirable-activity," both concepts that imply deeply normalized references to the dominant group, but rather in exploring ways in which more inclusive social policies can lead to greater congruence between these two forms of citizenship by fostering new forms of participation. While it is not the purpose of this paper to develop a full discussion of the theoretical implications of such debate, it is important to note from the outset that the actions of community groups themselves set the standards according to which the debate is engaged.

MULTICULTURALISM AS A CONTEXT FOR PUBLIC POLICY CHANGE

Multiculturalism has been a demographic fact in Canada throughout its history. For the past 27 years, however, we have codified a recognition of demographic diversity in a multiculturalism policy that has placed (until recently) increasing obligations on the federal government both to recognize rights of minority ethnocultural groups, and to implement programs to further those rights. I wish to argue in this paper, however, that however admirable and lofty the ideals it represents, multiculturalism is nearly empty as a public policy. Its elevation to independent status, rather than achieving the aim of creating greater equity, has allowed the majority of the Canadian policy agenda to develop independently of "multicultural" concerns. Instead of *multiculturalizing* every aspect of public policy, our peculiar system has channelled the concerns of *minority* ethnocultural groups away from the mainstream and into a narrow jurisdiction of what is now Canadian Heritage, so that they are neither considered nor recognized as part of mainstream Canada. Their concerns, which are fundamentally with issues of equality of access and participation in civil society, and with those issues such as employment, immigration, and education that affect their ability to participate fully and equally, are deemed to be those of "special interest groups."

I am by no means arguing to reject multiculturalism (cf. Bibby 1990; Bissoondath 1994) for unlike those who argue for an assimilationist perspective, I begin this paper from a position of supporting a pluralist perspective, and the *principles* expressed by the multiculturalism policy are strongly pluralist. But there is a difference between principle and practice, and the Canadian multiculturalism policy has not lived up to its practical objectives (cf. Kymlicka 1997). The most valuable aspect of the policy, nonetheless, has been to empower (primarily through funding) the minority ethnocultural groups to advance their own causes. It does so, ironically, however, in a very limited way. Multiculturalism is thus a policy of containment rather than one that promotes social justice. Minority ethnocultural groups are forced to pursue their issues along two, often contradictory, tracks; one, to gain basic recognition of the need to dismantle dominant notions of cultural status; and two, to change public policies in order to gain better access and fairness on the very grounds of their minority status. This paradox will not be overcome by designating them as "special interest" groups, but by giving them legitimate status.

The failure of the multiculturalism policy can be traced to Prime Minister Trudeau's original conceptualization following the release of the Pearson-commissioned *Report* of the Royal Commission on Bilingualism and Biculturalism (Canada 1969), which awoke politicians, policymakers and Canadians in general to the fact that Canadians "other" than members of the two majority linguistic groups did not enjoy either a sense of cultural security or full participation in Canadian civic life. Trudeau's now famous response was to state in the House of Commons that: "Although there are two official languages, there is no official culture, nor does any ethnic group take precedence over any other" (Canada 1971). It must be acknowledged that the official multiculturalism policy that ensued (Kobayashi 1993*b*) enshrined the notion of cultural diversity, placing Canadians ahead of practically all other countries in terms of recognizing and guaranteeing the rights of members of ethnocultural minority groups and these rights (but not multiculturalism itself) were subsequently enshrined in the *Charter of Rights and Freedoms*. But two fundamental flaws have regulated the development of multiculturalism policy since that time. The first is that the formal rights specified in the Charter and other human rights documents are geared toward *individual* expressions of equality. While it is true that rights are enjoyed (as life is lived) as individuals, it is usually membership in a group that compromises an individual's ability to enjoy those rights on an equal basis. The Canadian legal and policy systems remain quite inept at dealing with the concept of group rights as a means of bringing about greater substantive equality.

Second, the Canadian notion of equality remains rights-based rather than risk-based. That is, emphasis placed upon the specification of rights in themselves, rather than upon the substantive achievement of rights that might occur by ameliorating the conditions of civil risk that imperil full and equal participation for many minority groups. By "civil risk," I mean the full range of economic, social, cultural, and physical harms that result from the failure of human rights, brought about by systemic means of oppression and creating disadvantages for marginalized social groups. Such risk inheres in the standards and procedures according to which civil society is regulated, that is, in both the official and the unofficial ways in which multiculturalism (for one) is managed. In this sense, the limits to risk are constantly being negotiated through the institutional means of apportioning resources. Public policy in this sense is an exercise in risk management. Such risk management functions ideologically to determine what kinds of risk are more or less acceptable and what levels of risk will be publicly tolerated. The codification of such limits occurs in laws and policies, which specify an individual or a group's rights to access social goods. I have argued elsewhere that until we achieve the legislative and policy means to set risk before rights, the objectives of democracy are seriously compromised for all those members of society who for reasons of gender, "race," ethnicity, ability or sexuality, or other grounds of difference, do not set the terms for rights enjoyment. Social justice, therefore, requires a disruption, rather than a reinforcement, of those dominant norms that have allowed the civil risk to the well-being of ethnocultural minority groups to remain so high. Multiculturalism has failed us as an agent of risk reduction.[3] What this means is that governments have failed to make a commitment to ameliorate the effects of discrimination in our society, but I argue that they will not do so until they begin to recognize through public policy and legislation the huge risk that groups facing discrimination incur.

The comments made by Joe Clark to the CEC illustrate clearly the dominant view, and the dominant misunderstanding of multiculturalism, that the concerns of minority ethnocultural group members are separate and, for many subordinate, the problem of those ethnocultural groups alone, rather than of all Canadians. In other words, Trudeau was wrong; Canada does have official culture and it is that of the majority. This stark reality has fundamentally conditioned the development of the Canadian Ethnocultural Council as a nonprofit organization.

THE CANADIAN ETHNOCULTURAL COUNCIL

The CEC was established in 1980 as the only national umbrella group of ethnocultural associations. Its membership, which has varied somewhat over the years, currently consists of 33 associations, all of which must have a national rather than a local mandate. The national associations are in turn connected to a range of local ethno-specific social service and community organizations. The CEC thus operates at the meeting point of two nexes: one to the grass roots and the other to a collection of non-government and government organizations, most significantly the federal government (see Figure 1).

The member organizations represent a diverse set of interpretations of the term "ethnocultural." Some are clearly associated with a single national origin and "ethnicity" (the German Canadian Congress, the Portuguese Canadian National Congress);[4] others represent pan-regional linguistic or religious groups (the Canadian Hispanic Congress; the Council of the Muslim Community of Canada); multiple ethnicities within a single national origin (National Association of Canadians of Origins in India; National Association of Jamaicans and Supportive Organizations in Canada). Some claim "national" status without reference to an existing nation. For example, the United Macdeonian Organization of Canada was recently granted membership after several unsuccessful applications and despite strong protest from the Canadian Hellenic Congress, which claims to represent all Canadians of Macedonian background because they claim that Macedonia is a part of Greece. Similarly, there is both a Czech and Slovak Association of Canada, whose members are largely of Czech

Figure 1: Structural Relations of Ethnocultural Nonprofit Associations in Canada

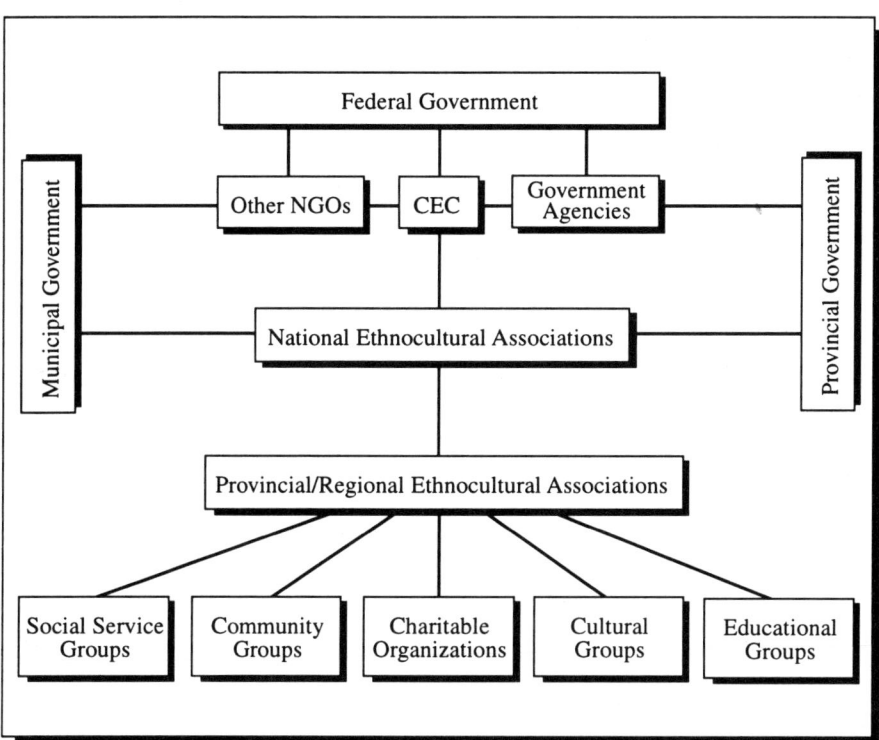

background, and a Slovak Canadian National Council. The diversity of membership represents the fact that the concept of ethnoculture is both flexible and contested, and perhaps more strongly rooted in the need for political representation than in cultural practice.

The mission of the CEC is as follows:

> ...to secure equality of opportunity, rights and dignity for ethnocultural communities in Canada. The CEC membership works by sharing information so as to develop a consensus on issues of concern to its membership and by advocating for changes on behalf of ethnic and visible minority groups (*Ethno Canada,* various dates).

Nothing could be further from the concept of ethnicity that guided the first secretaries of state for multiculturalism in the early 1970s.

The conflict between public notions of "red boots" multiculturalism and the CEC's carefully developed (if often conflict-ridden) political agenda has been apparent since the beginning. The association was founded at a time when there was great hope for the institution of a multiculturalism policy, but little established precedent. Since 1971, a series of junior ministers of state had administered small budgets that effectively fostered a sense of ethnocultural group interests in things such as "ethnic" food and dancing, reinforcing for some the notion of "other groups" and for others a more cogent image of a "third force."[5] The poverty of these cultural concepts was literally brought home during the period surrounding the repatriation of the constitution, when lobbyists for multiculturalism were partially successful in negotiating the inclusion of section 27 in the *Charter of Rights and Freedoms*. While this clause does not provide substantive guarantees, it requires the Charter to uphold the principle of multiculturalism. Since that time, the CEC's primary activities have involved lobbying and educational attempts to enshrine multiculturalism, envisioned and broadly interpreted as equality of access to all aspects of Canadian life, across a spectrum of activities, especially issues of labour, immigration, the media, public offices, education and, more recently, health and constitutional issues.

The post-Charter decade saw the CEC make considerable progress, and increase its visibility with government and the public in general. For one thing, the concept of the third force gained political resonance as a small but significant number of federal politicians recognized the significance of the ethnic vote in their election to certain ridings in the Toronto area. The CEC was active both in encouraging members of its representative communities to exercise citizenship through voting, and in cultivating, through personal contacts, those politicians who seemed most favourable.

The institution of Parliamentary Day became an opportunity for politicians and members of the CEC to meet to discuss their issues. Parliamentary Day was held each year during the annual general meeting, usually in May. Working on the assumption that the CEC represented a significant lobby, party whips played a strong role in providing a good turnout as the CEC representatives met for approximately one to two hours with each caucus.[6]

During the latter part of the first term of the Mulroney government (1986-88), these discussions focused on some very important legislative reforms, including the repeal of the *War Measures Act* (1988), redress for Japanese Canadians (1988), the reform of the *Broadcasting Act* (1989), the implementation of the *Employment Equity Act* (1986) and the Federal Contractors Program, the entrenchment of multiculturalism through the *Multiculturalism Act* (1988) and the creation of a full Department of Multiculturalism, to name the most significant. The CEC's ability to influence the direction of debates on these issues, and to promote full parliamentary discussion of the need to include multiculturalism as a legitimate concern, are clear indications that by the late 1980s the association was having a significant positive influence upon public policy.

Other issues that were less successfully pursued included protection of heritage languages (a *Heritage Languages Act* died on the Order Paper after the 1988 election), effective anti-racism and hate legislation, and achieving redress settlements for a variety of communities, including Sikh, Chinese, and Ukrainian Canadians. Perhaps the organization's most significant involvement was working with the Special Committee on Visible Minorities in Canada (SCVM), which produced the report *Equality Now!* (Canada. SCVM 1984) after consultation with over 1,000 groups and individuals across Canada. Following release of this report, the soon-to-be-defeated Liberal government established the parliamentary Standing Committee on Multiculturalism (a seven-member committee representing all three parties), which put in place the framework for structural multiculturalism, including a shift from heritage to human rights multiculturalism (Kobayashi 1993*b*). Many of its deliberations are expressed in the subsequent *Multiculturalism Act* (1988) which came into existence under the leadership of Gerry Weiner, the first full minister of multiculturalism.

Gerry Weiner's mandate was extended into the second Mulroney government, which was in power from 1988 to 1993. The second term, however, saw a closing of the "Red Tory window" through which we had glimpsed briefly a shift toward a strong human rights agenda in Canada. Although it is not within the ambit of this paper to examine in any detail the federal government's pulling back from human rights issues after 1989, surely the slowing down of economic growth and the riveting of national attention to constitutional issues are the two key explanatory features. When the Liberals again came to power in 1993, one of their first acts was to dismantle the Department of Multiculturalism. A much-downsized secretariat now exists under the ironically named Department of Canadian Heritage. There have been major financial cutbacks, sharp reductions of staff, and whole sections of the former ministry, including the Race Relations Directorate, have been demolished. The current secretary of state for multiculturalism, Hedy Fry, shares this portfolio with that of the similarly reduced Status of Women Canada. This paper now turns to a more detailed examination of the role of the CEC in affecting public policy during a period of cutbacks and pullbacks.

THE "THIRD FORCE" IN THE 1990s

Since 1993, the CEC has struggled. Lobbying efforts have been directed toward increasingly less sympathetic ears among federal politicians, the organization has experienced economic cutbacks and, recently, personnel difficulties in the national office. Yet the CEC has remained very active, levelling a constant barrage of critiques toward major public policy initiatives, or lack of initiatives, while undergoing significant shifts of orientation and priorities within its internal structure. There is a strong connection between the external economic and political environment, and these internal shifts.

The Appendix contains a list of briefs developed by the CEC between 1993 and 1998, representing the association's major public policy concerns over that time. These briefs fall into three major categories: (i) those that hammer away at a fundamental need to strengthen concepts of multiculturalism as a basis for public policies that meet a greater diversity of Canadian interests; (ii) those that address specific public policy issues, particularly related to labour and employment, immigration and refugees, racism, Aboriginal peoples, and constitutional issues; and (iii) those that shift attention away from federal government policy to forge stronger links with other NGOs.

Multiculturalism: The Great Fallback

No assessment of the CEC has meaning without a simultaneous assessment of the federal multiculturalism policy, for two reasons. The CEC is first of all a child of multiculturalism, having come into being when the policy was on the ascendancy, and having been closely tied throughout its existence to the Multiculturalism Department or Secretariat. Its fortunes are therefore fundamentally tied to those of the policy, in terms of both political and general public support.

A second reason is that the issues with which the CEC is primarily concerned are associated with multiculturalism in public discourse and in the processes by which public policy concerns are channelled through the federal bureaucracy. Council members are for this reason divided on whether they support the existence of a Department of Multiculturalism; some feel that it is advantageous to have at least one door on "the Hill" always reasonably accessible; others feel that their issues and concerns are ghettoized, and that greater progress would be made if multiculturalism could be integrated into every aspect of public policy.[7]

In any case, the single most enduring theme of CEC activities has been the need to gain widespread recognition of multiculturalism as a fundamental characteristic of Canadian society, rather than as a marginal issue that applies only to minority groups. Ironically, although little substantive progress has been made toward this goal, the CEC receives most attention, and is taken most seriously, when it sticks to a very literal definition of multiculturalism issues. In 1996-97, for example, the CEC produced 13 press releases. The only one to result in national coverage in *The Globe and Mail* (18 October) was entitled "Ottawa fails to sell multiculturalism."

In 1996, Canadian Heritage began to develop new guidelines following a review of the multiculturalism program, and released the so-called Brighton Report. The major points of the review include recognition of diversity (as opposed to fostering equity), and a revamping of the department's funding structure to support targeted activities rather than the general operation of ethnocultural community groups, along with greater accountability for funding. These changes have been received with some alarm on the part of ethnocultural groups most affected. They have two major concerns, one ideological and one economic. Ideologically, it is widely believed that the new approach represents a pulling back from pro-active programs on the part of the federal government, in favour of the kind of interpretive cultural commitments that characterized the Trudeau era. Kordan suggests that the new policy outlook presents ethnocultural diversity as a problem to be managed rather than as an ideal goal:

> The CEC is aware of the tendency that speaks of multiculturalism as a factor that contributes further to the fragmentation of Canadian society and the civic identity of Canadians. Although we are not prepared to say unequivocally that it is this sentiment which informs current government thinking in its recent initiative, there is this derived sense from the proposal that diversity is something that needs to be bridged in the process of creating a more cohesive citizenry. This, in our opinion, is false and dangerous thinking (1997, p. 137).

This issue speaks more broadly to the often difficult but symbiotic relationship between the CEC and the Multiculturalism Secretariat. Members of Council are deeply aware of the extent to which their fortunes rest on decisions made by the ministry, yet they are often deeply critical of policy directions. The new funding structure makes it much more likely that they will be adversely affected by the whims of bureaucrats making funding decisions informed by ideological perspectives that differ from those of the CEC, for whatever reasons.

Economically, therefore, while the new policy does not necessarily represent a diminishing of resources beyond what has occurred already, resources will be administered much differently. Groups fear a number of consequences — a loss of autonomy, a loss of control of the human rights agenda to one driven by government priorities, and, not least, financial pressures — because the need to undertake large projects in order to justify receiving multiculturalism grants will actually take away from the diminishing resources needed for day-to-day operation.

The CEC in the 1990s faces the conundrum that multiculturalism, the fundamental concept upon which the association rests, has not served it well. Most of the reasons for this fact lie outside the immediate concerns of the CEC for, while there may be different internal opinions about how the federal policy should be administered, papers and briefs of the CEC indicate very strong agreement that multiculturalism consists of two major objectives: (i) recognition and equal status for Canada's diverse population and (ii) overcoming the inequities that have resulted from historical discrimination. Exogenous factors include the current climate of fiscal restraint, although fiscal decisions are made ideologically on the basis of priorities placed on the issues in question. Therefore much more important than fiscal restraint is the pulling away from commitment to multiculturalism by a government that apparently is responding to opposition from the Reform Party and other voices against inclusive social policy.

The pullback became abundantly clear in 1997, on the occasion of the annual Parliamentary Day. By the early 1990s, the major parties had lost interest in attracting what was deemed ethnic support, no doubt in response to a general feeling that in times of fiscal restraint multiculturalism is one of the first luxuries to be cut and, more importantly, to competing messages from the Reform Party to the effect that multiculturalism is an unfair response to special interests, and to the Bloc Québécois demands to privilege the sovereign status of Quebec over that of "other" groups. Attendance at Parliamentary Day meetings dropped precipitously after the 1994 election. In 1997, the traditional format of caucus meetings was dropped in favour of small group meetings in the offices of individual Members of Parliament. The Reform Party refused to participate. The Bloc Québécois sent Osvaldo Nunez, Member of Parliament for Bourrasa, for a meeting with the entire delegation. The New Democrats and Conservatives sent regrets that they were unable to free up people for meetings. For the Liberals, Hedy Fry met initially with the delegation, which then split up into small groups to meet with an additional six Members of Parliament in their private offices. At one such meeting which I attended, we were told that the Liberal government was unwilling to support "multiculturalism" issues openly because of fear of reprisals from the Reform Policy. While this is a personal sentiment rather than an official government position, it reflects quite well what seems to be the dominant attitude on the Hill.[8] In 1998, the CEC executive decided to cancel Parliamentary Day. The annual meeting was held in Toronto instead of Ottawa, and the association began discussion of new avenues for conveying its public policy concerns.

Covering the Political Agenda: Public Policy Issues

The CEC position on a variety of public policy issues is consistent with its fundamental position on multiculturalism. That is, they begin with a premise of creating a multicultural society as defined above, and proceed systematically to address the public policy agenda. In a period of cutbacks, however, they have tended to take a somewhat more focused approach than in the past, when a greater effort was made to get across the idea that *every* public policy needs to be considered in terms of its advancement of multiculturalism. In this respect, their approach is very similar to that of the feminist activist groups, which take a similar approach to gendering the policy agenda.

In 1996, the CEC undertook a survey of the member organizations' opinions on public policy. Ten areas emerged as top priorities: multiculturalism, labour issues, racism, youth issues, national unity, immigration, health care, social services, education, and language issues.[9] Lobbying efforts to address these issues have focused on the following 15 issues presented to politicians at its last Parliamentary Day. The somewhat lengthy list is presented here in its entirety (but without the accompanying rationales), because it provides an excellent synopsis of the CEC public policy agenda:

> Access to professions and trades...What plan of action has your party developed to ensure that Canada will be able to benefit from its trade agreements and to eliminate barriers to the employment of immigrants in their professional field[s]?
>
> Armed forces... What will your party do to ensure that all sectors of the Canadian Armed Forces better represent the Canadian population and develop cross-cultural awareness training programs for their members?
>
> Canadian unity and identity... (1) What is the position of your party and what do you intend to do on this crucial issue?...(2) What is your party going to do to enhance and ensure multiculturalism's role and place in Canada's unity and identity?
>
> Citizenship... What is your party's position on changing the citizenship act, particularly on the above-mentioned issues? Will your party support public consultations on a new Citizenship Act?
>
> Culture... (1) How will your party respond to the CEC's call for a commitment to the four principles mentioned above? [access; representation; equity; self-determination]; (2) What is your party's plan of action to ensure the safeguarding, growth and dissemination of expressive heritage in Canada and abroad and enable the strengthening of Canadian identity?

Governor-in-Council appointments... What is your party's current policy on supporting Governor-in-Council appointments and do you have a plan of action to ensure that in the future such appointments will become more representative of the Canadian population?

Health... Will your party take measures to ensure that federally-funded health research requires that research questions be formulated to account/investigate the cultural, racial and linguistic aspects of health?

Heritage languages... (1) What concrete steps will your party take to ensure that young Canadians are encouraged and given the opportunity to become fluent in heritage languages and can thus later contribute to the economic prosperity of Canada and increase its competitiveness in the global market? (2) Would your party support the proclamation of the Canadian Heritage Languages Institute whose objectives are to encourage the preservation and use of heritage languages throughout Canada?

Human Rights Act... (1) will your party support an independent and comprehensive review of the Canadian Human Rights Act that would entail full consultation with the public, including community groups that are directly affected by the Act? (2) Would your party support a short-term package of reforms to the Canadian Human Rights Act to incorporate improved compensation measures, a permanent tribunal, a duty to accommodate, amongst others?

Immigration and refugees... (1) What priority will you give family class immigration in relation to independent/business class immigrants, in view of the shift in emphasis in the current policy to economic immigrants? (2) What specific and immediate measures does your party intend to take to address both the understaffing and the application backlog (as well as unequal processing times) between [sic] visa/immigration offices outside of Canada? (3) What specific measures will be undertaken by your party to ensure that national standards of fairness and efficiency are in place when immigration matters are transferred to the provinces?

Literacy... Despite jurisdictional issues, the CEC believes that the federal government should play a leadership role in the literacy issues by creating and promoting a National Literacy Policy. Will your party support this? How will your party address the special literacy needs of ethnocultural minorities to ensure that they can actively participate in our knowledge-based economy?

Multiculturalism... What is your party's commitment to establishing an Office of Multiculturalism Commissioner and having a Memorandum of

Understanding signed between the Minister of Canadian Heritage and the President of the Treasury Board to provide greater accountability for the implementation of sections 4 and 5 of the Canadian Multiculturalism Act?

Race Relations Foundation... What will your party do to clarify that the rewriting of the legislation will in no way erode the ability of the Canadian Race Relations Foundation to support action-oriented anti-racism projects as opposed to brokering information?

Royal Commission on Aboriginal Peoples... How does your party intend to proceed on the recommendations of the Royal Commission on Aboriginal Peoples?

Youth... (1) What is your party's plan of action to counter the high rate of unemployment faced by your ethnocultural minority Canadians? (2) What is your party's plan of action to involve ethnocultural minority youth in crime prevention? (CEC Parliamentary Day, 21 April 1997, "Issues to Be Discussed").

This list represents some major public policy issues that obviously cannot be addressed in depth here. Taken together, however, they convey a sense of the overall CEC philosophy, which I would summarize in the following principles: (i) an emphasis on inclusive and participatory democracy; (ii) a strong role for a centralized federal government; (iii) institutionalized multiculturalism as a fundamental feature of Canadian society; (iv) equity and diversity, with measures to achieve them, built into all public policies; and (v) public education as a means of promoting multicultural citizenship.

While the above represents a kind of wish list of the public policy issues that the CEC most wants to influence in principle, in practice the association's resources dictate a much more limited level of activity directed toward specific concerns. A review of activities for 1997-98 shows that attention has been focused very strongly in two general areas, immigration and labour (CEC 1998). This emphasis is driven somewhat by the public agenda, since Citizenship and Immigration Canada was in the midst of conducting hearings (to which the CEC made presentations) on possible revisions to the *Immigration Act*, just as Treasury Board had been involved two years earlier in revision of the *Employment Equity Act* and had absorbed a similar level of activity. But given the association's major priorities listed above, these two issues are likely to remain at the top of the agenda for some time to come.

New Directions

Economic pressures in symbiosis with a changing political context that challenges government dependency have brought the CEC to the point of crisis over the past two years. Faced with a major re-evaluation of its structure in order to comply with the new funding system, the association applied to Canadian Heritage in 1997 for one-time funding to engage external consultants to develop a strategic plan (Bouza and Associates 1998). The strategic plan calls for a highly risky move to consolidate finances in order to attract funding from sources outside government and for the association to marshal a much higher level of volunteer commitment. While these suggestions are in line with much of the thinking that guides the actions of nonprofit associations in the 1990s, there is considerable doubt that the CEC has the organizational infrastructure or the membership resources to undertake such a re-visioning. Its chances are further reduced because with a reduction of interest, even outright hostility, on the part of politicians, the member organizations are also beginning to show much less interest and commitment, and it grows ever more difficult to marshal volunteer resources.[10]

Intense discussions surrounding the restructuring issue did not result in a new agenda for *public* policy, but reiterated the current priorities, with emphasis on needs of multiculturalism policy, heritage languages, and education. When it came to policy internal to the association, however, there occurred an intense discussion, raising issues that had probably not been addressed systematically for some time. Working in small groups, members were asked to address six questions:

- What are the major desired outcomes for the ... strategic plan?
- What area(s) of internal capacity need to be developed in order to achieve these outcomes?
- Who needs to be involved, and in what capacities?
- What are the short-term and long-term benefits?
- What are the potential pitfalls?
- What can member associations do to facilitate this project?

Bearing in mind that these questions were asked of delegates from the member associations, rather than of members of the executive, and that the answers are based on consensus rather than on a quantitative poll of individual opinions, the following are the major findings.

- Members would like to achieve increased public and government awareness of their public policy concerns, particularly in the areas of multiculturalism, heritage languages and education, and national unity. They would also like to achieve a higher public level of understanding, acceptance and respect.
- The major emphasis for internal capacity is upon developing a strong body of volunteers who are dedicated to social issues, and who can bring a range of professional and community expertise, including lobbying and fundraising abilities.
- There needs to be equal involvement from all member associations, cultivated through frequent opportunities to get people together and by developing the capacities of individuals involved with the CEC so as to maximize their potential.
    1. Short-term goals are enhanced leadership and economic stability. Long-term goals have greater legitimacy in Canadian society and more effective capacity for communication.
    2. The greatest potential pitfall is public backlash against issues surrounding multiculturalism, and subsequent fragmentation, or isolation, of the CEC.
    3. Member organizations need to undertake grass-roots education programs with their own communities, develop capacity to participate fully in the CEC, including holding the CEC accountable for their concerns, respond to requests for information when approached by the CEC office, and develop community skills such as project management, communication, and lobbying skills.

While these responses, of course, represent to some degree the opinions of those individuals who attended the workshops, and while they are subject to the influence of the strongest personalities, I believe that they represent quite well the dominant views of the CEC member organizations.[11]

The challenge for the executive was to marshal the human resources provided by the member organizations in order to bring about a major shift in direction. Discussion among executive members and with delegates soon led to rejection of one of the major recommendations of the Bouza Report, which was to channel most of the financial resources for the coming year into a few months in order to kick-start an effective fundraising campaign. Instead, the association took the opposite approach, which was to reduce activities during the balance of 1998, while undergoing a period of reassessment. The latter course was dictated in part because the CEC had lost its program officer (due to financial cutbacks) and its executive director (due to resignation) over a period of several months, and it took some time to get things moving again under a new executive director hired in the autumn of 1998. There was also reluctance, however, to take the more risky route, especially when the association does not have a well-established history of private sector fundraising.

The major internal policy shift that the association has made in the past year is to work more closely with like-minded partners, thus sharing resources and increasing lobbying and educational effects. For example, the CEC cooperated with a coalition of federal public service unions to mount a conference on employment equity, worked with the Montreal-based Centre for Research and Action on Race Relations to submit an intervenor report to the Canadian Human Rights Commission challenging the definition of charitable status for ethnocultural association (see Appendix), partnered with the National Association of Japanese Canadians to seek funding for a major conference on anti-racism in the year 2000, and worked on several projects sponsored with its member organizations (CEC 1998).

The most significant recent activity is a project entitled "Healthy Aging in Caring Communities: A Cross-Cultural Approach," undertaken with funding from the Population Health Fund, Health Canada. The project involves working with local ethnocultural and aboriginal community groups to train volunteer health support workers and to provide opportunities for community meetings to discuss health issues in a cross-cultural perspective. Initial training sessions took place in Toronto and Vancouver, with follow-up meetings in Saskatoon, Winnipeg, and St. John's.[12] Funding for this project has provided a much needed boost to the association's resources. The more lasting effect, however, is that the project fulfils a number of goals with respect to public policy, through broadly based community involvement in communities across Canada.

These activities all strengthen the CEC's fundamental philosophy, while also allowing them to expand somewhat their limited resource base. They also show, however, that the association is developing a healthy distance from activities focused almost solely on the federal government, despite the fact that public policy concerns remain directed at the federal level. The Healthy Aging project provides a model for future projects — combining the objectives of funding, public policy development, and community access.

CONCLUSION: WHITHER DIVERSITY IN PUBLIC POLICY?

It is impossible to measure precisely the CEC effect upon national public policy. But this analysis shows a clear trend over the past decade, as the CEC has moved from being on the winning side on many of its issues during the late 1980s when multiculturalism and human rights were high on the public policy agenda, to the losing side as the end of the millennium approaches. Efforts of the CEC have focused on two major areas: entrenching multiculturalism as a principle of social equality and improving equality of access for communities represented by the CEC. Toward these ends, they have emerged over the past two decades as the major voice of minority ethnocultural groups, taken seriously by at least those politicians and policymakers who place a high priority on equality issues. Particularly over the past five years, however, they have to a significant degree lost sympathy in Ottawa. This loss reflects a lack of recognition, commitment, and understanding of equality issues on the part of current government, and a re-ordering of priorities toward deficit reduction, appeasement of the far right Reform Party, and a continuing (and probably correct) perception among politicians that Canadians in general are more interested in quelling First Nations' issues and maintaining national unity.

Despite its early promise, Canadian multiculturalism policy has been of very limited effect in countering the trend to marginalize the interests of minority ethnocultural groups, and because the CEC's existence is so dependent on the fate of this policy, its problems are very much those of Canadian Heritage. The current approach to managing rather than promoting the goals of citizenship diversity has resulted in a weakening of ties between the CEC and the Multiculturalism Secretariat, which many would read as emblematic of a general diminishment of commitment to social justice expressed through the Liberal government's diminished commitment to this department. While those (and there are many) who have been critical of the multiculturalism policy in the past may find reason to celebrate this scenario, it is an ominous development for the CEC because it plays directly to the aims of those who would abolish diversity rights along with the policy. The ability of the CEC and other similar organizations to create over the next while an effective means of operating further from the circle of official government activity will determine largely whether they are able to continue to have a future role in defining public policy.

These external factors are closely linked to a number of internal factors, most of which have not been addressed in this paper, with its emphasis on public policy, but which are also important. Although the association works hard to operate on a consensus model, it is an extremely diverse body, whose membership re-creates to some extent the international political arena. Diversity also occurs along racial and gender lines, an issue that has been the subject of intense debate around the council table. The limited resource base of the CEC is echoed in those of all its member organizations, so that it becomes increasingly difficult to marshal efforts from the ground up, which is clearly what needs to happen if a national organization is to build and maintain strength.[13] All of these internal factors have a direct effect not only on the CEC's capacity to effect public policy, but in its choices concerning which policies to address and how to do so.

Of course, the CEC is not alone in facing such dilemmas, and its experiences parallel those of many other organizations engaged in service delivery or policy advocacy. Women's groups, anti-racist organizations, and anti-poverty groups, to name but a few, are extremely vulnerable to shifts in government policy and the politics that drive such shifts. Recent years of budget cutting have highlighted how vulnerable are such groups to cuts in both the level and the form of public funding. These trends, and the attendant issues such as reduction in staffing levels that affect overall activity, reduction in the autonomy of nonprofit groups, shifts from independent to government-driven priorities, and a search for new forms of partnership and new kinds of activities are common features in the nonprofit landscape at the end of the millennium, as several other papers in this collection illustrate. The greater the degree of political marginality, and the smaller the resource base, the greater the impact of the external environment. Further work comparing both the ability of nonprofit organizations to respond to the changing policy climate, and the strategies invoked to adapt to change, would be very useful.

The road ahead for the CEC is not an easy one, but the strategic planning exercise surrounding the preparation of the Bouza Report in 1998 provided an opportunity to take stock of its future. While it is unlikely that the CEC will, or should adopt the corporate funding model that the report suggests, it has begun to recognize where its major strengths and potential lie. 1999 is no doubt a crisis year for the association as it embarks on a new direction that I predict will involve lessening allegiances to the once-vaunted notion of multiculturalism, weaker substantive ties with the Multiculturalism Secretariat, and stronger ties with the broader community of like-minded nonprofit organizations. This trend will mirror the current push to draw back on commitments to equity and equality and to represent the interests of minority ethnocultural groups as peripheral to the main national agenda. Partly driven by economic necessity, and ironically fulfilling the dominant ideology of the current federal government to encourage privatization, this direction is also an indication of the most recent shifts in civil society over definitions of citizenship. A fuller treatment of the CEC would therefore take greater account both of the philosophies of citizenship that drive its public policy agenda, and of the ways in which its public policy initiatives might be a basis for re-definition of Canadian citizenship values. In any case, the CEC priorities suggest increasing civil society activities to redefine citizenship participation, possibly with a stronger emphasis in future on more local spheres of metropolitan political involvement, especially in Canada's largest cities, which are most affected demographically by new immigration and where the streets are constant sites of struggles of expressions of cultural diversity.

If, as I have argued, the ability of the CEC to affect public policy is directly tied to the fate of multiculturalism policy on the Canadian political agenda, ultimately the CEC, like most nonprofit associations, exists to promote fundamental change in our ways of living and seeing the world. Their vision, articulated through a particular ideological lens, is one of re-visioning the way that Canadians view themselves and the ways in which Canadians interact with one another. Their vision of "citizenship-as desired-activity" (Kymlicka and Norman 1994) is one of equality and equal participation. Their status as an organization will in future depend very much upon their ability to move their agenda away from the margins, thus reducing the risk to inclusive social policies that their current status implies.

Notes

I wish to acknowledge a number of individuals who have contributed to the production of this paper: Kirsten McAllister and Cindy Tan provided expert research assistance; Keith Banting, Catherine Nolin Hanlon, Ransford Danso, Abbie Bakan, Linda Peake and Brian Ray contributed in various ways to the paper's development, and I owe them all a strong debt. Daiva Stasiulis provided an excellent and deeply perceptive critique of the paper. The Kahanoff Foundation and the School of Policy Studies, Queen's University, provided financial and administrative support that made the project possible. Finally, all the members of the Canadian Ethnocultural Council provided information, assistance, enthusiasm, and encouragement. This work is for them. The deficiencies are entirely my own.

[1] This paper is based on 12 years as a volunteer and representative to the Canadian Ethnocultural Council (CEC), as well as on intensive participant observation during 1998. The analysis is based on personal observations as well as on archival data collected from the CEC records, and focus group sessions with CEC member organizations.

[2] Section 27 of the Charter is an interpretive clause that specifies that it should be interpreted according to Canada's multicultural character, but multiculturalism is not guaranteed.

[3] For a full discussion of these two points, see Kobayashi and Ray (forthcoming).

[4] I recognize that there is diversity as well within these seemingly monolithic groups, especially if one examines their historical development. I am using the term "single national origin," however, to refer to their contemporary social construction and the way in which they present themselves as CEC members.

[5] The term was coined by Paul Yuzak, the first Senator who was of neither English nor French background, and it came into widespread usage toward the end of the 1970s.

[6] I participated in Parliamentary Day as a representative of the National Association of Japanese Canadians most years between 1986 and 1997.

[7] Interview with Irene Kamchen, Executive Director, 29 May 1998.

[8] "CEC Parliamentary Day, April 21, 1997, Issues to be Discussed" was distributed to caucus members in advance. Delegates received a briefing package entitled "On the Hill, Parliamentary Day, April 21, 1997." Notes entitled "Parliamentary Day 1997" were distributed after the meeting.

[9] Detailed members' opinions are provided in a document entitled "Canadian Ethnocultural Council Membership Public Policy Survey," dated May 1996; however, this is an internal document not intended for public use and I have therefore not provided any details here.

[10] My comments in this section are based on having worked closely with the CEC as a volunteer and official representative of the National Association of Japanese Canadians, during the period of evaluation. I attended several of the focus group sessions organized by Bouza and Associates as part of their investigations, and organized and ran workshops on organizational change during meetings of the Board of Presidents. This work is therefore based on participant observation in the fullest sense.

[11] In any case, organizations are run and directed by those on the spot, and often those with the strongest personalities. For this reason, I prefer to capture a sense of consensus rather than to attempt a method (such as opinion polling) that is more accurate quantitatively but less so in terms of actual practice.

[12] "Healthy Aging in Caring Communities: A Cross-Cultural Approach," Report by Sucy Eapen, Project Coordinator, May 1998.

[13] In 1994, the CEC produced a brief entitled "Gender Equity within the CEC." Various attempts have been made through council resolutions to improve gender and youth representation among the delegates, but motions that attempt to regulate the composition of delegations are consistently voted down, usually on the grounds that (a) better representation would be more costly; (b) the delegates represent the electoral decisions of individual national groups.

References

Abu-Laban, Y. 1997. "Ethnic Politics in a Globalising Metropolis: The Case of Vancouver," in *The Politics of the City: A Canadian Perspective*, ed. T. Thomas. Scarborough: Nelson.

Anheier, H. and M. Knapp. 1990. *Voluntas:* an editorial statement. *Voluntas* 1(1):1-12.

Bannerji, H. 1996. "On the Dark Side of the Nation: Politics of Multiculturalism and the State of 'Canada'," *Journal of Canadian Studies,* 31(Fall):103-28.

Bernd, M. and K. Patrick. 1996. "Non-Profit Organisations of Capital: Voluntarism and Collective Action of Corporate Interests." Paper of the American Sociological Association.

Bibby, R.W. 1990. *Mosaic Madness: Pluralism Without a Cause.* Toronto: Stoddart.

Bissoondath, N. 1994. *Selling Illusions: The Cult of Multiculturalism in Canada.* Toronto: Penguin Books.

Black, J. 1987. "The Practice of Politics in Two Settings: Political Transferability Among Recent Immigrants to Canada," *Canadian Journal of Political Science/ Revue canadienne de science politique*, 20(4):731-53.

Blanshay, L, in progress. *The Politicisation of Ethnocultural and Visible Minority National Organisations in Canada since the Post-War Period.* PhD dissertation, University of Glasgow.

Bouza and Associates. 1998. "Canadian Ethnocultural Council Strategic Action and Revenue Generation Plan, 1998-2001." Final unpublished report.

Brighton Research for the Corporate Review Branch of the Department of Canadian Heritage, Nadia Laham Director. 1996. *Strategic Evaluation of Multiculturalism Programs.* Unpublished report.

Calliste, A. 1996. "Antiracism Organizing and Resistance in Nursing: African Canadian Women," *The Canadian Review of Sociology and Anthropology*, 33(August):361-90.

Canada. 1971. *House of Commons Debates*, 8 October.

Canada. Department of Canadian Heritage. 1997a. *Strategic Evaluation of Multiculturalism Programs.* Ottawa: Supply and Services Canada.

_____ 1997b. *Multiculturalism - Renewed Program Design.* Ottawa: Supply and Services Canada.

Canada. Royal Commission on Bilingualism and Biculturalism. 1969. *The Cultural Contribution of the Other Ethnic Groups*, Vol. IV. Ottawa: Queen's Printer.

Canada. Special Committee on Visible Minorities in Canadian Society (SCVM). 1984. Bob Daudlin, MP, Chairman. *Equality Now!* Ottawa: Queen's Printer.

Canadian Council for Social Development. 1997. *Inclusive Social Policy: Ideas for Practitioners.* Ottawa: Canadian Council for Social Development and Carleton University School of Social Work.

Canadian Ethnocultural Council (CEC). 1987. "To the Back of the Bus." Brief presented to the Parliamentary Committee on the *Constitutional Amendment Act*.

_____ 1998. "1997/1998 Activity Report," submitted to the Biennial General Assembly, 23-24 May, Toronto, Ont. Prepared by I. Kamchen, Executive Director.

Castles, S. and M. Miller. 1995. *The Age of Migration: International Population Movements in the Modern World.* London: Macmillan.

Chui, T.W.L., J.E. Curtis and R.D. Lambert. 1991. "Immigrant Background and Political Participation: Examining Generational Patterns," *Canadian Journal of Sociology/Cahiers canadiens de sociologie*, 16(4):375-96.

Clarke, H.D., A. Kornberg and M.C. Stewart. 1985. "Active Minorities: Political Participation in Canadian Democracy," in *Minorities and the Canadian State*, ed. N. Nevitte and A. Kornberg. Oakville, ON: Mosaic Press.

Coleman, W.D. and G. Skogstad. 1990. "Policy Communities and Policy Networks: A Structural Approach," in *Policy Communities and Public Policy in Canada: A Structural Approach*, ed. W.D. Coleman and G. Skogstad. Toronto: Copp Clark Pitman.

Connor, W. 1994. *Ethnonationalism: The Quest for Understanding*. Princeton: Princeton University Press.

Dorais, J.-L., L. Foster and D. Stockley. 1994. "Multiculturalism and Integration," in *Immigration and Refugee Policy: Australia and Canada Compared*, ed. H. Adelman *et al*. Melbourne: Melbourne University Press.

Finkle, P., K. Webb, W.T. Stanbury and P. Pross. 1994. "Federal Government Relations with Interest Groups: A Reconsideration." Unpublished paper.

Fontaine, L. 1995. "Immigration and Cultural Policies: A Bone of Contention Between the Province of Quebec and the Canadian Federal Government," *International Migration Review*, 29(Winter):1041-48.

Guillaumin, C. 1995. *Racism, Sexism, Power and Ideology*. London and New York: Routledge.

Hammer, T. 1990. *Democracy and the Nation State: Aliens, Denizens and Citizens in a World of International Migration*. Aldershot: Avebury.

Helly, D. 1997. "Voluntary and Social Participation of People of Immigrant Origin: Overview of Canadian Research." Unpublished paper, The Metropolis Project, Citizenship and Immigration Canada.

Henry, F, C. Tator, W. Mattis and T. Rees, eds. 1995. *The Colour of Democracy: Racism in Canadian Society*. Toronto: Harcourt Brace.

Herman, R.D. and R. Heimovics. 1994. A Cross-National Study of a Method for Researching Non-Profit Organisational Effectiveness," *Voluntas*, 5(1):86-100.

House, E.R. 1992. "Multicultural Evaluation in Canada and the United States," *Canadian Journal of Program Evaluation*, 7(1):133-56.

Kobayashi, A. 1992. "The Japanese-Canadian Redress Settlement and its Implications for 'Race Relations'," *Canadian Ethnic Studies*, 24(1):1-19.

_____ 1993*a*. "Representing Ethnicity: Political Statistexts," in *Challenges of Measuring an Ethnic World: Science, Politics and Reality*, ed. G. Goldman. Proceedings of the Joint Canada-United States Conference on the Measurement of Ethnicity, Ottawa and Washington, DC: Statistics Canada and the US Bureau of the Census.

_____ 1993b. Multiculturalism: Representing a Canadian Institution," in *Place/Culture/Representation*, ed. J. Duncan and D. Ley. London: Routledge.

_____ 1996. "Japanese and Italian Canadians: Contrasts in Ethnocultural Strategies," in *Genova, Colombo, il mare e l'emigrazione italiana nelle Americhe*, ed. C. Cereti. Vol II. Rome: Instituto della Enciclopedia Italiana, Fondata da Giovanni Treccani.

Kobayashi, A. and B. Ray (in press). "Civil Risk and Landscapes of Marginality in Canada: A Pluralist Approach to Social Justice," *The Canadian Geographer*.

Kordan, B.S. 1997. "Multiculturalism, Citizenship and the Canadian Nation: A Critique of the Proposed Design for Program Renewal," *Canadian Ethnic Studies*, 29(2):136-43.

Kymlicka, W. 1995a. *Multicultural Citizenship: A Liberal Theory of Minority Rights*. Oxford: Claredon.

_____ 1995b. *The Rights of Minority Cultures*. Oxford: Oxford University Press.

_____ 1997. "Debating Multiculturalism." Unpublished paper presented at the annual meeting of the Canadian Ethnocultural Council, 20 April.

Kymlicka, W. and W. Norman. 1994. "Return of the Citizen: A Survey of Recent Work on Citizenship Theory," *Ethics,* 104:352-81.

Legare, E.I. 1995. "Canadian Multiculturalism and Aboriginal People: Negotiating a Place in the Nation," *Identities*, 1(4):347-66.

Lenk, A. and C. Andrew. 1995. "Decentralization and the Municipal State: The Case of the Community-Based Non-Profit Sector in Ottawa," *Canadian Journal of Urban Research*, 4(2):293-304.

Lijphart, A. 1995. "Self-Determination versus Pre-Determination of Ethnic Minorities in Power-Sharing Systems," in *The Rights of Minority Cultures*, ed. Kymlicka.

Marger, M.N. 1993. "Multiculturalism as Concept and Policy: A Comparison of the United States, Canada and Australia." Papers of the American Sociological Association.

McLellan, J. and A. Richmond. 1994. "Multiculturalism in Crisis: A Post-Modern Perspective," *Ethnic and Racial Studies,* 17(4):662-83.

Mentzer, M.S. 1993. "The Leader Succession-Performance Relationship in a Non-Profit Organization," *Canadian Review of Sociology and Anthropology/Revue Canadienne de Sociologie et d'anthropologie*, 30(2):191-204.

Minow, M. 1990. *Making All the Difference: Inclusion, Exclusion and American Law*. Ithaca: Cornell University Press.

Mouffe, C. 1994. *Democracy and Pluralism: A Critique of the Rationalist Approach.* Toronto: University of Toronto Press.

Phillips, A. 1995. "Democracy and Difference: Some Problems for Feminist Theory," in *The Rights of Minority Cultures*, ed. Kymlicka.

Rahim, A. 1990. "Multiculturalism or Ethnic Hegemony: A Critique of Multicultural Education in Toronto," *The Journal of Ethnic Studies*, 18(Fall):29-46.

Randon, A. 1996. "Constraining Campaigning: The Legal Treatment of Non-Profit Policy Advocacy Across 24 Countries," *Voluntas,* 5(1):27-58.

Richmond, A. 1994. *Global Apartheid: Refugees, Racism and the New World Order.* Toronto: Oxford University Press.

Salamon, L. and H.K Anheier. 1992*a*. "In Search of the Non-Profit Sector. I: The Question of Definitions," *Voluntas* 3(2):125-51.

_____ 1992*b*. "In Search of the Non-Profit Sector. II: The Problem of Classification," *Voluntas,* 3(3):267-309.

Sassen, S. 1994. *Cities in a World Economy.* Thousand Oaks: Pine Force Press.

Sharma, S.K. 1995. "Multiculturalism and Minorities in Canada: Some Reflections on Ethnic Conflict," *Social Action*, 45(1):11-23.

Stanbury, W.T. and M.J. Fulton. 1987. "Consultation and Public Participation Processes in Government Policy Making: A Conceptual Framework." Paper presented at the Conference on Consultative Process in Business-Government Relations, Max Bell Centre for Business-Government Studies, Faculty of Administrative Studies, York University, 24-25 April.

Stasiulis, D. K. 1982. *Race, Ethnicity and the State.* Unpublished PhD Dissertation, Department of Sociology, University of Toronto.

_____ 1994. "Deep Diversity": Race and Ethnicity in Canadian Politics," in *Canadian Politics in the 1990s,* ed. M.S. Whittington and G. Williams. Toronto: Nelson.

_____ 1997. "Participation by Immigrants, Ethnocultural/Visible Minorities in the Canadian Political Process." Paper prepared for Heritage Canada, presented at the Research Domain Seminar on Immigrants and Civic Participation: Contemporary Policy and Research Issues, Montreal, 23 November.

Stasiulis, D. K. and Y. Abu-Laban. 1991. "The House the Parties Built: (Re)construction Ethnic Representation in Canadian Politics," in *Ethno-Cultural Groups and Visible Minorities in Canadian Politics: The Question of Access,* ed. K. Megyery. Vol. 7 of the Research Series, Royal Commission on Electoral Reform and Party Financing. Toronto: Dundurn Press.

Taylor, M. 1992. "The Third Sector in International Perspective," *Voluntas*, 3(3):383-90.

_____ 1993. "The Politics of Recognition," in *Multiculturalism and the 'Politics of Recognition'*," ed. A. Gutmann. Princeton: Princeton University Press.

Ujimoto, V. 1978. "Postwar Japanese Immigrants: The Allocation of Time to Organizational, Social and Leisure Activities." Unpublished paper.

Waters, M. 1993. "Globalization, Multiculturalism and Rethinking the Social: Introduction," in *Racism and Migration in Western Europe*, ed. J. Wrench and J. Solomos. Oxford: Berg.

Young, I.M. 1990. "Polilty and Group Difference: A Critique of the Ideal of Universal Citizenship," in *Throwing Like a Girl and Other Essays in Feminist Philosophy and Social Theory*, ed. I.M. Young. Bloomington: Indiana University Press.

Zukin, S. 1995, *The Culture of Cities*. Oxford: Blackwell.

Appendix

CANADIAN ETHNOCULTURAL COUNCIL
INVENTORY OF CEC BRIEFS 1993-1998

1998 BRIEFS

1. May 1998. *Healthy Aging in Caring Communities: A Cross-Cultural Approach, Evaluation Report*, prepared by Elizabeth Kwan, 22p.

2. May 1988. *Healthy Aging in Caring Communities: A Cross-Cultural Approach*, report by Sucy Eapen, 45p.

3. 30 April 1998. *Canadian Ethnocultural Council Strategic Action and Revenue Generation Plan: 1998-2001*, Final Report, Bouza and Associates, 173p.

4. April 1998. *DRAFT, A Cultural Policy for a Multicultural Canada: Discussion Paper and Invitation to Comment*, 12p.

5. 2 April 1998. *CEC's Position on Detentions and Removals: Speaking notes for a meeting with the Standing Committee on Citizenship and Immigration*, Ottawa, p.3.

6. 11 March 1998. *Response to the Report of the Legislative Review Advisory Group entitled 'Not Just Numbers,' submitted to the Hon. Lucienne Robillard, Minister of Citizenship and Immigration*, 13p.

7. February 1998. *Factum of the Intervenor and Fact Sheet: the Legal Argument: Supreme Court Intervention on Denial of Charitable Status as a Charter Challenge.* Minority Advocacy and Rights Council, Canadian Ethnocultural Council and Centre for Research and Action on Race Relations, 21p.

8. 20 January 1998. *Federal Leadership on Access to Professions and Trades.* Submitted to Martha Nixon, Senior Director General, Operations, Human Resources Investment Branch, Human Resources and Development Canada, 5p.

9. 16 January 1998. *Report on Citizenship and Immigration Conference: New Selection for Economic Stream Immigrants*, 3p.

10. 14 January 1998. *Policy Institute and Academics: For CEC Partnership Possibilities*, 15p.

1997 BRIEFS

1. October 1997. *Canadian Unity and Identity: The Advantages of Diversity.*

2. 8 August 1997. *Remedy for Employment Inequity for Visible Minorities in the Federal Public Service: CEC Recommendations*, 4p.

3. 31 July 1997. *Response to an Independent Review of Canada's Immigration Act*, 8p.

4. 2 July 1997. *Backgrounder on Ethnocultural Youth Issues: A Review of CEC and Member Organization Activities.*

5. 30 June 1997. *Background of Past CEC Policy Resolutions.*

6. June 1997. *Mainstreaming Multiculturalism-Institutional Change, Final Report.*

7. 25 June 1997. *Governor-in-Council Appointments: Ensuring Participation*, p.6.

8. 20 June 1997. *Parliamentary Days: Issues, Questions and Responses.*

9. 15 June 1997. CEC Report on the 1997 Congress of Learned Societies, 69th Annual Meetings of the Canadian Political Sciences Associations.

10. 28 May 1997. *CEC Report on the 8th Annual National Prior Learning Assessment Conference.*

11. April 1997. *A Handbook on Anti-Racism Parenting.*

12. March 1997. *Multiculturalism, Citizenship and the Canadian Nation: A Critique of the Proposed Design for Program Renewal*, 8p.

13. January 1997. *Response to the Consultation Paper on Racial Equality by the Canadian Bar Association Working Group on Racial Harmony*, 14p.

14. January 1997. *Response to the McKenzie King Report to the Legal Education Committee of the Law Society of Upper Canada on the Accreditation of Lawyers with Foreign Training Experience*, 6p.

1996 BRIEFS

1. 27 July 1996. *Regulations and Compliance Mechanisms under the New Employment Equity Act*, 4 p.

2. July 1996. *Review of Citizenship Act: CEC Submission to the Standing Committee on Citizenship and Immigration*, 1p.

3. February 1996. *Ethnocultural Diversity: A Source of Competitive Advantage* (Conference Report).

1995 BRIEFS

1. December 1995. *Ethnocultural Diversity: A Source of Competitive Advantage Background Discussion Paper*, presented at the Conference on Ethnocultural Diversity: A Source of Competitive Advantage 15-16 Feb.1996.

2. October 1995. *The Advantage of Diversity: Global and Domestic Opportunities for Business*, Discussion Paper, Draft, joint project of CEC, The Conference Board of Canada and Canadian Heritage NOT IN CEC INVENTORY.

3. November 1995. *The 42% Solution: Making Equity a Reality*, (a Response to the Strategic Review of Multiculturalism Programs of the Department of Canadian Heritage), 37p.

4. 1995. *Child Abuse in Minority Ethnocultural Communities: An Exploratory Study* (submitted to the Multiculturalism Program, Department of Canadian Heritage and Family Violence Prevention, Health Canada).

5. 2 May 1995. *Brief to Senate Committee on Bill C-44* (proposed amendments to Immigration Act, Citizenship Act and Customs Act) 5 p.

6. 21 March 1995. *Bill C-53: Presentation on Bill C-53: An Act to Establish the Department of Canadian Heritage and Repeal and Amend Certain Other Acts* (to the Senate Standing Committee on Social Affairs, Science and Technology), 8 p.

7. 14 February 1995. *Presentation on Bill C-64 (Employment Equity Bill)* (to the Standing Committee on Human Rights and Status of Disabled Persons), 6 p.

1994 BRIEFS

1. December 1994. *Submission on Social Security Reform to the Standing Committee on Human Resource Development*, 9p.

2. 1 December 1994. *Presentation to Parliamentary Committee on Bill C-44* (Amendments to *Immigration Act* and *Customs Act*), 10p.

3. 31 October 1994. *Interim Presentation to the Standing Committee on Human Resources Development* (Social Security Reform), 9p.

4. August 1994. *Submission to Minister of Citizenship and Immigration on Canada's New Immigration Policy.*

5. 26 July 1994. *Brief to the Special Joint Committee Reviewing Canada's Foreign Policy*, 5p.

6. July 1994. *We are the Mainstream: A Cultural Policy for a Multiculturalism Canada.*

7. 2 June 1994. *Review of the Citizenship Policy.*

8. June 1994. *Integration for the Ethnocultural Communities' Perspective.*

9. May 1994. *Gender Equity within the CEC.*

10. 9 March 1994. *Submission to the Standing Committee on Human Resource Development* (Phase I Consultations).

11. January 1994. *Equality of Access and Equality of Outcome, Brief to the Royal Commission on Learning* (Ontario), 10p.

1993 BRIEFS

1. November 1993. *Report on the Conference: "Economic Renewal and the Ethnocultural Communities,"* 18p.

2. 15 October 1993. *Towards Equity: Review of the Canadian Judicial Process. Submission to the Dept. of Justice on the Review of Federal Judicial Appointments*, 6p.

3. September 1993. *Submission to the Ontario Government on Bill 79: An Act Respecting Employment Equity*, 10p.

4. August 1993. *In Support of the Aspirations of Aboriginal Peoples: Submission to the Royal Commission on Aboriginal Peoples*, 40p.

5. 21 June 1993. *Position Paper Submitted by the Canadian Ethnocultural Council to the Department of Employment and Immigration on the Proposed Immigration Regulation Amendments*, 4p.

6. May 1993. *Report to Statistics Canada: Comments on the 1996 Census Guide.*

7. 1 March 1993. *Brief to the CRTC on Structural Hearing* (Notice 1992-13), 13p.

8. 5 February 1993. (Second) *Submission to the CRTC, Notice of Public Hearing 1992-13, Structural Hearing*, 11p.

Contributors

Keith G. Banting, Director, School of Policy Studies, Queen's University.

Attah K. Boame, Graduate student, Department of Economics, University of Manitoba.

Laura K. Brown, Assistant Professor, Department of Economics, University of Manitoba.

Ram A. Cnaan, Professor, School of Social Work, University of Pennsylvania.

Raymond Dart, PhD candidate, Schulich School of Business, York University.

Katherine A. Graham, Associate Dean, Faculty of Public Affairs and Management, Carleton University.

Michael Hall, Vice-President Research, Canadian Centre for Philanthropy and Director, Kahanoff Foundation Nonprofit Sector Research Initiative.

Femida Handy, Assistant Professor, Faculty of Environmental Studies, York University.

Jane Jenson, Professor, Département de science politique, Université de Montréal.

Audrey Kobayashi, Professor, Department of Geography and Institute of Women's Studies, Queen's University.

Susan D. Phillips, Associate Professor, School of Public Administration, Carleton University.

Elizabeth S. Troutt, Assistant Professor, Department of Economics, University of Manitoba.

Brenda Zimmerman, Associate Professor, Nonprofit Management and Leadership Program, Schulich School of Business, York University.

Queen's Policy Studies
Recent Publications

The Queen's Policy Studies Series is dedicated to the exploration of major policy issues that confront governments in Canada and other western nations. McGill-Queen's University Press is the exclusive world representative and distributor of books in the series.

School of Policy Studies

Security, Strategy and the Global Economics of Defence Production, David G. Haglund and S. Neil MacFarlane (eds.), 1999   Paper ISBN 0-88911-875-2 Cloth ISBN 0-88911-877-9

The Communications Revolution at Work: The Social, Economic and Political Impacts of Technological Change, Robert Boyce (ed.), 1999   Paper ISBN 0-88911-805-1 Cloth 0-88911-807-8

Diplomatic Missions: The Ambassador in Canadian Foreign Policy, Robert Wolfe (ed.), 1998
Paper ISBN 0-88911-801-9 Cloth ISBN 0-88911-803-5

Issues in Defence Management, Douglas L. Bland (ed.), 1998
Paper ISBN 0-88911-809-4 Cloth ISBN 0-88911-811-6

Canada's National Defence, vol. 2, *Defence Organization,* Douglas L. Bland (ed.), 1998
Paper ISBN 0-88911-797-7 Cloth ISBN 0-88911-799-3

Canada's National Defence, vol. 1, *Defence Policy,* Douglas L. Bland (ed.), 1997
Paper ISBN 0-88911-792-6 Cloth ISBN 0-88911-790-X

Institute of Intergovernmental Relations

Comparing Federal Systems, 2d ed., Ronald L. Watts, 1999   ISBN 0-88911-835-3

Canada: The State of the Federation 1998/99, vol. 13, *How Canadians Connect,* Harvey Lazar and Tom McIntosh (eds.), 1999   Paper ISBN 0-88911-781-0 Cloth ISBN 0-88911-779-9

Canada: The State of the Federation 1997, vol. 12, *Non-Constitutional Renewal,* Harvey Lazar (ed.), 1998
Paper ISBN 0-88911-765-9 Cloth ISBN 0-88911-767-5

Canadian Constitutional Dilemmas Revisited, Denis Magnusson (ed.), 1997
Paper ISBN 0-88911-593-1 Cloth ISBN 0-88911-595-8

Canada: The State of the Federation 1996, Patrick C. Fafard and Douglas M. Brown (eds.), 1997
Paper ISBN 0-88911-587-7 Cloth ISBN 0-88911-597-4

John Deutsch Institute for the Study of Economic Policy

Room to Manoeuvre? Globalization and Policy Convergence, Thomas J. Courchene (ed.),
Bell Canada Papers no. 6, 1999   Paper ISBN 0-88911-812-4 Cloth ISBN 0-88911-812-4

Women and Work, Richard P. Chaykowski and Lisa M. Powell (eds.), 1999
Paper ISBN 0-88911-808-6 Cloth ISBN 0-88911-806-X

Equalization: Its Contribution to Canada's Economic and Fiscal Progress, Robin W. Boadway and Paul A.R. Hobson (eds.), Policy Forum Series no. 36, 1998
Paper ISBN 0-88911-780-2 Cloth IBSN 0-88911-804-3

Fiscal Targets and Economic Growth, Thomas J. Courchene and Thomas A. Wilson (eds.),
Roundtable Series no. 12, 1998   Paper ISBN 0-88911-778-0 Cloth ISBN 0-88911-776-4

The 1997 Federal Budget: Retrospect and Prospect, Thomas J. Courchene and Thomas A. Wilson (eds.),
Policy Forum Series no. 35, 1997   Paper ISBN 0-88911-774-8 Cloth ISBN 0-88911-772-1

Available from:
McGill-Queen's University Press
Tel: 1-800-387-0141 (ON and QC excluding Northwestern ON)
         1-800-387-0172 (all other provinces and Northwestern ON)
E-mail: customer.service@ccmailgw.genpub.com